Now with
Kung Fu Grip!

Now with Kung Fu Grip!

*How Bodybuilders, Soldiers
and a Hairdresser
Reinvented Martial Arts for America*

JARED MIRACLE

McFarland & Company, Inc., Publishers
Jefferson, North Carolina

LIBRARY OF CONGRESS CATALOGUING-IN-PUBLICATION DATA

Names: Miracle, Jared.
Title: Now with kung fu grip! : how bodybuilders, soldiers and a
    hairdresser reinvented martial arts for America / Jared Miracle.
Description: Jefferson, North Carolina : McFarland & Company,
    Inc., Publishers, 2016. | Includes bibliographical references and
    index.
Identifiers: LCCN 2016024110 | ISBN 9781476663500
    (softcover : acid free paper) ∞
Subjects: LCSH: Martial arts—United States—History. | Martial
    artists—United States—Biography.
Classification: LCC GV1100.A2 M57 2016 |
    DDC 796.80973—dc23
LC record available at https://lccn.loc.gov/2016024110

BRITISH LIBRARY CATALOGUING DATA ARE AVAILABLE

ISBN (print) 978-1-4766-6350-0
ISBN (ebook) 978-1-4766-2446-4

On the cover: *Fearless* aka *Huo Yuan Jia* aka *Jet Li's Fearless*, 2006
(Rogue Pictures/Photofest)

Printed in the United States of America

McFarland & Company, Inc., Publishers
    Box 611, Jefferson, North Carolina 28640
    www.mcfarlandpub.com

For my family. Sorry about the long absence.
For my teachers. What I don't know could fill a book.
Specifically, this one.

Table of Contents

Acknowledgments

Offering thanks should not be conflated with a suggestion of blame; any faults in the following pages are entirely my own. That said, I have to first recognize the hard work and patience of my doctoral dissertation committee as much of this research was done while in their charge. This illustrious group consists of a kung fu master, two boxers, and a man distinguished variously as an expert on honey, the history of kissing, and/or fossilized ordure. Thomas Green, Bruce Dickson, Larry Mitchell, and Vaughn Bryant provided me with the guidance to navigate graduate school without losing my sanity. The value of their mentorship cannot be overstated. Because graduate study offered me the access and funding needed to gather most of the information for this book, any meaningful contents found herein are due to their influence.

A debt of gratitude is owed to the Texas A&M Department of Anthropology staff for their tireless support efforts on behalf of all graduate students. In particular, Cindy Hurt and Rebekah Luza are actually cyborgs sent from the future on a mission to save us academic types from ourselves. Or at least that's how it seems when they answer the phone at three o'clock in the morning to call in a rental car and hotel because I've managed to strand myself in an airport. Again. Marco Valadez serves the dual function of navigator and ship's counselor. Thanks for always being a calm in the storm, brother.

My gratitude to the organizations and offices that provided funding for various portions of my research, including: the Texas A&M Office of Graduate (and Professional) Studies, the Glasscock Center for Humanities Research, and the Cushing Memorial Library and Archives. The staff at the Library of Congress, the American Folklife Center, the Smithsonian, and Cushing Library were most helpful in tracking down pieces of this puzzle. I would especially like to thank Rebecca Hankins, Steve Bales, Ann

Hoog, Megan Harris, Mari Nakahara, and the Library of Congress Prints and Photographs Division staff.

Thanks also to my friends and colleagues at Texas A&M and elsewhere for their support and commiseration over what turned out to be quite a long haul. Special thanks to Nick Mizer and Angela Younie for reading over portions of the early draft. My three surrogate families, the Peppers, the Mizers, and the Pepplers, opened their homes and refrigerators at crucial moments when being stranded in the heart of Texas was proving most challenging. Likewise, I have to thank a number of others who I am lucky enough to call friends: Michelle Franzen and Jacob Anderson for giving me a roof and think tank; Rachel Strack for title ideas; Tom Barton for reminding me to "cowboy up"; the families Green, Meng, and Zhang for all the kung fu and *guanxi*; and Tadashige Watanabe, Reiko Saito, and the rest of the Marobashi-kai for their kind patience.

I cannot adequately express my gratitude to those who agreed to be interviewed for and otherwise contributed to this project, especially "Professor Kaicho" Jon Bluming PhD., Russ Mason (whose *guanxi* is strong), Ben Fusaro, John Donohue (who was wise enough to stay out of the cage), Bubba Bush and the members of Brazos Valley Mixed Martial Arts (who can't seem to get enough of the cage), Ben Costa of Iron Crotch University Press, David McClung, Emily Egan of the Muso Jikiden Eishin Ryu, and the sundry others who asked to remain unnamed. I hope that I have told this part of your story with a modicum of accuracy. I owe a very special debt to the Smith family, without whose kindness and understanding none of this would have been possible.

Finally, thanks to my folks, who taught me that education is valuable for its own sake and who, as Dad says, probably let me "watch a few too many Jackie Chan movies" as a kid.

Preface

I defy you to locate a small town in America that does not have a Chinese restaurant. During the past few years, there has been a great deal of research into the origins of Chinese fast food as an American cultural institution. As we have come to learn, dishes like General Tso's chicken and kung pow shrimp are about as authentically Chinese as country-western music is Hawaiian. Another cultural mainstay of the American landscape that claims foreign heritage is the martial arts school. Whether these schools are housed in a strip mall, YMCA, or someone's garage, one is hard pressed to find a community without some sort of martial arts training on offer, whether taekwondo, karate, or (as is frequently the case in the United States) a proprietary system peculiar to the instructor. Like American Chinese food, these arts and organizations tend to be much more "American" than some of their exponents are aware. This book is the story of how a few of these arts made the leap from their homelands to become unquestionably American.

As an adolescent, I spent nearly every afternoon prowling the stacks of the local public library. One day I wandered past the sports section and a bright red cover caught my eye. It featured a black monochrome of an Asian man poised in an awkward stance, arms akimbo and hands in the classic "karate chop" position. The title was *Chinese Boxing: Masters and Methods* and the author was named Robert W. Smith. Few prospects are more enticing to a young man growing up in the sleepy and predictable Midwest than that of an outside world peopled with mysterious, exotic masters who may be willing to pass on their secret powers to an interested student. The cover may as well have been scientifically formulated to draw me in. One curious element, however, was the term "Chinese boxing." The Chinese didn't have boxing. Television had rendered me an expert on the ubiquity of high-flying kung fu to be found in China and boring old Western fisticuffs did not feature in these films.

1

What I found inside was a matter-of-fact author who was more than happy to address my confusion. "Chinese boxing" was simply the term he and others used to identify the multitude of Chinese fighting styles. He relayed fantastic tales of the type that filled my Bruce Lee–fueled dreams. He then proceeded to dismantle them in systematic fashion until it was apparent how imaginative they truly were. The majority of the volume was taken up with interviews, descriptions, and analyses of the masters with whom Smith had studied during his time abroad. By the time I finished reading, I no longer knew what to make of the pop culture images so prevalent in my teenage world of kung fu movies and Street Fighter arcade games.

Smith was one of several men and a few women who went to great pains to introduce the most authentic (relatively speaking) Asian fighting styles they could find to a Western audience. This book is also, in part, their story of collusion and confusion as they accepted the always-perilous challenge of translating cultural complexity from East to West. The greater scope of this work, however, has been to tease out trends in each generation's approach to the martial arts, both East Asian and Western. After sifting through historical material from the past century or so in three languages, interviewing famous—and not-so-famous—fighters, artists, and fans of the genre, and spending countless hours engaging in all elements of the martial arts industry on two continents, a few running themes emerged.

As will become apparent in the course of this narrative, masculinity is central to martial culture, no matter the location. While it may be manifest differently depending on the situation, I have yet to find an instance of martial arts being practiced, shown on-screen, or appearing in print that does not somehow refer back to systematized violence being used to assert or affirm masculinity. Before World War II, American men boxed and Japanese men practiced judo, karate, or another of the myriad styles available. In the postwar era, Americans shied away from boxing for a time, and instead adopted Japanese, then Chinese, Brazilian, Filipino, and any number of other cultural styles of fight training. The masculinity brought to these practices involves power, both physical and social. When karate first appeared in American movie theaters, in *The Karate Kid* (1984), it was the means by which a waiflike Ralph Macchio won the respect of his peers—and the girl. Within a few years, karate was just one more tool in the arsenal of Jean-Claude Van Damme, whose pectoral muscles alone probably outweighed Macchio.

The nature of belief was another matter that cropped up time and again. In my early interviews and correspondence I found that many who pursue the martial arts, whatever their styles, possess powerful beliefs in their systems and legendary characters. Other issues were repeated in the course of my research besides masculinity and power. Ultimately, though, the lesson to be taken away from this work is that the martial arts, across time and space, serve many more roles than simple violence. There are violent elements to these endeavors, but focusing on that single aspect is very much a forest-tree mistake. As is often said in certain circles of martial artists, practicing one of these arts purely for self-defense reasons would be akin to buying a high-performance sports car in the interest of hauling groceries: possibly excessive and certainly inefficient. Rather, it is best to consider the fighting arts as vessels for the transmission of culture in all forms. They are the stuff of myths and legends, folk tales, nationalist rhetoric, personal and collective values, and, in the final accounting, they simply provide a means of reflecting our own cultures back to us. In the words of David McClung, a well-known instructor and early competitor in mixed martial arts in the United States, "People are forgetting how to be human. Fighting helps with that."

A Note on Language

The Victorian swordsman-scholar-linguist Capt. Sir Richard Francis Burton preferred the verb "Englished" over the less prosaic "translated." This shows the degree to which the meaning of a word or phrase can be lost when searching for cultural equivalents. That being the case, I have attempted to minimize frustration for the reader by following standard modern Pinyin and revised Hepburn Romanization when presenting Mandarin and Japanese words, respectively. This guiding principle is ignored, however, when either an established alternate spelling is more common, such as "jiu-jitsu" instead of the more accurate "jujutsu," or when the words are in a quotation, where I have not altered the original spelling. Along the same line of thought, Japanese and Chinese names are generally presented in the traditional format—family name first—except where the individual is more commonly known in English elsewise.

Introduction

"To sit alone in the lamplight with a book spread out before you, and hold intimate converse with men of unseen generations—such is a pleasure beyond compare."

—Yoshida Kenko

When I was a child, I begged and pleaded with my parents to sign me up for martial arts lessons. Years of Ninja Turtles and Power Rangers left me with a burning desire to act out the fantasies I'd seen on screen. When they finally relented, I, like so many others, discovered a world of rigid practice and discipline that scared me away for some time thereafter. I still recall my first instructor, a world-renowned taekwondo champion who had once helped coach the U.S. Olympic team, thwacking us on the behind with a length of bamboo when he didn't like our execution. Or we didn't do enough knuckle push-ups. Or for pretty much any other reason. At the time, it didn't seem unusual that a Korean system of fisticuffs would be taught out of a dedicated studio in a small Midwestern town. Thinking about it as an adult, I began to ask some rather fundamental questions regarding how and why such a cultural institution found its way to corn-and-Bible country. The answer took several years, trips around the world, and a great deal of physical discipline to discover. Ironically, that answer was waiting for me in small town America the whole time.

This book focuses on the role of folk history and invented traditions within the realm of stylized fighting arts (otherwise known as martial arts) as a community of practice and consumption and as imported from East Asia to the United States over the course of the twentieth century and up to the present. The goal is to provide the reader with a contextualized cultural analysis of the major shifts and trends in the negotiation of the "martial artist" or "fighter" identity as it has developed in what is herein referred to as the "mainstream" and "middle-class" social set of Americans. By this

I mean the numerically and financially prevalent population that represents the hegemonic culture of a given era. As this is an interpretive analysis and not a scientific survey, a holistic approach to the material is taken in order to paint the fullest possible picture of any given historical moment. Likewise, this manner of study does not lend itself well to quantitative hypothesis-testing. Therefore, multimedia including films, television, graphic novels, newspapers and magazines, and popular books are used as source material along with archival evidence and personal interviews with current and former martial arts practitioners.

The questions driving this study are legion and, at times, complex. I will offer a shorthand version for the reader to keep in mind in the course of this journey. These will be addressed again in the conclusion. First, who are martial artists and why do they do what they do? A knee-jerk impulse may be to point to people who practice exotic fighting styles while donning unusual costumes, but that raises other matters for, say, boxers, wrestlers, and other Western traditions. It also problematizes the various levels of involvement since casual "white-collar" boxers who never spar are far removed from professional fighters. As will be discussed, many styles of Asian extract (or at least inspiration) were founded on American shores. Indeed, issues of nationality and "true" origins are impossibly murky in the context of American cultural institutions. This study is primarily concerned, therefore, with martial arts in America as they are practiced in modern times and how they came about. Second, is there social, political, or historical importance to the scholarly study of martial culture? I argue that there is; however, it requires a degree of background elaboration before that case can be succinctly made. Finally, how meaningful are depictions of the martial arts in both practice and media within the greater scope of American culture?

Here it is important to note the use of the terms "Western" and "Asian." Both of these are ambiguous, Asia accounting for roughly three-fifths of the planetary landmass, though both Asia and the West are only geographically defined in the blurriest of senses. This word choice is intentional. While the United States is the primary Western nation discussed in this book, the transnational nature of culture in general and fighting arts in particular causes even the idea of "American-ness" to be, at best, leaky. In the same way, although Japan is the site of most concern, it is a historical Japan that also spread into mainland China and Korea, and created the Manchurian puppet state. This, combined with the process of exotification in the mid-century American context, makes for an imaginary Asia or "the East" that is, by definition, vague and uncertain in terms of geographical and cultural distinctions. Therefore, "American" and "Western," while not fully interchangeable, are applied in many of the same contexts while "Asia" is used to refer simultaneously to the tangible landmasses of the Eastern Pacific Rim and an intangible imaginary. In short, the "Asia" to which many of my sources refer may as well be Shangri-La for all its historical or even geographic accuracy.

Influences

The impetus for the present project was a convergence of three different, though related, influential sources, which were then informed by several other works that comprise the nexus of my interpretive approach. First is the edited volume by Green and Svinth (2003), *Martial Arts in the Modern World*, and specifically the inaugural essay by Green, *Sense in Nonsense: The Role of Folk History in the Martial Arts*. Green hints at a number of factors that tend to influence the development of martial culture, regardless of nationality or time period. His work centers on the idea of martial arts as social tools, which I have adopted herein as the primary guiding influence for situating martial practices within local and global contexts. He also stresses that folk history is related to, though different from, scientific or historiographical research about the past as it is neither verifiable nor, indeed, does it *need* to be, as it serves purposes related to identity construction and social relations rather than attempting to establish an indisputable record of the past.

Second is an article by Clifford Geertz, *Deep Play: Notes on the Balinese Cockfight* (1972) in which the author stresses the value of not only close ethnographic observation, but in reading deeper meaning into such multifaceted activities as the Balinese cockfight. While a purely observational, etic (or "outsider") style of recording an event could be argued as more objective than Geertz's approach, he states convincingly that the "culture of a people is an ensemble of texts, themselves ensembles, which the anthropologist strains to read over the shoulders of those to whom they properly belong."[1] I would add to this that, even though Geertz is referring to definitively foreign cultures, the conversational state of folk history and modern international state of virtually every social group means that all such ensembles of text belong to specific groups regardless of geographic location. In order to examine any community of practice, that community's context in history must be taken into account, which cannot be accomplished without some degree of reading into the practice-as-text. Therefore, historiographical events can be utilized as a background against which to read and interpret practices such as engagement in the martial arts.

Third, Dunning and Elias (1986), in *Quest for Excitement*, make a strong case for the use of sport and play as means to negotiate violent intentions or sentiments that would be expressed through direct force if not for the complex web of social circumstances that prohibit outright warfare in most human interactions. As Dunning notes rather poignantly,

> [T]he existence of diametrically opposed ideologies which stress, on the one hand, that sport might form a substitute for war, and on the other that it is an ideal vehicle for military training in that it enhances the toughness and aggressiveness of those who take part, is further suggestive of the homologous character and perhaps of the interconnectedness of the two spheres.[2]

Here it is laid bare that sport (and, more specifically, fighting arts) are both tools for socially acceptable ways of avoiding warfare without surrendering conflict and a means of preparing for the physical and cognitive rigors of war through psychological and bodily conditioning of the individual and the group. The separation of intentionally harmful violence and playful violence is, it seems, an artificial one. This will become an important point later as I argue—based on an analysis of current and former professional fighters—that blurring the line between play and abject danger heightens the sense of realism, bonds the community of practice on a psychic level, and justifies the practice of martial arts in the minds of practitioners. The perception of real danger in rehearsal provides confidence and meaning for the individual due to apparent efficacy.

The above were formative, though not the only works on which this study draws. Others proved influential on the method and manner of analysis. In *Inventing Traditions* (1983), Hobsbawm sets out the meaning of the term "tradition" as it is intended herein:

> [A] set of practices, normally governed by overtly or tacitly accepted rules and of a ritual or symbolic nature, which seek to inculcate certain values and norms, of behavior by repetition, which automatically implies continuity with the past.[3]

Hobsbawm's concept of invented traditions is applicable to the context of folk culture within the martial arts. This will be seen in the construction of narratives about an imagined past among American karate students in the period after World War II. It also indicates the need for a perceived connection with an ancient past, even in cases where this may not be the case from a historiographical perspective. Invented tradition pairs with the idea of intangible culture to form "objects of knowledge." These are intangible traditions and practices that can be transferred, reinterpreted, and

generally modified in ways that suit a given social agenda. They are referred
to as "objects" because, just as physical objects can be invented and repur-
posed in different ways depending on time and location, cultural knowledge
operates in the same way.[4] Cultural, social, and historical background necessarily affects how objects are invented and implemented. That background is what may be termed a "texture of knowledge."[5] As an example,
the standard uniform associated with karate practice was designed in Japan
during the 1920s; the manner of wearing it was adopted by American servicemen after the Second World War as an object of knowledge, but without the texture of knowledge (that is, the cultural background that brought
about the uniform's implementation); it took on new meaning and was
subject to invented traditions as the Americans returned home and founded
their own communities of practice, where the traditions were integrated
based on a different set of social needs. The result of this rather abstract-
sounding process is the rainbow of martial arts accouterments seen in the
United States today, including red, white, and blue karate uniforms,
camouflage-patterned belts, and militaristic patches and stripes of every
order.

     The vessel for this intangible knowledge is as much the body as the
mind. In Western societies after the rise of secularism (especially in the
1920s), the mind and body have come to be seen as mutual opponents. The
body is commoditized and made a target for advertising based on a consumer culture in which ideal images are constantly changing in a perpetual
cycle of dissatisfaction.[6] As the body is commoditized as a necessary part
of transmitting the physical culture of fighting arts, it became apparent
through reading and interviews that discursive masculinity comprises a
common thread in all time periods and communities of practice regardless
of the combative style when discussing American martial artists. To that
end, I turn to Savran (1998) to bridge hegemonic discursive masculine
identity formation with Featherstone's society-level discussion of consumer
body culture. This establishes the greater part of the texture of knowledge
into which Asian martial arts were grafted over the course of the past century.

     In *Re-Situating Folklore* (2004), de Caro and Jordan show that folklore
as a shared cultural product cannot be defined in terms of "high art versus
low art" or "traditional versus nontraditional," but is instead in a constantly
shifting and fluxing arrangement with surrounding cultural and social elements—those that comprise the texture of knowledge—in order to remain
alive and relevant. Much of this project details the pertinent historical and
social settings in which fighting arts are constructed and reconstituted as

items of folklore in this dialectic dynamic. They further assert that folklore analysis is useful in identifying cultural frameworks that are made up of aesthetic qualities and into which items of folklore must be made to fit if they remain as a part of the greater cultural schema.[7] In this way the item itself—the object of knowledge—is simply a tool for the expression of a preexisting framework.

Finally, in order to understand the framework in which folklore-as-object-of-knowledge is expressed, I turned to the work of Joseph Campbell. Campbell analyzes what he calls the "monomyth," a self-contained framework that, taken in abstraction, describes virtually any narrative in cyclical terms. This proves useful in approaching the self-mythologizing (that is, the internal creation of a heroic narrative about the self) that I found to be critical in the establishment of identity among groups of martial artists. Creativity by means of an established textural framework, Campbell notes, is the cardinal feature of all heroic narratives, whether that product is a material object, a community, or even a new style of fighting art.[8] This explains much of the proliferation of martial arts styles, academies, clubs, and media in the United States since the Second World War. By viewing identity as a creative process of self-mythologizing (in terms of the personal self and the community with which one identifies), the need for narrative comes full circle, with the role of folk narrative in the collective creative endeavor as outlined by Green (2003). Martial arts are thus items of folklore as well as topics about which folklore is generated, objects of knowledge informed by a general cultural framework, and, ultimately, social tools.

Chapter Outline

This project is divided into five parts, each covering a different period of time and/or place that, taken together, may be seen as comprising a narrative arc in which the martial arts are the focal character. Chapter 1 discusses the history and role of the fighting arts in the United States from the end of the nineteenth century until just prior to World War II. As a more financially active public topic, much of the attention is given to boxing. The social context in which the act of boxing is placed as a predominantly male pursuit was heavily influenced by a movement known as "muscular Christianity." This movement is discussed at some length, principally as it shaped and was shaped by the Young Men's Christian Association (YMCA). In the same vein, public health reformers like John Harvey Kellogg (of breakfast cereal fame) are referenced as transitionary between a period of high religiosity and general secularization. All of this coincided with an epidemic of anxiety among white-collar urban men. Social commentators like Theodore Roosevelt renounced what they saw as the feminization of American men who no longer worked in physical professions and prescribed a number of curative behaviors, including combat sports like boxing. All of this led to boxing's golden age, which began just prior to World War II and ended within a decade thereafter.

The idea of a general social anxiety is referenced here not as an attempt to avoid more concrete causes, but to identify a collusion of factors that led to a sequence of events. Anxiety in this regard means the personal and public unease prevalent among men of the time as they were forced to redefine their place in the world amidst drastic social and political upheaval. The First World War introduced the American public to global conflict, setting the stage for what would come in later decades and establishing America as a potentially powerful military and economic force in the world. This had the result of simultaneously offering a path to adult manhood for young men living comfortable, white-collar existences while also threatening their ability to successfully achieve a personal sense thereof. At the same time, women of the era were discovering their own agency, intruding on historically masculine activities like exercise and smoking. Men had to locate a new means of establishing their prowess domestically, leading to an advertising culture that capitalized on this need. Such was the state of affairs in the United States from the turn of the last century until World War II.

Chapter 2 is concerned with roughly the same period of time, but deals with the social climate of Japan and East Asia. The twentieth century in Japan opened with the arrival of American gunships off the coast of the main island and the subsequent arrival of cultures and technology from the U.S. and Europe. As rapid industrialization took place, the Japanese looked to China as an example of potentially destructive effects from agreeing to unequal treaties with Western powers, and the general public as well as elite governmental leadership more or less unilaterally agreed to transform the nation into an imperial power lest it be conquered from the outside. Japan wrestled with the added issue of creating a national identity as it had been essentially a collection of independent states before the advent of the Meiji government at the end of the nineteenth century. One means by which extreme nationalists (who took power early on) sought to do this while inculcating young people with a fervent drive to conquest was by implementing, regulating, and drastically modifying both Japanese and foreign martial disciplines. Chinese martial arts are also discussed here. Their relatively lower popularity may be due to political influences such as a lack of personal contact in the postwar peacetime, and their role in the Boxer Uprising of 1900.

This chapter also provides a treatment of the most popular Japanese martial arts in the United States, particularly judo, karate, and aikido. The development process for each of these in Japan is discussed in relation to the context of a tightly controlled nationalistic system that selected official activities for schools and the military. Also of interest is the Japanese approach to boxing, which was short-lived and provides a contrasting example to the highly successful work of those who created and popularized other fighting disciplines. The pre-war period in Japan even saw boxing pitted against judo in mixed-style matches that preempted the modern mixed martial arts craze by eighty years or more. Luckily, sufficient sources are available to analyze boxing's failure in Japan in terms of the nationalist search for official martial systems. This is not the case for some other styles, which see only brief reference in the primary literature and are of little use to the present ends since even descriptions of lesser-known styles are hard to come by. Rather, the success of judo and karate as objects of mass appeal for the Japanese public receives the primary emphasis and shows how they were modified to match the desires of an expansionist regime.

Chapter 3 delves into the complexity of interaction between Allied servicemen stationed in Japan during the period of postwar occupation and their Japanese hosts, from whom karate and, later, other martial arts systems were learned and brought back to the United States. Misunderstanding abounded during this phase and men like Robert Trias, who opened the first karate academy in the mainland United States—in Phoenix, Arizona—in 1946, formed the first generation of creative mythmakers along with international promoters like Masutatsu Oyama, a Japanese of Korean ancestry who strongly supported the imperialist cause and described karate as an art for the improvement of men. It is during this time that the beginnings of uniquely American perspectives and adaptations of Asian martial arts can be seen; they eventually guided the development of identity formation by later generations of American fighters.

Focus is given here to the proliferation of myths and misunderstandings between Japanese martial artists and Americans who would go on to recreate these activities in the U.S. Oyama receives a great deal of attention because of his influential rhetoric, which labeled karate as an art for men. He went to great lengths to establish his own legend, which was quickly spun by media and even his own students into outrageous tales of fistic ability and accomplishment. To better understand how these tales became an inseparable part of his legacy, I consulted Jon Bluming, a pioneer in the world of martial arts and one of Oyama's closest and most dedicated students. Along with other material from the postwar era, Bluming's accounts of events are substantiated and help to place the legends and myths in context. On the American side, Robert Trias is viewed in the same light and for similar reasons. His own writing reveals the extent to which he weaved fiction into his teaching and, in so doing, generated a mythos for his followers to carry and build upon in later generations, which is precisely what took place.

Chapter 4 spotlights the topical experts whose voices in print and film media gave license to the general public for the normalization of Asian fighting arts in the United States during the 1960s and 1970s. One group, which included such colorful figures as John "Count Dante" Keehan, acted more as salesmen than fighters, advertising learn-at-home courses in comic books and magazines and vehemently perpetuating fantastic stories about themselves and the martial arts while also creating an extraordinary imagined Asia, home to mysterious masters of arcane power that could be acquired by individuals willing and able to risk their lives adventuring abroad—or by purchasing the advertised booklet. The other group included much more scholarly and grounded figures such as Robert W. Smith and Donn F. Draeger. These men ventured to Japan and other parts of East and Southeast Asia after the war to study the martial arts. They did so with a very clear mission that they would publish accurate information in the English language so that those in the West could be informed and educated. The life works of these two drastically different groups amalgamated with popular culture to form the landscape of American martial arts culture.

In an effort to avoid further apotheosizing or exaggerating the personalities profiled in this chapter, some personal information about them as people is provided to better understand who they were as real human beings. Although this section benefits heavily from the personal archives of Robert Smith, he and his colleagues are subject to the same critical treatment as John Keehan and his successors. This proved challenging in the course of research as it is exceedingly easy to dismiss all of Count Dante's claims as bogus while upholding Smith and Draeger as paragons of scholarly virtue. The truth is more complex than that, and so this chapter will give weight to lesser-known events, such as a disagreement between Smith and Draeger over a famous *taiji* master and Count Dante's long-term influence on martial arts publications and the slew of mail-order masters who followed in his wake.

Chapter 5 is concerned with the transformation of the martial artist identity as it has interacted with discursive masculinity from the 1970s to the present. The rise in popular martial arts films is seen to coincide with changes in male body image ideals which result from responses to society-level transitions in the place of feminism and hegemonic masculinity. The disestablishment of exclusively male social spaces led to a reactive hyper-masculinity in the media that continued to intensify until the 1990s, at which point it had reached unacceptable levels of expression and was supplanted with a turn toward rationalism. Rationalist trends in the fighting disciplines led to a newfound public acceptance of combat sports in the form of mixed martial arts, which is currently reaching levels of popularity reminiscent of boxing's golden age. Participation in mixed martial arts training is examined and found to be associated with the same needs for identity formation and social anxiety that have driven men to pursue combative arts since the beginning of the twentieth century.

It may seem incongruous to lump several decades together in this way, but the structure is necessary in order to tell the story properly. After an initial transference to American soil in the 1950s and 1960s, Asian martial arts went through a rapid boom in popularity and morphed into all manner of new forms, finding a place among the pantheon of American pop culture tropes. This happened as a single sequence of events that must be taken together to be fully coherent. What began as an invincible, mystical system of techniques from exotic lands (whether judo, karate, or another style) became fodder for cartoons and children's birthday parties, giving way to other systems that seemed yet more exotic and mystical. When many of those resources were exhausted due to globalization and cynicism, those men who had been navigating their masculine identities through more fantastical means then turned in the opposite direction and took to staging full-contact bouts in order to determine the most physically effective methods of personal combat. This movement has culminated in the present public fascination with mixed martial arts.

In the analysis and conclusion I pose the socio-historic narrative of fighting arts as they have been imported to the United States and adapted to fit changing social climates over the period of this project's concern. Ultimately, I argue that a contextual cultural analysis of the Asian martial arts in the American context reveals that a greater cultural framework is in place, cyclically drawing men into and away from particular martial arts styles at different times in a sequence of trends that are expressive of their masculinity as it must be renegotiated for each generation due to climate shifts. New mythical narratives are needed to accommodate a base desire for tradition and community.

Dramatis Personae

It is best to think of this as a narrative story in which Asian martial arts feature as the main character. Along the way, we will experience the turmoil of wars, see adventures in far-off lands, and meet some of the most intriguing and colorful figures of their respective generations. Because of the wide net cast for this study, much of the material has been trimmed down and limited to specific topics. While complete histories of, say, Filipino or African martial arts in the U.S. are certainly called for and would be utterly engrossing, the present volume is intended to provide context and groundwork for other such specialized recces. In this case, Japanese martial arts, specifically judo and karate, receive most of the attention, in large part because they were among the first to be established in America as products for mass consumption.

Some of the individuals who appear in this telling may come across as fictional for various reasons. Certainly the most epic of these men—or, at least, the one to elicit the most interesting responses when encountered for the first time—is John "Count Juan Raphael Dante" Keehan. His tale will be told in due course; however, it is important at this early juncture to remind the reader that the events and people to follow were and are very much real. Yes, Count Dante really did work as a hairdresser for *Playboy* photo shoots while also selling used cars, organizing "full-contact" fighting tournaments in Chicago, and marketing his own brand of cigarettes. Yes, he most likely did own a chain of pornography stores. And, indeed, he honestly was involved in the famous "midnight dojo fight" that left one dead and at least a few more seriously wounded after a sword-based conflict between rival schools.

Another figure who may seem to be based in some other world is Masutatsu Oyama, about whose life comic books, cartoons, and even a video game character have been created. Oyama and his karate school are now the stuff of legend. There was a significant cadre of Japanese and non-Japanese alike who ventured to his Tokyo academy to train for a thousand continuous days. It is also true that, in the 1960s and even now, one of the more extraordinary feats within his lineage is a grueling sparring session against fifty opponents in succession. We will also meet one of Oyama's senior students, among the most accomplished martial artists and athletes of his generation, who reveals the truth behind some of the stories told about his teacher. Among these is the popular story that Oyama once killed a bull with his bare hands. As with so many folk tales and legends, there is, in fact, a kernel of truth to it.

It is sometimes the case that martial arts personalities who pass into legend also attract a cult-like following. The founders of prevalent styles are unusually prone to such apotheosis. It is expected that certain less-than-flattering information about these individuals will upset some readers who hold unrealistically high opinions of these people. It is important to keep in mind that, despite their accomplishments, even the greatest of historical figures was still a human being, with all the unfortunate qualities that entails. Kano Jigoro, the founder of judo, for instance, altered his original curriculum and methods of practice to better appeal to nationalistic, imperial authorities. The material referenced strongly implies that, all positive intentions aside, Kano knowingly made concessions to the whims of authorities with less-than-peaceable intentions for his art. This should not be mistaken for an indictment of the man himself, who was, by even the most uncomplimentary accounts, an individual of the highest moral and professional caliber. The reality of politics simply necessitated compromise if judo were to survive.

Likewise, and perhaps more pertinent for the current trends in American martial arts, the history of Brazilian jiu-jitsu is portrayed in a way that does not pay obeisance to the near-legendary treatment enjoyed by the art itself and many of its historical figures. This is by no means intended to be insulting or belittling, but rather in keeping with the present search for facts to substantiate folk knowledge and rumors. It is necessary, when dealing with martial culture more than almost any other, to retain a strong sense of skepticism whenever material is uncovered due to the glut of lies, myths, and exaggerations. Brazilian jiu-jitsu is the trendy style at present, mostly thanks to brilliant advertising on the part of its early proponents. Some may be offended by having it pointed out that it is, in essence, judo with slightly different rules. The legend that traditional *jujutsu* was taught to a young Brazilian as thanks for the aid of his high-status father is explained as aggrandizement. In point of fact, the Japanese man was no mysterious master of the exotic East, but a down-on-his-luck judo teacher turned professional wrestler in a circus, trying to earn enough to scrape by. The well-respected Brazilian man was a boxing promoter in the same circus. The boy learned Kano's judo and marketed it under a different name. It rose to fame in the United States because of an absolutely inspired publicity stunt called the *Ultimate Fighting Championship*, the first of which was basically an advertisement for Brazilian jiu-jitsu.

In the same fashion as those who are offended by the implication that their idols were idiosyncratic and fallible are those individuals who feel slighted by the very idea that his or her martial art of choice had its beginnings in anything but legendary time. Coincidentally, backlash over suggestions that a martial art like taekwondo (which is sometimes purported to have a history dating back over two millennia) was actually invented in the 1950s by appropriating a foreign style (as is the case) and renaming the movements is evidence of how important the arts are for building and supporting personal identity. As will be seen, a belief in the extraordinary is one reason that so many people spend so much time on an activity that has little ostensible utility in daily life.

In all of the above cases, the reader would be well served to keep in mind that this is not a look just at the historical development of martial arts in the U.S., but a contextual analysis. As in all studies of folklore, what the community in question believes is equally important to what verifiably happened in the past. Because of this, I would urge the reader to keep in mind the difference between belief and fact. One may choose to believe in ideas and philosophies that have no basis in empirical fact without one arena harming the other. It is far from the purpose of this book to argue against any belief but that of the martial arts as useless pastimes. The arguments herein will make clear that, in many capacities, the value of the martial arts in America has been as cultural objects onto which beliefs may be grafted. Seeing value in unverifiable stories is not only acceptable, but common. It is, to a great extent, what makes humans unique among the animal kingdom. For the martial arts and belief, to echo the sentiments of Donn Draeger in his frequent admonition to young judo students, it is a matter of the singer, not the song.

1

The YMCA, Christian Muscle and Breakfast Cereal

Do you know, that is the root of the whole trouble—has been one of the roots at any rate—is people hearing things and then imagining some more and magnifying it and multiplying it.

—John Harvey Kellogg

Therefore I do not run like someone running aimlessly; I do not fight like a boxer beating the air. No, I strike a blow to my body and make it my slave so that after I have preached to others, I myself will not be disqualified for the prize.

—1 Corinthians 9:26–27

In the West, the twentieth century saw the creation of a "cultural ethic" that pushed men away from expressions of aggression and toward a new, congenial manifestation of their identity. Muscular Christianity—an informal social movement to express hegemonic Christian cultural values through the cult of sport—was the predominant influencing factor on that cultural ethic. Through muscular Christianity and institutions like the YMCA, American ideals of masculinity became more and more crystalized and extreme. This has proven problematic because the same men, lacking any traditional resources for asserting (or even conceptualizing) a non-aggressive masculinity, privately adhere to previous generations' attitudes and behaviors while simultaneously maligning those ideas in public due to new cultural expectations brought about by social upheaval from the 1960s through the end of the century. The formation of dichotomous selves was inevitable. A return to previous generations' expressions would be unacceptable as "contemporary men are increasingly being held accountable for violence throughout human history, judged guilty by virtue of their

Y chromosome," while a new conceptualization is nearly impossible since there are so few social arenas that men may claim with exclusivity.[1] For many of these men, the solution has been to look outside their own culture, to the "other," for recourse as they grasp for legitimacy in notions of the masculine.

This idea of looking as far afield as possible to discover oneself is not new or unique. The classic trope of the hero's journey demands that the hero figure venture away from home and face exotic danger to fulfill his/her destiny. The exotic has always presented an object of fascination, especially for Westerners, who ventured out of Europe and colonized all parts of the world despite hardship, loss of life, and resistance from every people over whom they sought control. As will be seen, this powerful drive for an external object or idea on which to hang the prospect of fulfillment or some manner of life purpose was a cultural ethic that found some of its staunchest opposition in the inward-focused China of the early twentieth century. It also led to a violent clash with the imperial Japanese, who overhauled an entire nation's economy and infrastructure—and, indeed, its very basic values—in what proved to be among history's more astonishing transformations.

Perhaps it was the inward focus of these East Asian societies that drew the fascination of Americans in a repeat of the immemorial tale of forbidden fruit being the sweetest. Maybe it was a natural next step for Americans, having recently completed the agenda of Manifest Destiny, to look yet farther in that direction. I would propose that it is, as in so many areas of social history, a mixture of the two along with other, as yet unidentified factors that brought about the events to follow. In any case, the tale begins where another had just left off. The end of the Victorian period left American culture with a desire to explore, conquer, collect, catalogue, and face the barest fronts of nature and civilization. Even Christian religious life, ostensibly inward-looking, contemplative, and peaceful by this time in history, found its expansionist, aggressive, virile side. These same personality types, hinging on male power and prowess, first ventured into the world of East Asian fighting disciplines. We will therefore begin with the Christian religious life of men.

Muscular Christianity

The notion of male social hegemony in Western Europe and North America has been treated as a given by many popular social theorists since at least the 1970s. This leads to a simplistic view of the relationship between individuals and their gender identity, as well as assuming that such identities are somehow unified and even, to some extent, organized. In pragmatic reality, "constructions of differing political, regional, national, and more recently, sexual identities among men have always worked to undermine any sense of a unified phallic front."[2] When considering subcultures and folk groups, it is particularly important to include the personal and cultural shifts that take place over time, especially in the interest of avoiding the gloss that "all men do this" or "all women think like this."

During the Victorian era in England and then spreading to other parts of Europe and North America, such a cultural shift took place in the form of a movement now known as muscular Christianity. Far from seeking to emulate the image of Christ as a gentle lamb, muscular Christianity stressed the value of physical prowess, confidence in the religious realm, and the ability to exert control over both one's personal life and one's surroundings.[3] Crusader-like, adherents of this movement sought ways to prepare themselves for the rigors of negotiating a world filled with iniquity, seeing life as a daily battle in which the result was either stronger conviction or a weakening of the self. Writers (notably Charles Kingsley) expressed this struggle by depicting the male body in action as a "point of reference in and determiner of a masculinist economy of signification and (all too often) degradation."[4]

Kingsley (1819–1875) was a prolific novelist, evangelist for the Church of England, and close friend of both Charles Darwin and George MacDonald. Probably most well-known in the present for his novel *Westward Ho!* (1855), he was a proponent of both early evolutionist thinking and the importance of religious faith in the lives of young men inclined to seek adventure beyond the borders of their homelands. In *Westward Ho!* he sets forth the story of Amyas Leigh, a restless English youth who follows Sir Francis Drake on a voyage to the New World, ventures to the Caribbean with gold-hungry privateers, combats the Spanish Armada, and falls in love with Ayacanora, an exotic Indian woman. In many ways, *Westward Ho!* was at least as influential on the times in which it was written as it was reflective of them. English men with a desire to establish themselves in the world, earn respect, and make their fortunes may not have universally embodied the exaggerated virility of Amyas Leigh, but they certainly saw an element of themselves in his swashbuckling. While not stated explicitly, none of the events in *Westward Ho!* would be possible without a fit and vigorous masculine physique.

In the United States, too, this attitude that the male body could be a tool of either piety or degeneracy grew prevalent. Emerson and other nineteenth-century moralist writers advocated habits of self-denial, discipline, and abstinence as means of strengthening one's manliness. At the same time (or perhaps as a consequence), "they consistently labeled the 'weaker' and more sensual impulses 'feminine' or 'effeminate' and attempted to expurgate them from their definitions of self."[5] Defining the self through the body and one's mastery over it became the hallmark of muscular Christianity. Both the ability to deny physical desire and to build up physical power were upheld as central to the survival and propagation of their beliefs.

In daily life, the stress on physical, body-centered understanding of the self in relation to both the world and spirituality resulted in an increased social emphasis on sports and adventure as a signifying practice of the masculine. Religions founded in the nineteenth century reflect this trend; the doctrine of the Seventh-day Adventists includes abstinence from habits perceived to be unhealthy, avoidance of alcohol and caffeine, a vegetarian diet, and regular exercise. The Young Men's Christian Association was founded in London in 1844 with similar views that Christian piety should be seen in the daily behavior choices of the adherent. In its early days the various sports clubs housed within the YMCA were somewhat controversial given the views of both some members and outsiders that an overemphasis on sports could lead young men down a path of vanity, causing them to focus too much on the body and personal achievements and victories.[6]

This attitude was prevalent from the beginning, as the YMCA was founded chiefly to spread an evangelical Christian message to young men living in urban centers, usually far from their families and perhaps in the city for the first time to seek their fortunes.[7] As muscular Christianity was then in its infancy, the general view among the YMCA's early membership indicates a markedly different concept of recreation than it would later come to embody. During this early era of its existence, the YMCA was not at all geared toward recreation of any kind. The organization's newsletter, *The Watchman*, even suggested as late as 1877 that, as far as recreational pursuits were concerned, there may have been some situations in which keeping around a set for checkers or chess might be appropriate. Such measures would only be deemed suitable after consulting the local leadership, with the stipulation that game pieces should remain under lock and key.[8]

Over time, it became apparent that the organization would need to diversify its means of engaging young men or risk losing them to more entertaining activities offered by busy population centers. If not downright militant, the YMCA's approach to spreading the gospel and Protestant morality did become more assertive. By the 1890s silent reading rooms and Bible study groups became second-tier to networking with a more high-powered audience of businessmen and civic leaders. This assertiveness was public enough that the *Atlanta Constitution* referred to the YMCA in 1885 as "the business side of religion."[9] The collective decision to court successful entrepreneurs and other public personalities was due, no doubt, to an effort at recruiting new membership of a particular demographic; when middle- and upper-middle-class young men moved to large cities to chase business success, the attraction to an informal and open group of accomplished movers and shakers would have been difficult to resist.

The question then became one of how to draw in membership from the higher rungs of the social ladder. The solution came in the form of a single man, Luther Halsey Gulick, Jr. A physician with a degree from Columbia, Gulick represented a new breed of American man. He was born in 1865 to missionary parents serving in Hawaii and received something of a global education, traveling with his family as they spread the Gospel. He was greatly concerned with the state of physical health among America's burgeoning white-collar workers. Muscular Christianity was a natural marriage of Gulick's twin passions for religion and health, and while at Harvard he reconceptualized the Greek ideal of the scholar-athlete to fit a Christian mold. In 1886 he created a physical education program for the YMCA, initiating a significant departure from the established activities of the organization at that time.[10]

For Gulick and other physical education reformers, the goal of cultivating young men for service to church and society required not only mental, but also physical preparation. This message was readily absorbed by much of the active YMCA membership, such as a clergyman who wrote in *The Watchman* in 1885 that he almost never fell ill thanks to regular physical exercise, thereby allowing him to continue evangelizing:

> [The gym] used to be considered a wicked place, a place for pugilists to get a muscle, a training school for manufacturing Heenans. Now what do you see there? College professors swinging dumbbells, millionaires turning somersaults, lawyers upside down, hanging by one foot, doctors of divinity with coats off punching a bag, sending out blows as if in a controversy, and the bag an opposing bishop, dyspeptics on a rope ladder, old age dancing itself young. Ah! It's better than all the curatives of earth, better than all the plantation bitters, and all the other board fence literature in creation.[11]

The editorializing here indicates the moralistic criticism of combat sports common at the time. "Heenan" is a reference to John Heenan (1834–1873), a bare-knuckle prizefighter as popular for his colorful, lower-class background as for his ring victories. The child of Irish immigrant laborers, Heenan grew up to become an enforcer for Tammany Hall; in many ways, he was an avatar of all that the YMCA found threatening. He was not a pure American, having strong ties to Europe. He was a blue-collar worker and did not seek to improve himself through study, preferring to seek manual occupation. Perhaps most important, though, his devotion to professional pugilism placed him in the midst of a world of gambling, corruption, and law-breaking. Most states had begun outlawing prizefights in the 1850s, finding that the surrounding culture of alcohol and free-spirited revelry clashed with Victorian-era morals and religion.[12]

Men like Gulick, with respectable backgrounds and academic achievements, lent credibility to the idea that exercise was more than a simple tool for lowly prizefighters to damage one another for public spectacle and a few dollars. As demonstrated by the clergyman's reference to professors, lawyers, and other high-class occupations behaving like fighters and athletes, the late nineteenth century marked the beginnings of what grew into a national obsession with health and fitness. Gulick and his followers transformed the now expansive YMCA from a purely social club to one that promoted men of industry to make their bodies stronger as a part of the overall person, including the study of "the manly art of self-defense."[13]

The YMCA's initial objections to physical education programs were ultimately pushed aside, and as a worldwide organization it has taken on the mantle of social athletics, the ministry portion of its activities becoming less of a focus. The early members tended to see sport as a two-way street, at once drawing in young men who would normally have avoided blatant evangelism and purely devotional meetings, as well as strengthening the bodies of those same young men who could then serve more effectively abroad as missionaries. This attitude resulted in a feedback loop: Muscular young men were recruited through athletics, made physically capable by participating in them, and sent off to serve as teachers at other locations where their virility would attract more young men. This concept appealed most to medical professionals and those who favored an interpretation of the Bible that called for care to be taken of the body as a "temple of the Holy Spirit."[14]

Spreading Democracy

The success of Charles Darwin's evolutionary model had a profound influence on at least some advocates of the emergent Christian masculinity.

George MacDonald, author of such classics as *The Princess and the Goblin* (1872), appears to have applied the concept of natural selection in his telling and re-telling of fairy tales. In MacDonald's world, the central hero—Curdie, a young man from a family of miners—must overcome the forces of evil both through his physical agility and spiritual enlightenment. When pitted against opponents and situations equal to his strength, Curdie overcomes them through new spiritual insights. MacDonald is one example of a writer who suggested, as many would later, that the model of natural selection could be used to explain the success of Christianity in its spread around the world.[15]

As Hoganson convincingly illustrates, the dedication of many nineteenth-century American men to following a particular ideal of Darwinian social and financial success was not limited to religious institutions like the YMCA, but was instead a broader cultural conception of what constituted masculinity. Progressing from the Victorian era into the twentieth century, individual achievement came to the center of male social life. Accompanying this general focus on the individual's success was a gender-specific orientation of men toward aggression and ultimately violence. Like Curdie conquering his goblins with spirituality in one hand and a sword in the other, successful masculine leaders of the American state were perceived, in the eyes of the public, as builders of peace only through warfare.[16] The nineteenth century was transformative for American masculinity in this regard.

However, it is apparent that the transformation was one of enactment rather than the underlying schema of what constituted the masculine. Passion, for instance, was considered an essential part of manhood at both the beginning and end of the century, but there was a drastic change in the ways in which it could be suitably expressed in public and the subjects about which it was acceptable to be passionate.[17] In his classic *American Manhood* (1993), E. Anthony Rotundo explains that, at the beginning of the nineteenth century, two young men in a physical dispute would be marked with "a badge of evil" for demonstrating a lack of self-control. By the start of the twentieth century, however, the same young men would receive nods of approval from their seniors for behaving in a way to build character and show personal resilience.[18]

Nor were such activities limited to youth; men across the social spectrum found a need to express their individual achievements and capabilities in the aftermath of the economic depression of 1893. As the nineteenth century came to a close, more and more men had followed the model of early YMCA membership and moved into white-collar careers in the interest of upward mobility. The depression halted this mobility, though, and with it the sense of self-worth gained through financial success. It became unpleasantly apparent at that time, then, that a man with a passion for his work was susceptible to economic decline outside of his control. With such a tenuous thread supporting masculine identity, attentions turned to elements of individual life that could be more readily controlled. This led to a growing concern over the physical health (or lack thereof) among urban, white-collar professionals.[19]

Rather suddenly—at least, that is, as suddenly as any sociocultural transformation can occur—the American public developed something of an obsession with health, vitality, and personal resilience. This shift is palpable in YMCA history as Gulick and others spread their muscular Christianity ever farther. Public concern over the popularity of pugilism and other athletic endeavors was silenced by a newfound appreciation for neo-primitivism that viewed life as a Darwinian struggle for survival. The culmination of this metaphoric worldview was seen in warfare and military culture as fertile soil for building stalwart men of a truly masculine nature. The nation could not afford to be constantly seeking new war fronts, however, nor could all men serve, so sport came to be seen as a proxy for the struggle of man against the world.[20]

If the confluence of militarism, the cult of sport, muscular Christianity, and the generalized fear of urban living as degenerative to the vital forces of the American man were to be manifest in human form, that form would not be altogether different from Theodore Roosevelt. After surviving a sickly childhood, Roosevelt undertook a lifelong project of personal development, both physical and intellectual, that came to epitomize the new breed of American masculinity: powerful in body, confident in deed, and willing to pursue personal passions at the risk of self, family, and fortune. He followed the upper-middle class pattern established by prior generations of Anglo-Americans on the East Coast by receiving a university education, but broke with bookishness in order to practice "the strenuous life" of woodsmanship, pugilism, ranching, and other bodily pursuits in the interest of building up both health and character.[21]

The desire of Roosevelt and others to build up their bodies through neo-primitivism included recreational sports, camping, and dabbling in the labor careers of the lower classes. It also led Americans, for the first time in decades, to consider the larger world as a potential source of useful material for the development of the new masculinity. In a curious historical episode, Roosevelt—avid as he was about combat sports—crossed paths with Yamashita Yoshiaki, an expert judo instructor from Tokyo's newly founded Kodokan institute (more about the Kodokan and judo in later chapters). Roosevelt's time as president had caught up with his health and he was seeking a new avocation to aid in weight loss. After a demonstration of Yamashita's impressive abilities, Roosevelt retained him for private lessons.[22]

Just as the new willingness to engage in sport was a continuation of underlying cultural values of male passion, the seemingly progressive outlook on foreign cultures as a source of useful tools for building character extended only as far as underlying traditional values held. Roosevelt, despite his interest in foreign politics and military expeditions, was still an evangelical at heart, as indicated by a letter he wrote in 1908 to a student volunteer leader: He wrote that "men of ability to lead the aggressive forces of Christianity" were needed more than ever.[23] Not simply symbolic, it has been convincingly argued that the martial metaphor for building masculine character gave ample justification for warfare in the early twentieth century.[24] For Roosevelt and other civic leaders, foreign military expeditions went hand in hand with efforts to spread Christianity overseas. As a new generation of young men sought to assert themselves, they had learned the lessons available on the sports field; in particular, they had come to value competition as the preferred engine for character-building, with national warfare being the ultimate form of competition.[25]

Commercialization

As new generations took up the mantle, muscular Christianity has morphed over time. The image of the sport-playing, athletic young man well-equipped to somehow evangelize the audience through the use of his body is plainly seen in modern organizations like the Fellowship of Christian Athletes, Upward Sports, and Athletes in Action. The latter is an international organization that, along with planning camps and competitions for young athletes, hosts a number of high-profile events featuring famous current and former professional athletes, all in the interest of furthering a religious message. Like the early YMCA, these groups are focused on minors and college students. Similarly, commercial efforts in the muscular Christian tradition have also targeted youths, but that was the end result of prior decades in which the American public at large were undertaken with a health and fitness craze, the echoes of which can still be perceived in modern magazines and the proliferation of gym franchises that promise to make the consumer more fit, happy, energetic, and sexually desirable.

At the beginning of the twentieth century, American men were in the grip of a crisis. Social commentators became critical of the negative effects that burgeoning urban, white-collar jobs had wrought on a once virile and active male population. Following the Civil War and through the 1893 depression, psychic damage was perceived as an epidemic among upper-class professionals, a cure for which could be found by supplementing the "neurasthenic effects of sedentary jobs with the healthy effect of manual work ... suggested to the elite that some working-class activities might help prepare them better for the future."[26] Thus groups like the YMCA, known for bringing together such men, turned to reformers like Gulick to imbue their membership with the physical vigor needed to combat neurasthenia, the supposed nervous disorder from which so many elite men were suffering.

An impressive array of treatments was developed to supplement the positive application of physical exercise. In keeping with the neo-primitivism of Roosevelt and others, camping became a valuable tool for escaping the stresses of urban life and returning to a more "natural" existence in the wilderness (though, it should be noted, in a controlled setting with modern equipment and for a short time). Drawing on Anglo-American perceptions of Native American culture, men sought to experience a more elemental mode of being because "there were fewer robust heroes to serve as models for younger men, and the apparent closing of the frontier meant that young men had to search for new tests to replace the challenges of the wild West." Lacking a frontier to conquer, the rising individualism of the twentieth century meant that men could now negotiate their notions of masculinity through personal challenges with the out-of-doors. Boys were offered the same opportunity through new organizations like the Boy Scouts of America (founded in 1910) which, like the YMCA, was imported from England with the express purpose of allaying social problems.[27]

As individual men now embarked on a mission to defeat their personal neuroses through sports and wilderness adventuring to build healthier bodies, they also focused on the fuel for those activities. Naturally, men were not alone in their newfound gastronomic interests given that women have, historically, been charged with preparing meals in many American homes. Consequently, a number of food reformers were women like Catharine Beecher (1800–1878), sister to Harriet Beecher Stowe and advocate for public moral education. As a Calvinist, Beecher believed that moderation and temperance were the keys to a spiritually and physically healthy life, but also realized that the public might dismiss her argument as religiously motivated. Instead, she urged men and women alike to consume less food because "in proportion as man becomes elevated, this lowest species of enjoyment gives place to higher and more refined pleasure."[28] Dietary discretion was important not for religious reasons, but because the social elite did not seek out such base pleasures. In appealing to the American desire for upward mobility so prevalent among the new individualists, Beecher and those like her were able to forward their position that everyone should eat less and move more in order to resolve social woes.

Remedies for bodily problems were not so disparate that all reformers focused on individual concerns. Indeed, many such health advocates were like cereal inventor John Harvey Kellogg (1852–1943). Seen as somewhat radical at the time even among like-minded Seventh-day Adventists, Kellogg was a physician who supported vegetarianism, physical exercise, and various "water cures" to rid the body of toxic substances from exercise and food that "must be hurried out of the system with great rapidity." In keeping with this philosophy, he founded a sanitarium in Battle Creek, Michigan, where members of the upper-class could stay to have their neurasthenia treated through holistic methods. Realizing that not everyone would be able to undertake such involved treatment, Kellogg and his brother also marketed one of the first commercial breakfast cereals (to clean one's inner regions) and called on all levels of society to bathe frequently to clean one's outer parts (he believed that clogged pores led to kidney disease and hysteria).[29]

Taken together, physical exercise, a controlled diet, and neo-primitivism formed core elements of a new kind of American life in which the individual took on an adversarial tone with the outside world. The psyche was constantly being assaulted by neurasthenic urbanity, the body by disease and weakness, the personal character by corrupting influences of modernity. These changes were negotiated by emphasizing the role of competition as a means to invigorate the personal and collective strength of American males. Competition was added to previously non-competitive pursuits (spelling bees, Sunday school lessons, art displays, etc.) in order to encourage participation and to heighten the effects of character-building. With the emphasis now being placed on competition as a positive social mode for men and boys and the general desire for greater physical wellbeing, two individual sports, both once-maligned, took hold of Americans' attention: boxing and bodybuilding. Pugilists were no longer seen as brutish avatars of human cockfighting, but as the possessors of profound self-discipline, self-denial, controlled diet, and the mental toughness needed to overcome the neurasthenic onslaught.[30]

Strongmen and Fisticuffs

Tom Manfre, 1953 Mister World bodybuilding champion, recalls meeting his inspiration, the legendary Charles Atlas, who told him, "God was good to me, and I'm sure He'll be good to you." Atlas was the stage name of Angelo Siciliano, who arrived in New York at the turn of the twentieth century a malnourished child and proceeded to build himself up through daily exercise and careful nutrition. Advertising his transformation from self-described "97-pound weakling" to muscle man, Atlas took advantage of a personal narrative from his childhood in which a more physically gifted fellow pushed him down and kicked sand in his face at a beach. Printing ads with the story in comic books and magazines, Atlas' company sold an at-home training regimen that both reflects and had an influence on changing public perception of the male body.[31]

If Atlas, with his exhortations to trust in a higher power, represented an older breed of muscular Christian, the new breed of the 1920s could be seen in the wake of his success. As commercialization took hold, two major shifts occurred in the Western conceptions of masculinity. First, the commercial ventures coincided with a secularization of manliness. No longer was it necessary for a "real man" to also be a churchgoer. Second, the hallmarks of masculinity continued to be muscular; however, the focus slipped from practical (that is, sports-based) physical prowess to more visual depictions of masculinity. For instance, in their important study of male body image as portrayed through action figures, Pope, et al. (1998), found that both the toys' muscle size and definition increased dramatically over time. In their study, the researchers measured the dimensions of action figures' physical traits to see how they compared with real human bodies. As one example, the authors note that the GI Joe Extreme figure, "if extrapolated to 70 in. in height … would sport larger biceps than any bodybuilder in history."[32]

At the same time, bodybuilders found success in the film industry, with stars like Arnold Schwarzenegger and Sylvester Stallone portraying tough men of action on the silver screen where the previous generation knew stars like John Wayne and Kirk Douglas. In the popular media, muscles were growing larger. This would snowball over the decades into a major point of frustration for American men, who could not hope to reproduce the perfect bodies portrayed in media. This proved especially troublesome for generations of boys who grew up with comic books and action figures with such prodigious musculature. The psychological impact of having childhood heroes whose bodies one could never hope to grow into has been largely understudied, but there can be little doubt that it was a significant contributing factor to the proliferation of body image and eating disorders, illegal anabolic steroid usage, and the public fascination with bodybuilding that took off in the waning years of the century. The question then becomes how, in the course of less than one hundred years, male bodies in America went from something clothed and ignored out of modesty to objects for public fascination and critique.

After 1900, the nation placed greater emphasis on the "muscular" and less on the "Christianity." This may be tied to increasing levels of immigration leading to greater ethnic diversity in the urban centers, but it is just as likely related to a commercial turn in the public commentary on health and fitness. To be sure, it is possible to make money on religious activity, but astute entrepreneurs of the early twentieth century saw an even greater potential for wealth in the rising desire of Americans to be healthier. It was as a direct result of this turn in public interest that strongmen and bodybuilders made the leap from circus sideshow acts to mainstream fitness gurus, taking on the status of media idols. Simultaneously, pugilists, also a once-marginal group of athletes whose income and social status revolved around their participation in spectacle, came to be considered paragons of health, embodying the virtues of the new American individualism: self-discipline, personal courage, a strict diet, and physical ability.

Bederman (1995) points out that the drive toward neo-primitivism in the interest of building character was directly responsible for the rise of the muscle and fitness culture that arose from those more general panaceas espoused by Kellogg and others. This development is reflected in the idealized male body. During the late nineteenth century, American preference for depictions of the male form in art and media tended toward a lean, wiry form. In the early years of the twentieth century, the form morphed into a still thin, but more muscular shape, like that larger prizefighters. The connecting logic here is reasonable given the premises. Assuming that neurasthenia was a genuine threat to the overall wellbeing of middle- and upper-class urban men, that the condition came about through lack of physical activity combined with a unique type of stress caused by white-collar work, and that lower-class men did not suffer from these conditions, then the solution must lie in imitating the lower-class. This could certainly be accomplished through diet (lean foods and not too much), but also by turning to the appropriate pastimes, like pugilism. In order to live like the supposedly healthier members of the urban lower class, it would follow suit that a healthy man should look like them as well. Manual laborers, by virtue of daily activity, were more muscular than their managerial

A barn-side advertisement along Highway 99 shows health as a commodity in the years prior to World War II (Prints and Photographs Division, LOC).

counterparts. Greater muscle, in short, indicated physical and psychological wellbeing.[33]

Unlike earlier reformers whose attentions centered on indirect methods for the curing of physical and psychic ills, such as chewing food slowly, consuming specially treated mineral water, or adhering to a rigorous bathing regimen, fighters and strongmen had the advantage in advertising of demonstrable feats. Either a boxer won in the ring or he did not. A strongman, regardless of actual bulk, could lift prodigious amounts of weight or bend rigid objects. The public took notice of these feats such that even the YMCA, now fully supportive of the movement to attract young men by offering physical education and sports programs, was hiring retired prizefighters, religious or otherwise—more often otherwise—to serve as fulltime directors of its gymnasiums under the assumption that, however else they may feel about the Association's activities, competent former pugilists at least knew how to train young men to be strong and fit.[34]

The feats of strongmen had always been attractive to crowds of gawkers, thus making them a natural fit for circuses and other traveling entertainment venues. But as their abilities came to be associated with physical health, the scrutiny took on a scientific bent. Before long these performers' training methods were being discussed and replicated in educational institutions like Harvard, where George Windship and other medical school students developed means of molding male bodies into the shape now preferred by the general fitness-seeking public and, perhaps more important from the physicians' perspective, capable of recreating their displays of bodily power. Windship makes for an excellent case study of early popular strongmen because he stood 5'7" and managed to lift a thousand pounds, lending demonstrable credence to his claims and, like the later Charles Atlas, providing a narrative of accomplishment that would draw public interest, particularly from boys and men of small stature.[35]

The 1920s, Secularism and Print Media

By the advent of the Gilded Age, widespread public practice of religious austerity in the interest of improving self and society was well out of fashion, even as evangelical institutions like the YMCA, thoroughly rooted in urban America, went to great lengths in the transformation of their methods to appeal to a younger audience. Individualism was the order of the day and a successful man, both in life and business, relied on his personal improvement. Competition was so heavily embedded in all aspects of social interaction that even recreational endeavors like sports and reading centered on training the individual to reach greater levels of achievement. This can be seen in the movement toward boxing as a spectator sport and a means of personal development. Likewise, print media of the time at once reflected and influenced the zeitgeist of personal development: intellectually, financially, and physically.

While upper-class men sought to emulate the activities of their blue collar counterparts, those of the growing middle class found themselves— many for the first time—able to afford a modicum of leisure. Indeed, because of the highly competitive nature of industry in the 1920s, these men came to identify themselves at least as much by their recreational pursuits as by their primary occupations. With such limited time to relieve stress and build the individual's capabilities, the sacrifices of traditional religious life became less of a concern for a large number of those working in the cities.[36] This proved problematic in terms of pastimes that involved solely intellectual participation since the neurasthenic condition was considered a direct result of "brain work" that had come to occupy the days of men in the middle and upper classes. The solution was to spend one's off hours developing the body and attempting to follow programs of self-cultivation through bodily and neo-primitive outdoor hobbies.[37]

In direct response to this very apparent public turn away from communal practice of austerity and toward individualism and competitive recreation, the YMCA continued to transfer resources to its physical education divisions, building more gymnasiums and hiring more directors whose theological backgrounds were less robust than their biceps. Although the evangelism of the organization was not as pronounced, Gulick and his followers maintained that they had simply "taken the gymnastic work of the world and remodeled it so that we can use it successfully."[38] Despite this, the gymnasiums themselves showed the slowly widening rift between the original evangelical zealousness of the founding YMCA membership and its "physical work" with young men in the urban centers. In addition to directors who were frequently unschooled Christians (and in some cases, not religious at all), the buildings tended to feature separate entrances, were disconnected or wholly separate from the main compounds, and usually had almost entirely different memberships.[39]

As early as the 1890s, YMCA circulars like *Young Men's Era* were paying for their print runs through advertising while also offering non-religious advice articles, mostly aimed at self-improvement to the end of personal profit. Hopkins notes, "At the moment it was appealing most strongly to the virtues of honesty and integrity, the *Era* was advertising patent medicines, real estate, and gold mining stock."[40] The Association, then, was as much subject to as it was an agent of social reform. As the twentieth century rolled on, secular publications followed suit, becoming sounding horns for the various recreational communities of consumption that were now a major factor in bestowing men with a sense of their own masculinity (or, at least, how to achieve it). What would have been considered effeminate one century prior was now a hallmark of American masculinity; certain acts of recreation took on the patina of manliness and, therefore, reached new levels of popularity in the public sphere through both personal involvement and consumption of mass publications.[41]

Here, then, was another crossover point between the waning muscular Christianity of the previous generation and a commercialized, industrial approach to masculine consumption that came to replace it. Even YMCA circulars featured advertisements and articles urging men to improve their minds, bodies, and bank accounts. In the popular press, *Physical Culture* enjoyed a healthy circulation among men from all walks of life. Founded by bodybuilder and self-improvement guru Bernarr Macfadden in 1899, the magazine—in keeping with the widespread fear of neurasthenia—was initially aimed at overcoming disease, but soon covered topics such as training muscles to be larger and more powerful, improving relationships with co-workers, and maximizing profits. Interestingly, advertisements for various programs to improve one's English indicate that a large portion of the readership was immigrants.[42]

By the 1920s, bodybuilding was among the physical pastimes most closely associated with the new masculinity and self-improvement trend. Insofar as larger muscles were seen as a means to personal success in life and business by indirect competition with other men, pugilism offered a much more straightforward method of overcoming adversaries. With pugilism no longer the topic of nearly universal condemnation, men all over the United States were flocking to YMCAs and private gymnasiums to study the "manly art of self-defense" and to emulate the physical feats and physiques of prizefighting champions. Boxing offered many men a unique sort of personal interactivity as they looked on professional fighters as avatars of masculinity, successful in their goals through personal improvement and occupied full-time in what was, to most men, a recreational endeavor.[43]

The drama of prizefighting, literally embodied by champion fighters and (re)enacted by communities of consumption at the newsstand and the

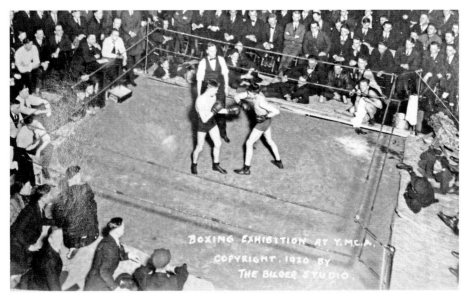

Boxing Exhibition at YMCA (Prints and Photographs Division, LOC).

boxing gym, gave American men a fantastical release from the mundane existence of office work and an alternative social hierarchy in which personal physical accomplishment allowed even the lowest member of a corporation to win social prestige by virtue of his participation. In what amounts to the physical manifestation of a modern myth-making, men laboring under the dual stress of "brain work" and social pressure to make their muscles larger and stronger found an escape by means of acting out the roles of champions at the gym, reading magazines dedicated to masculine topics (including pugilism), and participating in communities of men in order to share narratives of struggle and success by reflecting on the admirable qualities of mythologized professional fighters.[44]

From the end of the nineteenth century through the 1920s and 1930s, the rugged individualism that arose from the muscular Christian imperative that men become stronger and more capable helped usher in a new era of public focus on personal achievement, which, coincidentally, contradicted the idea of being reliant on a deity or religious institution for worldly success in business or one's personal life. Self-improvement came to be seen as the means by which one could most efficiently utilize one's free time. To combat the psychological dangers of "brain work," the development of the body through exercise and boxing came to be considered the manliest of activities. The new male physical ideal was larger and more muscular than it had been in the previous century and public interest in prizefighting was now more acceptable as men projected themselves onto the bodies of favored champions. Boxing and bodybuilding provided an escape from the hazards of the hierarchical workplace and redefined what constituted masculinity.

Challenges to Masculinity: Women and Suffrage

On a number of fronts, twentieth century American society can best be described as revolutionary. Religious piety and abstinence gave way to a new consumerism. Collective concern for the community was upended by individualism and a newfound need for self-improvement. Elements of lower-class life became the topic of upper-class recreations. Given this pattern, it is perhaps unsurprising that newly minted standards of masculinity were immediately threatened by the "new woman." It has been suggested by some experts that contestation is one of the defining elements of masculine identity due to the supposed hegemony often attributed to male social roles. Likely because of this, masculinities are also fluid, varied, and sometimes contradictory. These are highlighted in challenges from the "new woman," not only due to the power implications of female enfranchisement, but because of the peripheral activities in which such women participated.[45]

Bodybuilding and pugilism offered the same central attraction to men: power. Whether that power was literal (e.g., the ability to lift heavy objects), social (intimidation, respect from peers), or mythic (acting out one's personal narrative in the boxing ring or projecting onto other pugilists), the main goal was the acquisition of personal capability. An evolution-inspired way of thinking about this change is: Social behavior holds that the focus on men's physical growth stemmed from their desire to display sexual dimorphism. Over the course of the nineteenth century, more fathers began to work away from the home, leaving their heirs' upbringing to others. Consequently, the generation of boys who would become the consumer base for physical culture in the early twentieth century was, to a great extent, raised by women. In such a situation, those boys would always associate their mothers with authority—a complex in direct contradiction to their fathers' worldview in which women were meant to be obedient. Increasing one's size and physical formidability afforded men the chance to apply the new American competitiveness to the body, which could be more readily controlled than the variegated social revolution happening around him.[46]

This came in the wake of America's nationally traumatic 1917 entry into the First World War. The country was split over the propriety of their erstwhile neutral homeland to enter into a foreign dispute in which the government and people had mixed interests. Americans of German and English dissent disagreed over which side to support, and even the sinking of the RMS *Lusitania* did little to clarify the public's feelings. Eventually the U.S. came to the aid of the Entente Powers and declared war on Germany, albeit as an independent actor and not a formal member of the alliance. This proved a nationwide learning experience given that Americans had never previously engaged in what many termed a "total war." Both technologically and strategically, too, World War I was a new frontier for servicemen as they emerged from an era of more or less direct warfare into battlefields featuring terrible new killing machines, airborne combat, trench fighting, and open landscapes. Despite a costly victory over the Germans, public anxiety on the home front continued to intensify with the return of veterans, whose experience was little understood by their friends and families.

Adding to this anxiety about the place of male power in the world was the effect of the new individualism on women. Despite the arguments of traditionalist commentators like Beecher, American women attained suffrage in 1920 after decades of public demonstrations and legal arguments. This is a clear indication of the degree to which women had the same autonomy as men. Individualism came with assertion of the self in social settings, too, and the 1920s saw the introduction of a consumer fitness industry almost entirely separate from that aimed at men. Women were wearing more revealing swimsuits for the first time and appropriated traditionally masculine behaviors like smoking and drinking. This pattern drove men to greater levels of idealized sexual dimorphism; the perfect American male physique grew larger and more muscular.[47]

Not all emphasis was given to appearance, however, as empowered women were also encroaching on the male monopoly on organized fighting. A few exceptional cases aside, the boxing ring was the province of men, a sort of refuge from other arenas in which women were now appearing, including the fitness realm. Legal issues as regarded female prizefighting in earlier decades would continue to be unresolved until much later in the century, but that didn't prevent women from negotiating other methods of self-defense practice, such as *jujutsu*, which was most popularly introduced to the British by railway engineer William Barton-Wright in 1898. The world at large took note of its potential after the Japanese victory over Russia in 1905. The Japanese government trumpeted its application of *jujutsu* tactics as the means by which a small nation could overcome a giant one just as a larger body may be defeated by a frail one.[48]

The reason for this rhetoric was well-founded. The *jujutsu* (a Japanese term literally meaning "gentle method or technique") of which Westerners were then aware was known in Japan as Kano *jujutsu*. The same system, once completely formulated into a comprehensive curriculum, would take on the name judo, meaning "gentle Way," as will be discussed further in the next chapter. It is an important distinction to make, however, as the older, medieval styles of *jujutsu* in Japan featured all manner of fistic techniques, including grappling, striking, and a broad range of weapon skills. Most of these maneuvers were eliminated in Kano *jujutsu* for being too dangerous and uncivilized in what the creator described as a more peaceable age of humanity. Kano *jujutsu* emphasized less dangerous wrestling holds, locks, and throws intended to disable an opponent without causing undue injury to either party. This is the system studied by Barton-Wright and is clearly visible in the few photographs and descriptions of women practicing the art from this period.

Women fighting for their right to vote took note of this feat and sympathetic male experts took to training women in the art, even producing instructional booklets and, later, short films to educate women on their potential to overcome male size and strength. When both British and American press outlets announced that groups of suffragettes would begin receiving an education in *jujutsu* en masse, it marked the first time that the women's movement and the Japanese grappling method were publicly unified.[49] Predictably, this was disconcerting for men who had lost their monopoly on the vote in 1920 and their hold on the household a generation before, and were in the process of losing exclusive hold of the "breadwinner" position in society at large. One response, as demonstrated by prizefighting's popularity in the 1920s, was to dedicate more time and attention to the "manly art of self-defense" as a simultaneous escape from the outside world and a supportive community in which masculinities could be constructed, negotiated, expressed, and validated.[50]

Barton-Wright's legacy did eventually continue in a rather unusual fashion, even by the standards of martial arts pioneers. Upon his return to London, he abandoned his engineering trade and opened an academy for the study of martial arts and physical health. In what may have been the first instance of a Westerner instituting his own take on Asian martial arts, he combined the methods of fighting he had accrued in his world travels and called his new system Bartitsu. Inviting expert instructors from every fighting system available, the Bartitsu School of Arms and Physical Culture opened its doors in 1900 and offered courses on Barton-Wright's proprietary method, along with Kano *jujutsu*, French savate, boxing, wrestling, fencing and cane fighting. Other physical culture offerings included the patent medicines and therapies of the day, such as electrotherapy and a full range of stretching and fitness exercises. The club eventually suffered too many financial losses and was forced to cease operations, but not until two other curious historical interactions took place.

In 1900, Sir Arthur Conan Doyle published the Sherlock Holmes story "The Adventure of the Empty House," in which the famous consulting detective faces down his arch nemesis, the fiendishly brilliant Professor Moriarty, at the Reichenbach Falls. At the edge of a sheer drop, the two struggle to pitch each other over the edge. Holmes proves the victor, later attributing his survival to training in "Baritsu," an obvious misspelling of Bartitsu. This would lead to increased public interest in the Asian martial arts generally, but was especially positive for Barton-Wright's school, at least in the short term. Conan Doyle may simply have learned of Bartitsu from newspaper reports of the various London demonstrations held as a public relations measure, though the description given in his writing likely indicates that the author witnessed the system himself, perhaps even participating. Unfortunately, barring the appearance of any further documentation, the matter will remain a mystery worthy of his most popular character.

In order to bolster his club's offerings and to distribute the teaching load of such a large operation, Barton-Wright invited Japanese *jujutsu* experts to instruct at the institute. They rotated through, leaving after varying lengths of time, with the exception of one named Tani Yukio. Tani was nineteen when he first arrived in London in 1900 with his older brother, who soon returned to Japan. Tani taught at the Bartitsu School until 1903, after which he set out on his own. Desperate for money and finding that *jujutsu* is not a sufficiently pliable skill to qualify for other vocations available in Edwardian London, the young man retained the services of an entertainment promoter and took to engaging in public challenge matches against Western opponents, usually the largest available in order to demonstrate his skill at grappling. In 1904 Tani was able to accrue enough capital and students to open a *jujutsu* academy of his own, teaming up with another Japanese expatriate. The school was in operation only two years before closing. He went on to publish an instructional book on the art of grappling and, in 1918, became the first professional instructor of the London Budokwai, Europe's oldest Japanese martial arts organization, which remains open to this day, having produced many Olympic medalists in judo.

Boxing's Golden Age and the Great Depression

On July 2, 1921, the great American heavyweight Jack Dempsey (otherwise known as the "Manassa Mauler" and "Kid Black") fought Frenchman Georges Carpentier, widely touted as the best boxer in the world. It was a decidedly asymmetrical meeting. Dempsey's prowess was overwhelming and the European was clearly outmatched from the start. While an impressive show of force on Dempsey's part, the fight itself is not the reason for this event to be considered truly momentous. The match's promoter, Tex Rickard, had an outdoor stadium constructed to house the spectators, charging varying amounts for the different seating levels. It was built to hold 80,000 attendees; some estimate that as many as 91,000 turned out. This marked the first time that a sporting event drew in more than a million dollars in ticket sales. Thanks to the work of the RCA Corporation, the fight's commentary was also the first nationwide radio broadcast. Boxing, as both an amateur and professional sport, had entered its golden age.[51]

Pugilism's popularity can be credited to a few chief factors: neo-primitivism, the aforementioned transformation in ideals of body image, scientific efficacy, and the onset of the Great Depression. Partly due to the changing status of women in American society and the autonomy that came with it, many men sought refuge in the world of the boxing gym and the shared culture of the public fight-performance. Sociologically, it is important to point out that identity-based communities draw not only on what the group's constituency has in common, but on what it does not. To strengthen the unity and resolve of a consumptive community, it is necessary to draw a clear delineation between self and other, in-group and out-group.[52] In the case of American boxing, the neo-primitive variety of masculinity espoused by Roosevelt and others found its fruition in an almost tribal mentality whereby men could act out fantasies of a supposedly simpler life in which fights, though more physically strenuous than mundane office work, afforded a more animalistic, natural outlet for nervous energy.

Boxing, like bodybuilding, transforms the body. In the 1920s a culture

This undated photo from the famous **Piping Rock Club** shows upper-class boys being tempered through boxing (Prints and Photographs Division, LOC).

of mass consumption seized the public as more people moved into urban areas, or at least attempted to imitate the urban lifestyle. A significant part of this new consumptive mode involved marketing via magazines, newspapers, radio, billboards, and motion pictures. These new methods of reaching the public also loosed a powerful ability to influence the individual's perception of self and body. While companies now offered cures for nervous psychological disorders caused by modernity, they also generated a new kind of anxiety in which the consumer had to constantly self-monitor for imperfection, where images of perfection created by advertisers served as the measuring device. In this way, "advertising became the guardian of the new morality." This, naturally, and for the first time on such a scale, created the classic circular process of profitable marketing. Men were shown standards of perfection that they did not meet, and worked to correct their flaws (e.g., by becoming more muscular); advertisers then offered a yet more extreme measure of perfection, spurring the individual on in a Sisyphean quest for an ever-distant ideal.[53]

Advertisers were able to commandeer much of the muscular Christian legacy during the Gilded Age because American involvement in the First World War sounded the death knell of muscular Christianity as a major political and religious movement. The reasons for this decline were twofold: the push for America to enter the war and subsequent backlash and the contradictory message of the movement itself. It was perhaps inevitable that theologians seeking to increase the masculine composition of young men in order to resolve the effeminacy of white-collar work would push for them to go to war. During the period leading to and during World War I, many preachers publicly supported sending soldiers to Europe so that they could learn and act out their masculinity. In this case, it was not uncommon for patriotic and religious messages to be mixed, as preachers "wrapped themselves in the flag" and "characterized America's cause as God's cause." Even during peacetime, these same clergymen encouraged boxing as a "moral equivalent of war."[54] Immediately after the war, a sympathetic public supported critics who blamed muscular Christian advocates for leading the nation to war and, in a moment as symbolic as it was literal, pulled down the YMCA statue, "Christian Student," on the Princeton University campus in 1929.

The message of muscular Christianity was also internally conflicted. For decades, churches and organizations like the YMCA had been imparting to young men that they should surrender themselves to the service of God; that they would be at their most useful if physically fit, psychologically sound, and fully self-sufficient; and that the religious community would be the best place for the cultivation of these qualities. Developing self-sufficiency, however, led men to avoid relying on others and added to twentieth century individualism, inherently drawing the self away from both the religious community and its message of total reliance on a higher power. Whether consciously or not, men who followed the precepts of a muscular Christian worldview found that traditional principles of irrevocable human fallibility and weakness did not fit well with their stated goals of becoming autonomous supermen.[55]

Boxing offered an outlet to men seeking a physical form of expression, which was validated by means of scientific, empirical evidence. As the influence of religion receded from public life as the primary source of personal fulfillment for the masses, it was replaced with secular offerings of a more rationalized nature, including psychology and physiology. Boxing, also called the "sweet science," represented a test of skill and principle wherein the outcome could be observed, measured, and studied. While health reformers of the nineteenth century, such as Kellogg and Beecher, were forthright about their religious affiliations, the corporate-based sources of information with which they were replaced tended to focus on scientific (or, more often, scientistic) language to sell their wares. A 1927 advertisement for Bran Flakes features an image of a woman who is clearly exhausted, stating that she "could be beautiful" if only she had the "natural bulk" lacking in her diet. Similarly, a 1931 Shredded Wheat ad pictures a father and son next to copy that calls the cereal's fiber a source of strength. Rather than the vague claims made by religious reformers, the impersonal corporate products could be tested. Indeed, a doubting individual could consume Bran Flakes and, with some certainty, the evidence for "natural bulk" would be rather apparent.[56]

Bodybuilders were able to sell their products in the same way. Beginning in the 1920s, Charles Atlas, the famous "ninety-seven-pound weakling" who recompositioned his body through diet and exercise, sold his at-home training course through magazines like *Physical Culture*. As with the above cereal advertisements, any skeptical reader could try Atlas' program and, provided he followed it strictly, reading the fine print, would likely see an increase in strength. In the print itself, this is explained by Atlas as simple adherence to scientific physiology: "You sow the seeds of disease, and you MUST reap the penalty of poor health as a result of your disobedience of Nature's unalterable laws."[57] While Atlas himself was a religious man, he had learned to keep this hidden, instead drawing attention and revenue by relying on public trust in provable, science-like rationalism.

In 1933, *Physical Culture* added a subtitle describing it as "The Personal

Problem Magazine." This solidified the aim of the publication to help the individual become lean, muscular, and psychologically sound. It ran articles and advertisements promising to cure all manner of ailments, improve the physique, and reveal ways of emulating movie stars. The image of the well-fed man as a symbol of wealth was dead and supplanted with the new marks of opulence; having the time and resources to exercise, buy expensive health food, and tan on the beach demonstrated one's success.[58] Macfadden, the magazine's publisher, held contests for the "World's Most Perfectly Developed Man," which were essentially the earliest of what would now be considered bodybuilding competitions. First among the champions was none other than Charles Atlas.[59]

Carrying newfound fame under his belt, Atlas teamed with partners in the advertising industry to expand his reach. After the crash of 1929, marking the onset of the Great Depression, Atlas' Dynamic Tension system remained the most popular of its kind. This may have been due to the growing anxiety brought on by such monetary and social challenges, leading each individual to seek out ways of negotiating a new world of hardship. This would reasonably allow for the continuing success of self-improvement products in the years leading up to World War II. Regardless of the causes for its initial success, though, the marketing experts behind Atlas found an even more eager audience than the adult health and fitness set by pandering to young men via comic books. Exact years are disputed, but some time during the 1930s Dynamic Tension began to appear in the back pages of popular graphic novels, offering to teach readers with less-than-powerful physiques to recreate Atlas' personal myth of self-improvement. By running these claims as follow-ups to narratives in which muscle-bound superheroes overcome impossible odds by demonstrating their perfection, the message was clearly that awkward youths entering a world of financial uncertainty could achieve the status of perfect men like Atlas—who actually held such a title—through hard work and time.[60]

Many of these same young men, seeking fame, fortune, and masculine character, set out to build themselves not just through Dynamic Tension and similar programs, but by joining boxing gyms in record numbers. During the two decades leading up to the Second World War, it was common for 8000 to 10,000 new professional prizefighters to be licensed annually. These numbers are roughly three to four times recent years' averages. Such an influx of fighters invariably resulted in an abundance of talent, which, in turn, attracted even larger audiences through more and more exciting displays of fistic aptitude. An apt comparison, both artistically and temporally, would be the golden age of pugilism to that of jazz: Both arts burst onto the national landscape after years of quiet development, both public performances of a percussive nature in which the artists must improvise to be successful.⁶¹

In terms of fight-as-performance, it drew (and continues to draw) on traditional notions of physical conflict as a source for and protector of masculine honor. While older generations were concerned with personal disagreement as a source of fights, organized boxing during the golden age simply required the motivation of the gym, neighborhood, ethnic group, or internal psychology.⁶² The same can be said of bodybuilding and nutrition practices, with the stage being daily life and the performance falling on each member of the audience. In the years leading up to World War II, masculinity, then, transformed from a communal to an individual performance. It went from religiously based to consumer-based, seeking ever greater levels of differentiation between men and women.⁶³

A sense of control over one's physical environs through the use of the body is clearly a significant part of the Western idea of masculinity. Presented with the possibility of transforming one's own body to match an unrealistic ideal (as with Charles Atlas' comic book advertisements that helped spark a bodybuilding boom) or through the application of social violence to achieve certain ends by negotiating the personal myth and communal need for a uniquely masculine sphere, it would appear that neither option is especially appealing. Rather, returning to the idea of muscular Christianity, it may be necessary to look outside the immediate cultural milieu to locate an alternative model of masculine expression that could be seen as both acceptable and legitimate. In this case, I propose that the model in question resulted from Western interpretations of certain historical peculiarities of late nineteenth and early twentieth century Japan.

2

Karate, Boxing and Other Japanese Creations

Even if it seems certain that you will lose, retaliate. Neither wisdom nor technique has a place in this. A real man does not think of victory or defeat. He plunges recklessly towards an irrational death. By doing this, you will awaken from your dreams.

—Tsunetomo Yamamoto

DANIEL: I thought it came from Buddhist temples and stuff like that.
MIYAGI: You watch too much TV.

—*The Karate Kid* (1984)

A list of well-known Japanese cultural traits written today would likely contain the word *bushido*. Literally meaning "warrior path," it evokes images of proud samurai fighting for their ideals and defending traditions of the type dramatized in the Tom Cruise film *The Last Samurai* (2003). Certainly this notion of the warrior class as guardians of tradition and possessors of admirable qualities is prevalent in both Japanese and American popular culture; however it is a case of what Hobbsbawm and Ranger term an "invented tradition."[1] In historical reality, *bushido* was not a codified set of beliefs, despite Inazo Nitobe's well-intentioned effort to interpret his own nation's social background for a Western audience through such a proxy.[2] In fact, the concept could not have existed during the heyday of the samurai, the Warring States Period (roughly 1467–1573 CE), because archipelago-wide, multigenerational warfare was the direct result of a total lack of federated identity. There simply was no Japan and, therefore, no Japanese identity for the samurai to guard.

Nitobe's goal in writing his *Bushido* (1972) seems to have been to explain how Western democratic principles could thrive in Japan even though his understanding of democracy relied on the existence of a core religious conviction (Christianity) to hold the democratic society together. His conclusion was that samurai ethics of honor and social obligation drawing on Confucian, Buddhist, and Shinto world orders passed on to the modern Japanese all the cultural properties necessary to reach fully democratic integration. Interestingly, Nitobe's sentiments, although no doubt well-intentioned, gave Japanese right-wing nationalists a tool to justify the morality of their expansionist policies in Asia and further fueled the drive to deify the emperor.[3]

During the Meiji Restoration (1868–1912 CE), Japanese national identity underwent significant overhauls along with virtually every other facet of the country, such as the construction of railroads, the introduction of electricity, replacement of the warrior class with a conscripted military, and the change to Western fashion in street wear. As might be expected, this was a time of social conflict and upheaval, different factions vying over influence in all areas of life, even athletics. The Meiji government established Western-style public education in 1872. By 1885 the mandatory system of school gymnastics (*gakko taiso*) was replaced with military gymnastics exercises (*heishiki taiso*).[4]

The movement toward militarism in public institutions was driven by a desire to expel the powerful foreign influence that had come on suddenly and created for the Japanese something of an identity crisis. Some members of society—particularly those who benefitted economically and socially from the arrival of foreign interests—adopted Western styles and modes wholeheartedly while others objected in various ways, sometimes picking and choosing the areas of conflict and acceptance depending on their circumstances. For example, in 1898 Ishikawa Yasujiro, a journalist with the *Mainichi* newspaper, introduced the term *haikara* ("high collar") to indicate those Japanese who had given themselves over to foreign influences, the term being a reference to the collars of the Western-style shirts favored by such individuals. The other side of the coin included men known as *bankara*, an amalgam of "collar" and *ban*, meaning "barbarian." The *bankara* man was one of action, adventure, and social conservatism through which he rejected Western fads and clung to a perceived Japanese ideal.[5]

Youths were inspired by their nation's performance against a much larger and ostensibly powerful foe in the Russo-Japanese War, prompting a wave of nationalistic fervor in boys' magazines and other popular media. One such magazine, started in 1908 by Oshikawa Shunro, was dedicated almost entirely to his romantic ideals regarding adventure and shunning materialism. Oshikawa pushed "a social Darwinistic view of society and believed that conflict would serve to expel decadence and overcivilized

Note the Western fitness equipment and military-inspired uniforms at this Japanese school (Prints and Photographs Division, LOC).

effeminacy." The stories he published went so far as to suggest that students administer beatings to those tainted with *haikara* aesthetics.[6]

In keeping with the move toward social Darwinism, the national government introduced *budo*, the overall category that refers to Japanese martial arts, to the school system. By 1931 all students at the middle and normal school levels were required to practice either judo (a jacketed form of wrestling) or kendo (fencing in armor using a bamboo pole to represent a sword). It is important to distinguish between *budo* and *bujutsu*. Generally (though, like most generalizations, there are a number of exceptions), *bujutsu* is used to refer to classical Japanese martial skills. This encompasses the methods of warfare developed primarily during the Warring States Period and, in most cases, the Edo Period (1603–1868 CE), including strategy, the use of various weapons, means of swimming in full armor, etc. *Bujutsu* is a word formed from the characters for "war" and "skill." *Budo*, a combination of the Chinese ideograms for "war" and "way" or "path," chiefly refers to those martial arts (or ways) developed during and after the Meiji Restoration. Such modern martial arts include judo, aikido, kendo, and karate, as well as non-competitive styles less common in the West, such as *kyudo* (Japanese archery) and *iaido* (the art of drawing a sword from its sheath). The *budo*, as indicated by the use of "way" rather than "skill," are primarily aimed at self-cultivation and often have little if anything to do with practical fighting ability.[7]

The formation of *budo* can be linked to the 1876 ban on carrying swords, which had been a signifier of status among the warrior class. Removing the swords from daily interaction heightened the sense of identity crisis among the once-powerful clan lords. In 1895, one of the ways they responded was by organizing the Dainippon Butoku-kai (Greater Japan Martial Virtue Society) with the goal of preserving traditional martial arts in a way that could be overseen and controlled by sympathetic experts. If the Butoku-kai represented one method of conserving tradition by institutionalizing technique, then the work of Kano Jigoro (1860–1938) represented another formed mainly around modernization and re-invention.[8]

Kano was an educator with a keen interest in both the unarmed fighting arts of Japan (frequently referred to as *jujutsu*) and modern scientific rationality. He grew up the scion of a fairly well-to-do household; his father insisted that he receive a thorough education that included instruction in foreign languages. Naturally bookish and somewhat meek as a youth, Kano desired to build his self-confidence in the style of Charles Atlas. Seeking to increase his masculine virility—or at least to avoid being roughed up by larger men—Kano, against his father's wishes, looked for someone to teach him the then-dying art of *jujutsu*. At the time, it was widely held that *jujutsu* was an activity for tough young men and had an air of the lower class. Kano was eventually able to locate one instructor and then another.

In 1882, after training in two of the old traditional methods, Kano founded his own organization, the Kodokan, "Place for the Study of the Way." Here he began to develop a new style, which he came to call judo, by having his students engage in rigorous sparring matches to test the validity of different techniques. As a modernist and a devotee of educational methodology, Kano saw his new creation as simply another step in the development of *jujutsu* and, therefore, the best way to perpetuate the tradition. Kano reasoned that if he took rough-and-tumble techniques of war and reconstituted them in a congenial, school-like setting (one of his mottos was "mutual welfare"), his trainees would progress more quickly and efficiently. Instead of the hermetic methods of direct bodily contact used to impart knowledge in the older systems, pupils were given a lecture explaining the principles of a technique, then allowed to practice with a partner as the instructor provided individual corrections. In this manner the new judo demonstrated the nationalist concept called *wakon yosai*, adoption of Western technology while retaining the Japanese mind.[9]

The main problem with preserving the spirit of *jujutsu* in the modern age, as Kano saw it, was overcoming the hurdle of its lowbrow reputation.

After Kano eliminated weapon techniques, strikes, and the more dangerous throws, holds, locks, and chokes, his new judo could easily be demonstrated to and engaged in by members of the public without fear of substantial injury. In the process of crafting judo out of *jujutsu*, he intentionally and mindfully applied Western principles of scientific reasoning and the latest in exercise physiology to render a highly cohesive curriculum.

One apocryphal tale passed around judo clubs has Kano inventing the technique known as *kataguruma* (literally "shoulder wheel") by checking out a book on European wrestling at his school library. *Kataguruma* is known in Western wrestling as the "fireman's carry." In another, he visits a rival *jujutsu* school, where the proprietor offers to convert to the new judo if Kano is able to make a show of strength by breaking a roof tile. Excusing himself to the restroom, Kano finds a mallet, which he conceals in his clothing until the demonstration, then utilizes to satisfactory effect. These folk tales are intended to characterize him as a man of unusual cleverness and cunning. Such stories likely came about only decades after his success.

Kano's figure, fictive or otherwise, continues to loom large in the martial arts world. Judo's founder, however, may very well have been denigrated by his contemporaries as too *haikara* for the good of Japanese martial arts. He was active in international sporting groups and functioned as Japan's first liaison to the International Olympic Committee. In the 1920s and 1930s, Kano's work to replace the combat-oriented, secrets-laden classical fighting arts with the idea of *budo* was co-opted by nationalists like those at the Butoku-kai. In 1931, as military expansion proceeded in Manchuria, boys' magazines and the popular press pushed for a "return" to conservative ideals like "self-abandonment" and "devotion to the nation-state," ultimately leading to the federalization of judo and kendo into *gakko budo*, school martial ways, which comprised part of the social realignment needed to engage in total war.[10]

By utilizing the school system and popular press to raise an entire generation of young people to associate masculinity with an "unchanging spiritual ethos" that "sought to sustain the myth of an essential masculinity while concealing the socially constructed nature of gender identity," the national government and conservative right-wing groups were able to construct a new interpretation of what it meant to perform the masculine.[11] A central part of this idea was the assertion that modern *budo* was actually the often-centuries-old *bujutsu*, with only a slightly more up-to-date mode of practice. By seeing that young men were trained in these skills with a nationalistic fervor in mind, *budo* study led to the martial arts' inevitable

Mass martial arts drills were common in prewar Japanese school life (Prints and Photographs Division, LOC).

link with "Japaneseness." Indeed, as of World War II it was assumed that the *budo* were "timeless."[12]

Origins of Japanese Nationalism

Although it is often assumed that the Meiji Restoration was a sort of reset point for Japanese culture that happened suddenly and without warning, historical evidence would indicate the contrary. The Tokugawa leadership, in control since the start of the seventeenth century, was in a state of irrevocable political impotence by the 1850s. Well aware of what was then taking place in China, many Japanese officials were hesitant to respond openly to the appearance of American warships in 1853, fearful that they would be subject to a second Opium War. These conservative types chose to entertain the American commander, Matthew Perry, with an indirect show of force. Sumo wrestlers (easily some of the most powerful combat athletes in the world, even now) were asked to put on an exhibition of their art in the hopes that the Americans would be intimidated and reconsider any plans they had of exploiting the Japanese for their resources. The display failed at its intended purpose, prompting one crewmate to comment that it was "a very unsatisfactory trial of strength … any wrestler that I have heretofore seen of half the muscle would have laughed at them."[13]

Without the authority of a strong central government, the ruling samurai class fractured into several political movements, each with a different solution to the potential crisis of foreign intervention. Among these were the *shishi* ("gentlemen with purpose") who, even if vaguely, idealized the concept of a traditional Japan in which the emperor reigned with absolute sovereignty. Such a place had never existed, but perception being more important than documented reality, these lower-class imperialists responded to the wave of foreign influence by immersing themselves in the Confucian classics and, in a trend later reenacted by twentieth century nationalists, underwent vigorous martial arts training. Although this group was small, they were able to effect a significant impact on official discourse through acts of extremism. This eventually coalesced in the 1865–1866 Satsuma-Choshu insurgency in which the samurai of two powerful domains were convinced to rebel against the national government in order to restore what they believed to be the proper place of the emperor. The rebels were defeated by the government's new, Western-style military. Those who survived were executed, imprisoned, or sent to live in exile far from the capital.[14]

Despite continuing trepidation, the national leadership reformed itself into a quasi-republic under the technical control of Emperor Meiji in 1868. A young man with a fondness for exotic foreign goods and ideas, Meiji allowed an unprecedented influx of foreign products, people, and philosophies, much to the delight of profiteers on both sides of the Pacific. The samurai class was essentially disbanded. In an openly symbolic maneuver, topknots and the wearing of swords in public were officially banned (not that this deterred devotees). Westernization arrived so quickly that in only a few years, a vocal preservationist movement emerged. In 1878 Ernest Fenellosa, a Harvard graduate, came to Japan as a university lecturer. He teamed up with his student and colleague, Motoori Norinaga, to push for the promotion of "traditional" Japanese art and aesthetics. While not necessarily as influential as they had hoped at the time, their concept of East Asia as a unique cultural entity in which Japan was possessed of a yet more unique national tradition would be echoed by political agitators as justification for the unification of East Asia under their rule. In effect, decades before the events that led to American involvement in World War II, the seeds of Japanese nationalism had been planted, in part, by an American.[15]

This is also important because of how Japan was perceived overseas. Although Westerners had been aware of the island nation's existence for centuries, the Tokugawa shogunate's isolationist policies left most people with very little information or interest in Japan. What claims could be found were, like those about East Asia in general, highly suspect and often fantastical. When the nation opened itself to the world at the end of the nineteenth century, then, Americans jumped at the opportunity to exoticize it, often attributing the Japanese with a lifestyle "somehow simpler and healthier" than that of Americans. Despite the initial lack of awe at Japanese demonstrations of martial skill, it seems that at least some Americans were impressed with the notion of *bushido*, which was no doubt encouraged by the publication of Inazo Nitobe's eponymous book in 1900. That no codified or coherent universal notion of *bushido* can be found from earlier than the modern period is perhaps further indicative of the degree to which it was formulated under heavy Western influence, especially since Americans had already been looking back at their own imagined traditional past since at least the mid-nineteenth century.[16]

Ultimately, those Tokugawa leaders who feared a repeat of China's experience with economic aggression by foreign powers were vindicated with a series of "unfair treaties," which gave Western nations control of valuable trade rights and numerous domestic commercial products. Even after critical politicians were able to gain favor in the Japanese Parliament, it wasn't until after meaningful and surprising Japanese victories against the Chinese (1895) and Russians (1905) that Westerners began to take them more seriously, as much because of their potential for trade as for the military threat on mainland Asia. Unfortunately for the Western powers occupying China, the Japanese discovered the profits that could be reaped through postwar indemnities and now looked for potential targets to spread the empire.[17] At the same time, in a fashion again mirroring the past-looking neo-primitivism in America of the early twentieth century, the Japanese, accepting that they could function successfully in the world without necessarily copying Western ways, looked to the (typically imagined) past for traditions that could help generate a cohesive national identity.[18]

Judo, Karate and the Japanese Nation-State

The founding fathers of the Meiji state were aware of the need to quickly generate a national identity in order to prevent a national fracturing. The danger of sectarianism was demonstrated in the Satsuma and Choshu regions during a short-lived rebellion a few years before. The Satsuma Rebellion was caused by disaffected samurai who claimed loyalty to the emperor and took a violent stand against the new national army. (The conflict would later be depicted very loosely in the plot of 2004's *The Last*

Samurai.) To that end, the aforementioned *heishiki taiso*, military-style gymnastics, were adopted as the core of public schools' physical education curricula. The engineer behind this move was Mori Arinori (1847–1889), the first Minister of Education. Although born into a samurai family, he was a thoroughly modern bureaucrat who fully embraced *wakon yosai* and was an outspoken critic of including the older *bujutsu* in public education, as was common practice in the early years of the school system. Mori's agenda included excluding swordsmanship from school life for fear that it would encourage the continued wearing of swords in public. He and others supported the implementation of a national police force in the interest of maintaining domestic tranquility and believed that a citizenry carrying weapons in public would inevitably be prone to violence.[19]

This was the social milieu in which Kano, himself a professor of education and keen adopter of modern ideas, developed judo. The influence of Mori's educational philosophy is evident when considering that Kano's system does not feature armed training and is expressly peaceful in its stated purpose. There is, too, evidence to indicate that Kano's molding of judo was largely dictated by government responses to his repeated requests to have it integrated with the established physical education curriculum in teacher training colleges. His entreaties to have judo considered for official inclusion were rejected three times before finally gaining acceptance in 1911. In that time he seems to have made alterations to the practice and techniques of his martial art, finally managing to strike a formulation that pleased the National Institute of Gymnastics, a governing body formed in 1883 to evaluate the effectiveness of physical education methods. The leadership of the Institute was comprised of three physicians, two of whom were German. In effect, judo's most formative period saw it transformed to pass approval by an organization more German than Japanese.[20]

The purpose of national identity was still foremost in the minds of Japanese educators, however, and judo's success depended on a demonstrated ability to inculcate students with a sense of social unity despite being an ostensibly individualistic activity. To that end, Kano set about altering two damaging public perceptions: that the martial arts are dangerous and that Japanese styles originated in China. The safety aspect was simple enough to negotiate. Kano implemented padded flooring, a scientific method of lessening impact upon falling, and included a series of resuscitative procedures. The issue of history called for educating the public through a series of publications and lectures in 1889 in which Kano asserted that, contrary to popular understanding, the martial arts of Japan were only ever linked to China because it encouraged acceptance of their efficacy. At the same time, he attempted to appeal to the controlling upper classes within the educational hierarchy by linking *jujutsu* with a classical Confucian upbringing.[21]

While attempting to penetrate the school system proved challenging, Kano experienced much more success when dealing with the newly formed military. The Naval Academy adopted judo into its physical training regimen as early as 1887. This connection opened the way to other institutes of higher learning and by 1898 there were regular intercollegiate tournaments. The Tokyo Metropolitan Police Bureau formally adopted judo as its unarmed physical training following a famous 1888 mixed-style match between Kano's Kodokan organization and the Totsuka school of *jujutsu*, held at the behest of the police superintendent in order to identify the most effective technique for police officers. The match also served as inspiration for one of Kurosawa's early films, *Sugata Sanshiro* (1943). By the time of the Russo-Japanese War, then, an entire generation of police cadets, naval officers, and many of Japan's educated elite had spent time studying judo. To this they brought their own notions of how it might be used to further the cause of nationalism and cement the Japanese identity.[22]

In response to the needs of the demographics most widely employing judo, Kano created various elements of practice now commonplace in many martial arts around the world. As everyday clothing would be irreparably damaged during the course of rigorous practice, he experimented with an official uniform, likely inspired by the tough hemp coats (*yakki*) worn by Japanese firemen of the period.[23] The older systems of *bujutsu* recognize technical competence through idiosyncratic systems of licensing, but with little outward recognition. Following Western pedagogical practices and almost certainly with the police and military in mind, Kano devised a system of ten grades to identify the level of a practitioner's ability and experience. His reasoning for the implementation of recognized levels centered on the concept that frequent acknowledgment of achievement would motivate students to continue applying maximum effort. These grades were later associated with the color of cloth belt worn as part of the uniform so that unfamiliar trainees could more easily distinguish between accomplished judo players and fellow neophytes.[24]

Following the technical and ideological adaptation that allowed Kano's judo to be accepted by the police, military, and ultimately middle and upper schools nationwide, the erstwhile tradition-bound Butokuden embraced the practice of judo as a new form of *jujutsu* along with kendo, another recent invention. A socially and politically conservative organization by design, the Butokuden membership reveled in the Japanese victories over China and Russia and, subsequently, provided training to physical culture educators in order to spread martial arts through the school system. This took place through their education branch, which was established in 1905 (the year of the Russo-Japanese War) and became a fully accredited college in 1912. In 1919 the college was made almost fully autonomous and took on the name Budo Senmon Gakko, Martial Arts Technical School.[25]

With its modern pedagogical approach, standardized uniforms, simple grading system, and clear technical corpus, judo became the template for Japanese martial arts of the twentieth century. This is most apparent in the adaptation of Okinawan karate to Japan. The Ryukyu archipelago that now comprises Okinawa prefecture lies almost equidistant between Japan, Taiwan, Korea, and China. Historically, the islands formed a sovereign kingdom with its own language, customs, and royal family. The region was annexed by the Japanese over the course of the nineteenth century, but maintains a separate cultural identity even now. Karate refers to the indigenous martial arts of the Ryukyus; however the name, manner of practice, and even costume are somewhat recent inventions.[26]

As with judo, karate as it is widely known today was shaped and propagated by a schoolteacher. Funakoshi Gichin had studied the martial arts of his homeland for a number of years and, much like Kano, sought to systematize and update the disparate styles into a single, coherent corpus that could be promoted as physical education. At the same time, the Japanese military was seeking conscripts among Okinawans to fight for imperial expansion in China. One physician conducting exams noted in 1903 that, although many of the islanders lacked the proper nutrition and exercise to be of much use, those who practiced karate were in excellent condition and advised the incorporation of the martial art into the local schools, which subsequently took place.[27]

Having previously been known as *te*, or "hand," the unarmed martial art spread by Funakoshi and his followers required a Japanese name in order to serve its function in the government-run schools. They chose to call their art karate, applying the Chinese ideograms for "Tang" and "hand." Historically, the martial arts of Okinawa are known to have come from China, and the use of "Tang" reflects that understanding. Karate predominantly employs percussive techniques. While some historical research has uncovered grappling methods within older schools of the art, the pragmatic fact is that karate is best considered an art based around punches, kicks, and other striking motions. Funakoshi would later change the character "Tang" for another with the same pronunciation, but meaning "empty."[28]

The karate program was successful enough in Okinawan schools that Funakoshi was invited to demonstrate his exercises at the Butokuden (the Butoku-kai's headquarters) in Kyoto in 1916 and was summarily made the official Okinawan representative to the organization. Naturally, this impressed Kano and many others, resulting in another demonstration by Funakoshi, in 1922. This time he traveled to Tokyo and performed for the Ministry of Education.[29]

It is important to recognize the relationship between Okinawa and Japan in terms of culture and governance. Okinawa is to Japan, in many respects, what Hawaii or perhaps Puerto Rico is to the United States. While officially a part of the Japanese nation, Okinawan culture is markedly, undeniably unique as a combination of Chinese, Japanese, and Southeast Asian cultures. The Okinawan language is distinct, as are its social practices, and a great many native Okinawans have been vocal in recent years about their desire to operate as a sovereign state. This is probably not made any less vehement by the presence of a large number of American military men and women, whose often-poor treatment of the locals in the past few decades has served as a reminder to the Okinawan populace of their historical treatment by the Japanese as second-class citizens. The potential for a peculiarly Okinawan style of martial arts to be officially adopted by the national government, then, was too great an opportunity for Funakoshi to squander. Becoming such a visible part of the Japanese landscape would have meant more than personal success or the survival of his art form. If Funakoshi could bring karate to the Japanese masses, it would thereby earn respect for his people and their culture.

The path to official acceptance having been paved by Kano, Funakoshi's karate was quickly absorbed by Japanese universities after a few alterations to make it palatable to the nationalist government. Technical terms were transliterated into Japanese, training was held in a *dojo* (Japanese-style practice space), judo-type uniforms and rank belts were incorporated, and the primary mode of exercise was made to resemble military drills, with students lined up by seniority and executing movements together as dictated by an instructor. The older modes of *te* practice in Okinawa usually involved personalized instruction in small groups or individually. It generally took place outside, sometimes in secluded settings to avoid revealing the methods to observers, and did not have any sort of official ranking system. The idea of a uniform would have been completely foreign to older generations of Okinawan karate practitioners as their exercises tended to involve stripping down to one's bare essentials, clothing-wise. The purpose was twofold: to reveal any minute errors in posture or alignment and to alleviate the unpleasant heat generated by vigorous movement in a tropical environment.

The thoroughly "Japanized" karate, with its uniforms and rank structure, appealed to university students and, by 1932, every institute of higher education in the country had a dedicated *dojo*.[30] This was approximately the same time at which Funakoshi created a list of somewhat vague values supposed to guide the karate player in his moral development. These values (such as "seek perfection of character") are very similar to Kano's guiding principles of judo, conformed to the needs of extreme nationalists, and reflected the moral education demands placed on teachers by the National Institute of Gymnastics.[31] In point of fact, the list of values that Funakoshi passed along to all clubs under his direction was as pliable as one may imagine. Consider, for instance, the first of these: seek perfection (or completion) of character. How one chooses to define both perfection and character may result in any number of possible outcomes. Okinawan conceptualizations of a positive character likely differed from those of the imperial Japanese government, and so by instituting such an open set of moral principles Funakoshi was able to offer a perfectly vanilla package with which the state authorities could do as they pleased.

Nationalism, Adventurism and the Masculine Ethos

With the national education system placed in a position to inculcate Japanese youth with imperialistic fervor through both intellectual and physical training, the increasingly extremist government turned its attention to expanding its sphere of influence. Those rapidly taking hold of the nation's reins had an agenda of increasing expansion abroad, social and economic conservatism domestically, and an overall belief in the natural superiority of the Japanese over foreign cultures. In the years following the annexation of northern China and Korea as an outcome of the Sino-Japanese War, colonies of settlers had been encouraged and funded to move into Manchuria. By some estimates, there were as many as 134,000 Japanese living in Manchuria as of 1920.[32] In keeping with Japan's move toward total mobilization of society in the interest of expansion, popular media encouraged young people—especially boys—to idolize the continental adventurers who left Japan with visions of overthrowing the Manchu and Chinese governments, not as a means of hostile conquest, but to aid their Asian brethren in overcoming corruption and the taint of Western powers that also sought to control the fragmented Chinese territories.[33]

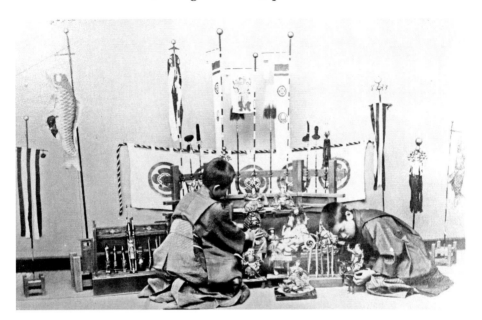

Boys of all social classes were encouraged to adopt an invented samurai ethos (Prints and Photographs Division, LOC).

Until the 1930s, despite what, in retrospect, appears to have been a unilateral move toward militarism and imperialistic expansion, the Japanese government established during the Meiji period did support multiple political parties, often fostering debate over the nation's future. By the time of the global economic crisis that followed the New York stock market crash of 1929, however, a weakened economy and stagnant political system led the general public to favorable treatment of military leaders, whose ability to act without inhibition from the civilian government was established by the nation's guiding documents. Only the emperor had the absolute authority to rein in military ambitions, and he lacked either the willingness or political clout to do so.[34]

Japanese media outlets responded to the sudden global depression with an optimistic push for the public to become active agents of recovery. Popular boys' magazines of the 1930s touted slogans like *risshin shusei*, "establish yourself and go into the world."[35] The messages were clearly aimed at encouraging young men to head for Manchuria, where the Japanese military had established a puppet state to give the appearance of autonomy despite total colonial control. This wasn't simply a response to social anxiety over Japan's conscribed situation as an island nation; as in the U.S., the 1930s depression coincided with disastrously poor farming conditions

Children raised after the Meiji reforms were imbued with a powerful brand of patriotism (Prints and Photographs Division, LOC).

that coalesced with an already weakened market, leading to all-time lows in agricultural output and profits. The Japanese saw expansion into China and Korea as perhaps the only way to avoid total domestic collapse.[36]

Japanese adventurism in mainland Asia increased sharply between groups of organized settlers sent to expand the agricultural base needed to feed both those in their homeland as well as the continental military and the popularity of romantic adventure stories published in boys' magazines like *King*.[37] Since at least the end of the nineteenth century, Japanese men who sojourned throughout mainland Asia on a quest for personal achievement and wealth were referred to as *tairiku ronin*, continental *ronin*. The use of the word *ronin* tied such professional adventurers to the newly minted concepts of samurai ethos and *bushido* as it historically applied to samurai left without masters. Literally meaning "wave man," the term harkens back to a time in Japanese history in which one's entire existence was defined by direct relations to superiors and subordinates in a highly Confucian ethic of social orientation. During the twentieth century the image of the *ronin* as a free-spirited traveler would become romanticized through magazines, novels, and films, most notably Kurosawa's *Shichinin no samurai* (*Seven Samurai*) (1957). These narratives later served as inspiration for American westerns like *The Magnificent Seven* (1960).

Glorification of a newly conceived samurai ethos fit well with the popular practice of martial arts and aggressive adventurism being promoted in public schools and entertainment media, and through quasi-governmental organizations such as the Butokukai. Even assuming that there had been, at some point, a united ethical and moral standard followed by the samurai class, its implementation on a popular scale would still be markedly recent as members of that social class comprised approximately five percent of the total Japanese population.[38] The samurai imagery, then, like the martial arts, was co-opted by those interested in promoting expansion abroad in order to attract and excite a young male audience. This trend worked to great effect as indicated by both the number of young men going overseas and the success, despite economic hardship, of magazines featuring *tairiku ronin* stories. By the 1930s the government was conscribing soldiers at such a rate that the demographics of settlers in Manchuria became unfavorably skewed. The solution was to recruit from the juvenile age set and in 1932 the national government began coordinating large groups of male teenage volunteers to fulfill the need for labor and military presence, their time in Manchuria being split between agriculture, education, and combat drills.[39]

The appeal of braving what was depicted, more often than not, as the untamed Asian steppe was not limited to adolescents. Men of all ages and social classes found themselves swept up by the romanticism of liberating their Asian brethren from the shackles of local warlords, communists, and Westerners. One of the more interesting examples, whose work went on to have a substantial influence on the relationship between Japanese and American martial artists, was Ueshiba Morihei (1883–1969), the progenitor of aikido. Stylistically, aikido is difficult to categorize because of its multitudinous forms and unusual means of engagement. It is neither entirely a method of grappling nor of striking, but falls somewhere in the middle. Forty-one years of age, Ueshiba met with and became a follower of Deguchi Onisaburo, a cult leader who had charge of a colorful offshoot of Shinto. In 1924 Deguchi, Ueshiba, and a small band of settlers went to Manchuria and Mongolia with the goal of establishing their own theocracy, with Deguchi as the *de facto* head. Although the ensuing events were not well-documented, it is commonly agreed that the group's religious zealotries were met with unwelcoming reactions by the indigenous population. Several of the party members, including Ueshiba, were stood up before a firing squad only to be rescued in dramatic fashion, at the last moment, by Japanese imperial order.[40]

It is tempting, in an analysis of the origins of Asian martial arts exoticism in the U.S., to point to Ueshiba's highly spiritual approach to the martial arts as a major contributing factor. This would be largely erroneous, however. Ueshiba's aikido has never enjoyed the demographic popularity of karate or judo and certainly his Shinto-infused philosophy does not translate well enough for much public engagement via mass media. The sole high-profile American film star to utilize aikido in any meaningful way is Steven Seagal, who was purportedly given his initial on-screen parts thanks entirely to the work of his martial arts students who also happened to be film executives. Seagal's mainstream success was short-lived, due, perhaps, as much to his unusual personality and choice of activities as to his ability to draw an audience. Ueshiba's supernatural beliefs are part and parcel of aikido, even for those who practice the art without believing the rhetoric of universal harmony and mystical energy fields. Consequently, it is difficult to put on a film screen, and performances are generally unbelievable as far as fistic efficacy is concerned.

Negotiating Masculine Nationalism

A number of high-ranking military officials frequented Ueshiba's martial arts academy in the 1930s, beginning a relationship (particularly with the navy) that continues to the present day. This is intriguing given that the other two modern martial arts most promoted by the education and military spheres (karate and judo) differed from Ueshiba's style drastically on the subject of the supernatural. Karate, as Funakoshi formulated it, was inoffensive to Japanese sensibilities and even its moralistic mottos could easily be plied to whatever ends required by the practicing body. Judo, due to Kano's keen interest in things modern and Western, was powerfully rationalistic. Techniques that failed to be functional in sparring were generally eschewed, in the process eliminating any sense of supernatural powers that may be ascribed to a given judo player. Aikido, however, not only recognized, but relied on a belief in the cosmic power known simply as *ki*, or "energy." Ueshiba was known to have stated on at least a few occasions that aikido was not intended for combat purposes, even going so far as to suggest that families might practice it together and thereby improve their relations and health simultaneously.[41] Emphasis on the supernatural, spiritual, and non-combative elements of the style may have been useful in terms of the sociocultural mission of the developing Japanese government, but did little to make a more masculine and aggressive citizenry that could be pointed toward Manchurian expansion.

The formulation of Ueshiba's aikido was influenced by combat techniques which were then rendered non-combative. Video comparison of the Japanese imperial army's bayonet drills, adapted to Japanese needs from European methods, shows a marked similarity with aikido's staff techniques. It would seem, based on an examination of Ueshiba's life and development as a martial artist, that much of his treatment of the four-foot stick is derived from his time serving in the Japanese army. It is a curious historical point, then, that he chose to adopt tactics aimed at war for his highly peaceable martial art. Strange, too, is the fact that these skills are rooted in European bayonet usage. Much like judo's complex history with German advisors, aikido would seem to have at least a small degree of Western basis. Still, this is far from the first portion of the aikido curriculum to be fashioned from modern innovations since Ueshiba's main teacher, Takeda Sokaku, appears to have invented his own martial art to begin with. In point of fact, then, when Ueshiba invented aikido he was merely following in the same line as his own instructors, military or otherwise.

If aikido lies at one end of the fantastical spectrum by functioning entirely around the assumption of a mystical energy field, its greatest possible opposite would likely be boxing. The golden age of pugilism in America was the 1920s and 1930s, but in Japan, too, it had become an established, if radically different, pastime. Boxing's brief rise and decline in imperial Japan serves as an excellent rounding point to the examples of Japanese (and "Japanized") martial arts as utilized by nationalist leadership. It also illustrates the degree to which practice of combative arts can lead to a deep psychological affiliation with the community of practice, whether local or national.[42]

There is little about boxing that could be mistaken for an indigenous Japanese development. From the costume to the arena and the individualistic nature of competition, there is little left to be imagined that its origins lie in the West. As with many such cultural transplants, however, Japanese boxers and enthusiasts made efforts to adapt the art to their own social requirements. Boxing was introduced to the island nation at the beginning of the twentieth century through two simultaneous avenues. Japanese who had experience with the style overseas returned and established the first clubs, while foreign visitors took an interest in setting up mixed matches between boxing and *jujutsu*. One of the first Japanese to bring pugilism to his homeland was Uriu Sotokichi, who learned to fight while attending the U.S. Naval Academy in the 1880s. The mixed matches, known as *merikan*, were popular in the 1910s, but waned in public interest as anti–Western sentiment took hold in the 1920s. The usual format for these contests was to have a gloved, often foreign boxer (American sailors are most prevalent in the newspaper articles) follow one set of rules while attempting to strike a jacketed Japanese *jujutsu* practitioner, who generally won in short order due to the boxer's prohibition on grappling.[43]

The Japanese military took an interest in boxing and experimented with its application as an educational device during the 1920s. In this case, the sport being so much more foreign than even karate, the expertise of a foreigner was necessary. The individual chosen was Captain Warren Clear, an American army officer stationed in Tokyo. This was primarily in reaction to the experience of Japanese military officials who had observed British army trainees being made into "he-men" through the inclusion of boxing in their basic training. As previously established, the imperial government was interested in breeding the most aggressively masculine populace possible, even if it meant seeking outside aid. This, however, led to immediate adoption of *bokushingu*. Just as karate's very name had to be altered to fit nationalistic tastes, *bokushingu* was replaced in the 1920s by *kento*, which combines the Chinese ideograms for "fist" and "fight."[44]

The decline of boxing in Japan by the time of the Pacific war was a result of several factors. Despite efforts to appeal to Japanese sensibilities by referring to the art as *kento*, much of the argot consisted of loanwords, giving the activity a *haikara* aesthetic that nationalists found unpalatable. Many of the more technically savvy fighters on the international circuit who achieved a measure of success were actually ethnic Koreans whose country was colonized by Japan beginning in 1876 and officially annexed in 1910.[45] This, too, almost certainly agitated the *bankara* groups. Finally, the nature of the sport, with professional fights and the associated glamour of fame, may have appealed to some young men, but certainly did not gain favor with the imperial government that desired systemization, safety, and a communal mindset in its physical education, as established by the National Institute of Gymnastics. These issues amalgamated to cut short boxing's run in imperial Japan. It would, however, see a postwar rise under radically different social circumstances.

China and Martial Art as Cultural Identity

While Japanese nationalism was building and the leadership sought suitable means of constructing a singular identity, including mandatory practice of carefully chosen martial systems, China was in the throes of domestic turmoil in which indigenous fighting arts would play a key role. The post-World War II spread of Asian martial arts to the Western world was directly shaped by the radically different socio-historical events in China during the nineteenth and early twentieth centuries as compared with those in Japan. There were three primary reasons for this. First, the practice of Chinese martial arts during this period was dictated from government officials to the public, rather than the Japanese case in which practitioners like Kano and Funakoshi appealed to state authorities in a bottom-up pattern. Second, while the history of Japanese martial arts was rewritten to give them an upper-class patina, the Chinese styles were already widespread and commonly practiced by the public, preventing such a whitewashing. Finally (and certainly most important), Japanese sentiments like *wakon yosai* encouraged exchange with foreign cultures in an era when China was simultaneously occupied and fractured by several foreign powers, leading to a great deal of anti-foreign activism, most notably during the Boxer Rebellion of 1900.

Although constructing and navigating folk history is a challenge, distinguishing between real and imagined historical narratives is particularly difficult with regards to Chinese martial culture. Much of this obfuscation can be attributed to the dissemination of faulty information during the nineteenth century when certain scholars attempted to formulate a coherent story marrying common political ideologies with popular versions of martial arts narratives. These ideologies were reactionary to the violence—both social and physical—brought about by foreign incursion. Between the collapse of the central government and the territorial conflict involving Western powers and Japan, everyday life in China during the nineteenth century was less than placid. This landscape provided ample employment for agencies of professional custodians of an antagonistic nature. At the same time, secret societies sprang up all over the territories with the shared goal of ousting the foreign interests and restoring Chinese sovereignty, frequently touting combative training as the preferred method.[46]

While the best-known of the violent groups is likely the *Shenquan* "Spirit Boxers," other organizations with similar methods of operation appeared both before and afterward, including the Big Sword Society and the Red Spears. The *Shenquan* combined their martial practice with belief in the supernatural, providing a strong contrast with the highly rationalistic Japanese interlopers in the northern climes of what came to be Manchuria and Mongolia:

> The distinctive ritual of these Boxers was a type of spirit possession whereby in theory any member could become a god. Opening the door to universal deification, the ritual had important egalitarian implications. The Spirit Boxers, with few local gentry to restrain them, spread rapidly across the North China Plain, launching aggressive attacks against foreign targets in their midst.[47]

Neither the spiritual belief from which this manifestation sprang nor the physical arts that they practiced came into being solely as a result of perceived foreign threats. However, when triggered, intensification took place and what began as "self-defense organizations" became aggressively violent and centralized the importance of the supernatural.

Combining martial practice with supernatural belief structures in this way led to a search for historical justification, which some scholars found in *Epitaph for Wang Zhengnan* by Huang Zhongxi (1617–1669). This work, framed as a piece in honor of Huang's son's teacher, is also a flamboyantly anti–Manchu work that references a Buddhist monk from India teaching fighting skills at the Shaolin monastery in legendary times (specifically, an imagined version of the sixth century CE). He characterizes this style and Buddhism as "external," stressing their inferiority in the face of native Chinese "internal" fighting arts and Taoist beliefs. As Henning notes, this marks the first time that martial arts in China are (1) referred to as "internal" and "external" and (2) claimed to originate with the temple at Shaolin. In this light, it is clearly a response to foreign occupation by the Manchu regime and it was a simple matter for nineteenth-century martial cults like the Spirit Boxers to graft this invented tradition onto their existing structure of anti-foreign supernatural martial practice.[48]

As these groups were, to some extent, organized parties, historians have been able to accumulate an impressive quantity of information about the constitution of their membership. Perry notes that Western Henan province saw more violent action from the Red Spears than did Northern Henan. The members in the west tended to be more "authoritarian" and came primarily from the ranks of "local bullies" and "demobilized soldiers" while those in the north were more likely to be land holders. Interesting, too, is that the lands in the west were under consolidated ownership while those in the north were more equally distributed. This points to two matters that establish the context of the Boxer Rebellion and push against foreign encroachment in general: that, while violence was widespread in all regions, the west, under greater European influence, was more forcefully subject to riots and banditry than the Japanese-occupied north and that the composition of those struggling for sovereignty were mainly from the lower socioeconomic classes, although the northern groups were primarily farmers while those in the west had an established history of violence.[49]

In both cases, the organizations that went on to rebel against foreign powers were preparing their members to do so by teaching them fighting skills of one variety or another. Unlike Japan, where Kano and Funakoshi were attempting to draw patronage from the government by associating their systems with classical Confucian education and upper-class young people at the universities, the Boxers, uninterested in government attention, drew on the peasantry to spread their fighting styles, which quickly led to an association of martial arts with lower-class interests. This is not unique in Chinese history, as demonstrated by the great sixteenth century vernacular novel *The Water Margin* (also known as *All Men Are Brothers* and *Outlaws of the Marsh*) and other later popular works. In most cases, foreigners are depicted as causing trouble for the otherwise peaceful Han Chinese, who then utilize martial skill (and often supernatural power) to enact justice for the common man.[50]

Intriguingly, vernacular novels about extraordinary martial arts heroes were both contemporaneous and analogous with Japanese popular magazines that treated Manchuria and Mongolia as fronts for exploration by adventurous young men. Also influenced by works about the Chinese Song period bandits of *The Water Margin*, Japanese boys' magazines like *King* applied the same messages of liberation via fighting prowess and stressed violence in the interest of common welfare, but to the exact opposite ends as those of the Boxers. Japanese colonists were depicted as freeing an oppressed people from cruel local warlords, just as the heroes in vernacular Chinese novels did. Both literatures focused on the inevitability of victory when supporting a righteous cause.[51] Unfortunately, the conflict between colonizer and colonized being incommensurate, the Boxer Rebellion of 1900 was short-lived due to the pairing of tactical styles.

Many of the Chinese fighters who took part in the uprising were fervent believers in the virtuous nature of their cause, as well as the efficacy of their martial arts and supernatural beliefs, which included claims of invulnerability to bullets. As expected, advanced military technology won out. The battle was particularly sanguine in Shandong province, where the fighting arts are rooted in local tradition and are even more commonly practiced than elsewhere, both currently and historically. It was in Shandong, too, that social pressure to reform the government and reestablish sovereignty were extremely high as the region "had been hit by three disasters all at once: floods, famine, and the Germans."[52]

The Boxer Rebellion did not last long, nor was it successful in terms of freeing the Chinese from oppression by unequal treaties with foreign powers. However, it is indicative of the zeitgeist in occupied China at the turn of the last century and serves as an indicator of the domestic troubles at stake during the 1911 Revolution. The Revolution, having only been partly successful given the circumstances, ended in a still-fractured China, though now regional warlords, in many cases, acted as independent states without a strong central government. Realizing the power of applying martial arts as tools of social empowerment and control, it was common practice to hire expert instructors to train one's private army. This transformation can be seen by looking again to Shandong where, in the period from about 1917 to 1927, Feng Yuxiang (1882–1948) came to power and mobilized the elite Big Knife Unit to secure local peace and, later, to combat Japanese forces.[53] While most of these men had been members of various Boxer organizations, there were also Boxers who saw the warlords as simply another threat to the common good. One such reactionary group was the Red Spear Society, who swore to oust foreigners, warlords, bandits, and gamblers alike.[54] This was, therefore, a period of tremendous social unrest, but also one in which the martial arts flourished, if not in terms of stylistic development, then certainly with regards to the sheer popularity of their practice.

It was at this time, too, that official standards of martial arts instruction were established. Ma Liang (1878–1947), leader of a garrison in Shandong, headed a gathering of martial arts instructors and published *Zhonghua Xin Wushu, New Chinese Martial Arts*, in 1917 with the aim of providing basic instruction in several methods of training that could then be regulated and instituted throughout the country. The manual was not adopted, but did see official consideration by the National Assembly the following year. In 1919 the interest in martial arts as physical culture had grown so large that Guo Xifen produced *History of Chinese Physical Culture* which, as Henning points out, is responsible along with *Epitaph for Wang Zhengnan* for propagating the historically inaccurate legend that Chinese martial arts sprang from the Shaolin monastery.[55]

Nineteen twenty-eight was a watershed year in China. Chiang Kai-shek's Nationalist government was finally established as the controlling power in Nanjing, effectively putting an end to the era of local warlords, while in the Japanese-controlled north, Mongolia, and Manchuria, banditry remained commonplace despite the efforts of the sympathetic Kwantung Army. That same year, a Kwantung Army officer, apparently acting of his own volition, hatched a plot to blow up a train carrying Zhang Zuolin, a former warlord and supporter of Japanese rule. The officer's thinking seems to have been that the assassination of an influential character in Zhang, blamed on anti–Japanese nationalists, would spur the Japanese colonial government into pursuing more aggressive policies in Manchuria and, perhaps, an outright war to firmly determine the fate of northern China. The assassination did not have this effect; if anything, the Japanese became more controlling in their administration of the puppet state.[56]

That same year, the Nationalist government established the *Zhongyang Guoshu Guan*, Central Martial Arts Institute, with the purpose of bringing together the leaders of the nation's vast array of styles so that they could be preserved and propagated under a single controlling body. This movement found a measure of success and, in 1930, the Ministry of Education mandated that all public schools provide instruction in Chinese martial arts. Within three years of announcing the policy, the Central Martial Arts Institute, much like the Butoku-kai in Japan, opened the Central Martial Arts Physical Culture Specialty School to train educators in the use of martial arts as gymnastic exercises. The school's curriculum included methods of unarmed combat, wrestling, saber and bayonet, and the usual academic subjects such as history, geography, etc. Similar centers were constructed elsewhere, forming a nationwide network of government-run martial arts schools. Their goal was to breed a generation of strong, independent Nationalist citizens who could stand up to foreign demands for control.[57]

The need for a strong citizenry was becoming more urgent as the Japanese Kwantung Army continued to expand throughout the 1930s. It is generally accepted that outright war between the two nations began again in 1937 (called either the Second Sino-Japanese War or the War of Anti-Japanese Resistance, depending on one's perspective) with the Japanese push south to Hangzhou. Violence followed attempts at peaceful negotiations by the League of Nations, which demanded multilateral talks in the interest of demilitarization in 1933. Japan sent a legation, angered as both the government and general public were by the implication that colonization of the Asian mainland by Western powers was acceptable while an Asian power was considered wrong in doing so. Matsuoka Yosuke, Japan's foreign minister and head of the contingent, was so offended by the claims made at the meeting that he and his attendants walked out and formally withdrew from the League. For the first time in over fifty years, Japan chose isolation in the face of perceived foreign threats.[58]

In those areas still held by the Nationalist party, martial arts training intensified, but also saw the inevitable struggles of attempts to unite as diverse a field as the hundreds of systems found throughout China. The Central Martial Arts Institute found that the mentality fostered by secret societies like the Spirit Boxers and the Red Spears led to divisiveness, secretiveness, and internal political misgivings. An unwillingness to share the full teachings of one's system was naturally tied to the anti-foreign rhetoric of the secret societies and would become almost inextricably linked to the now-nationalized practice of Chinese indigenous martial arts. This attitude even spread overseas with emigrant Chinese labor communities.[59] These elements of Chinese martial culture (secretiveness, anti-foreign attitudes, and desire to remain independent from other styles even within the same organization) will be seen later as hallmarks of the Chinese fighting arts that ultimately stymied their spread within popular culture overseas until at least the 1970s.

The further development of martial arts in Manchuria and Mongolia was limited by Japanese invasion and occupation. Although they were widespread in practice by groups like the Red Spears, they were used less as a means of cultivation than as a social tool for building resistance against an imposing foreign nation. The Nationalist government also understood the martial arts as an effective means of building a strong, unified polity and enculturating young people with the values and beliefs of the Party, but was able to do so through an organized network of schools, legitimizing instructors with government backing and a singular aim toward defending the nation from external threats in the form of Japanese aggression and unfair Western treaties. The program was so readily accepted that the Nationalists sent a team of top martial artists to perform at the 1936 Berlin Olympics. This marked the highest moment of achievement for Chinese martial culture, however, as war with Japan beginning in 1937 kicked off a tumultuous period in which survival became every individual's daily concern until well after the end of World War II.[60]

Comparing Chinese martial arts with Japanese, it is evident that aikido, like karate and judo, whatever the initial aims of their founders, came to be associated with militarism and national expansion during the years leading up to the Second World War. Although some elements of these modern martial arts are no doubt practical in terms of physical antagonism, the technological state of warfare in the twentieth century rendered such skills an inefficient use of time compared with firearms practice. Rather, the purpose of popularizing and systematizing Japanese martial disciplines was to accomplish two intertwined goals: the inculcation of young people with nationalistic ideals who would serve the expansionist cause and the fostering of a nationwide group identity where there had been none prior to the Meiji period.[61] This government-mandated spread of the martial arts to the general populace resulted from a bottom-up structure in which individuals like Kano and Funakoshi appealed to the controlling powers for official recognition, which contrasts sharply with the Chinese pattern in which the Nationalist government sought out martial arts experts to provide the means of instruction, seeing value in the use of martial arts toward nationalistic ends.

These goals were shared in the Chinese context, though, coincidentally with Japan as the main target of anti-foreign aggression in the light of colonization. In the 1920s and 1930s the nation split under Japanese expansion, with Manchuria being established as a Japanese puppet state and serving as a stronghold for intended conquest of the entire mainland. Martial arts were both a practical physical tool as well as a social one in this arrangement as the central government collapsed, leaving local warlords and the wealthy to employ strongmen for the purpose of quelling unrest. By 1928 the Nationalists unified most of the south, formed an effective government, and dedicated significant resources to the growth of martial culture as a part of the educational system, again, just as was taking place in Japan at the time and with essentially the same ends in mind. The unstable political terrain in China, however, gave way to outright war with Japan in less than a decade and, combined with internal struggles among members of the Central Martial Arts Institute, led to a pause in the cultural development of Chinese martial arts until years after the chaos of the war was concluded and Chinese culture began to spread overseas.

The impact of the Boxer Uprising on Chinese social relations with Western powers should not be underestimated simply because of its brevity. The effects of the Uprising continued to be fodder for popular culture in the following decades, even seeing reference in much later works such as Trevanian's classic 1979 novel *Shibumi*. The recovery of some Chinese martial arts in the West has been slow in coming. The style known as Plum Blossom Boxing, for instance, was quite popular in the nineteenth century due to its strong rhetoric centering on independence and brotherhood. But that same rhetoric made it a popular choice for the violent Boxers and it was later nearly wiped out by the Maoist government, likely for related reasons. In recent years there has been a great deal of interest in preserving the Plum Blossom style and its history as a folk art. I would conjecture that it will be a matter of years before Chinese folk martial arts take their turn as objects of fascination among Western audiences. This was seen to a limited extent with the success of Hong Kong martial arts films in the 1970s. For good or ill, though, Chinese martial arts have, until somewhat recently, lacked the kind of central organization and commercial promotional power needed to draw in an American public with a notoriously large wallet but short attention span. Consequently, it was the Japanese martial arts that first drew mass consumption in the West, but only after being accessed directly by American servicemen.

3

U.S. Occupation and a New Manly Art

They only want authority over others, to raise their own rank, and paste
gold on their face pretending to be a Buddha.
—T.T. Liang

While bearing resemblance to the original, it should have stylization;
this makes it art, and is what delights men's minds.
—Hozumi Ikan (quoting Chikamatsu Monzaemon)

Responses to War

Despite the focus on efficacy of the arts in both China and Japan during the imperialist era, it should not be presumed that during times of war,
martial arts somehow cease to be used as social tools. But it's evident, particularly from the example of the Sino-Japanese theater of the 1930s and
1940s, that resources which might otherwise be applied to the propagation
and growth of the martial arts in terms of cultural artistry tend to be
directed elsewhere. This was clearly the case in China, where war with the
Japanese stymied the Nationalist regime's efforts to maintain a functioning
public education system and, therefore, the standardization of martial disciplines administered by the officially sanctioned bodies. In Japan, where
the fascist solution to a weak populace was mandatory martial arts training,
war with China and then the Allied Powers only heightened this reactionary policy of physical indoctrination. In the West, boxing's golden age
of popularity was cut short by the inevitable resource scarcity of war. As it
had in Japan, though, the war brought about new images of masculinity,
tied more tightly than ever to violent images and physical power. Popular
press and especially graphic novels reflected the dreams of young men all
over the U.S. and elsewhere in the face of the first truly global threat to

Western civilization. Within the areas of conflict, fighting arts served more immediate functions, certainly with regards to survival, but also as a means of psychic bonding, social cohesion, and much-needed recreation in the most stressful of environments.

China, having again fallen into a state of political and social tumult after over a century of foreign incursion, extraordinary Japanese military aggression, several revolts and rebellions, serving as a war zone during the course of the Pacific theater, and undergoing its own civil war between the Nationalists and Communists, was at last stabilized—to some extent—by the founding of the Communist government in 1949, as well as the retreat of the Nationalist state to Taiwan, which was no longer among Japan's holdings as a consequence of the nation's surrender. The new People's Republic of China was quick to place martial arts instruction under the Physical Culture and Sports Commission. The All-China Traditional Sports Festival of 1953 saw over 100 martial arts styles represented. By 1959 the Commission not only organized and standardized the curricula of a great many martial traditions, but published a manual of rules to govern competitions between and within various arts.[1]

At this point Chinese martial arts were not especially associated with masculinity, nor do efforts by early members of the Communist leadership seem to have been focused on the development of an aggressive type of male citizenry. Indeed, the rules for martial arts competition published in 1959 include special provisions and even entirely new forms for female competitors, indicating that women were participating in great enough numbers to warrant consideration of different physical abilities.[2] During the period of 1953 to 1965, too, the Physical Culture and Sports Commission quietly made what would turn out to be one of the most influential decisions in the recent history of martial arts by interpreting the Party's mandate to spread the Chinese martial arts among the people as license to create a new method. After a few years of development, they unveiled a simplified form of *taijiquan*.[3] It would go on to become the most commonly practiced style of *taiji* worldwide and feature heavily in Western practice of Asian martial arts.

In Japan, where withdrawal from the League of Nations was only one act of isolation brought about by increasing tension between the fascist government and foreign powers, domestic production couldn't keep up with the demands of fighting on mainland Asia, let alone the new problems raised by the outbreak of war with the U.S. and its allies in 1941. At that time Japan, despite being one of the most developed of the industrialized nations, had only about one-tenth of the American productive ability, and most of it was dedicated to war with the Chinese, as well as holding fronts in Korea, Taiwan, and swaths of Southeast Asia. The strategy of engaging the Allies in a Pacific war relied on the notion that, while larger and more productive, the Western forces would be mostly aimed at fighting in Europe. The Japanese military further reasoned that, to a man, their troops were superior, physically, mentally, and psychologically, thanks to the amount of careful attention given the public education system since the Meiji period. American soldiers, out of shape, overfed, and undertrained, would be met in a draw by the smaller, but more efficient, Japanese units.[4]

Although professional boxing in the United States suffered greatly from a siphoning of talent for the war effort, the pastime remained popular among troops on both sides of the Atlantic as a shared cultural element and even served multiple simultaneous social roles. In Nazi prisoner of war camps, for instance, the Allied prisoners often engaged in athletic contests (particularly foot races) to remain mentally occupied and physically healthy. International agreements with the YMCA allowed for limited amounts of sporting equipment to be provided for these ends, the German rationale apparently being that busy prisoners are less apt to cause trouble. In an interview with the Veterans History Project at the Library of Congress, former POW John W. Baber explained that, in a unique moment of cultural intersection, some American captives, having been furnished with boxing gloves either by the camp staff or the YMCA, enthusiastically engaged in boxing matches for a mixed audience of German and Allied troops. The German soldiers not only attended these contests but, in photographs liberated from the camp where Baber was held, are seen to be socializing with the prisoners while one of their own acts as referee. Both prisoners and jailors are smiling.[5]

Wrestling was also a popular combat sport among American servicemen during their deployments and seems to have been most common among sailors, who organized boxing tournaments with equal interest.[6] The nature of maritime service may have favored wrestling over boxing as an entertainment medium due to the limited availability of equipment and international standard of rules. The danger of debilitating injury is much higher for boxing than wrestling, too, and many sailors worried about losing pay or opportunities for shore leave if they weren't able to work. Regardless of other considerations, however, recruits had fresh experience with grappling due to the orientation of close-quarters combat training at the time. It was common in all branches of U.S. armed forces to refer to hand-to-hand combat methods as "judo," despite a marked inconsistency of techniques with the curriculum of Kano's Kodokan school. Even so, the drills do appear to have been primarily based on or inspired by judo training and included "throw[ing] them with their rifle" and "disarm[ing] an attacker."[7] Raymond Van Skiver, a military policeman during the war, recalls practicing judo as part of his training under a Corporal Swallow, who "claimed to have had training and experience." In their practice matches no one received notable injuries; however, a tooth was chipped during an informal practice session because "we were boxing at the time."[8]

U.S. servicemen, then, retained a cultural interest in combat sports even when facilities, equipment, and training were in limited supply. Although some of these activities were intended to prepare for the occupational hazards of soldiering, most veterans' descriptions center on boxing and wrestling as enjoyable escapes from the stresses of training and war. Unlike Japan, where fighting arts were mandatory for young men, and China, where they were standardized and endorsed by governments, men of the Western world viewed the fighting disciplines as recreational entertainment. This would come to factor strongly into their interpretations of the Asian martial arts. The succeeding generations of Western martial arts consumers took the recreational attitude to heart, creating a cultural space in which dichotomous messages not only cohabitated, but somehow became mutually reliant. This is still the case today. On one hand, the martial arts are engaged in for discipline and follow a militaristic mindset. On the other, they are the stuff of recreation and children's television. The story of how this came about is complex and features some of history's more colorful individuals.

After the War

In 1946 the Allied General Headquarters ordered that all Japanese cease practicing martial arts and dismantled the Butoku-kai. Given their recently acquired nationalistic flair, the occupying forces saw *budo* and *bujutsu* as potential threats that needed to be eliminated in order to begin reconstruction. Two years later the Kodokan was permitted to reopen and host tournaments, but instruction in public schools was prohibited. During the 1950s various national organizations were founded in order to oversee the revival of the arts and in 1957 kendo was reintroduced to the education system. Now thoroughly "sports-ified," the global spread of judo took off during the 1960s. It was featured as an Olympic event for the first time at the 1964 Tokyo Olympics.[9]

Although judo was certainly the first Japanese martial art to reach a large-scale global audience, others soon followed. As discussed previously, the case of karate is notable in that it was brought to the Japanese mainland from Okinawa—until very recently, a place as culturally Japanese as Puerto Rico is American—by Funakoshi Gichin at the beginning of the twentieth century, amidst the movement toward conservative nationalism. Sponsored by Kano, Funakoshi went on to reshape karate into a package that would appeal to the Japanese. His students took to wearing a lighter weight version of the judo uniform, adopted Kano's colored belt rank system, and began practicing in specially designated dojo. The names of techniques were changed to forms not so foreign to the Japanese language.

The second generation of Japanese karate practitioners included an instructor of Korean descent, Masutatsu Oyama. Oyama founded his own style of full-contact karate called Kyokushin that became immensely popular among male audiences looking for a rough-and-tumble style, both domestically and overseas. Oyama was a prolific writer and one of his volumes, *The Kyokushin Way* (1979), lays out much of his worldview as regards women, masculinity, nationalism, and his generation's perception of tradition. "Karate has already conquered the hearts of young people throughout the world," he wrote, "these people have turned to karate in the hope of realizing a dream shared by all people—at least by all men—of being strong."[10] Oyama portrayed a character of unrelenting and unrivaled machismo, denigrating those focused on material comfort of "the white-collar job, the little house in the suburbs, the family, and the little happinesses.... [A] man should seek more challenging battles and should try to expand his visions and aspirations."[11] At the same time, however, his was a uniquely Japanese brand of manliness, equally at home with outright violence and with "sitting on the root of a pine on a cliff overlooking the bright expanse of the Pacific Ocean" contemplating the words of Confucius: "He who is pure in body is like the god of energy."[12]

For Oyama and many like him, the total surrender of self to the imperial experiment was a mistake to be rectified not through the abandonment of absolute dedication, but through a change of course in one's focus thereof. The Japanese term for this is *ikigai*, that which makes life worth living.[13] For men of the first postwar generation, Matthews found that work was almost universally upheld as one's *ikigai*. Their sons, however, often expressed a desire to seek personal experiences for personal development, "Yet ... work and self have in common the fact that they are not family—as if preserving a non-family realm as the prerogative of masculine *ikigai* in Japan."[14] The connection with Oyama's view here is clear: Modern men who wish to be masculine must have something other than

Oyama breaking bricks for the camera (Robert W. Smith Collection at Cushing Library, Texas A&M University).

a family to which they are fully devoted.

Full devotion for devotion's sake can be traced to the merging of Zen Buddhist philosophy with the Japanese aesthetic. Since the end of the Warring States Period (roughly 1457–1573 CE), "monastic practices in Zen temples and a popular interest in artistic practices have been subsumed by the notion of a religio-aesthetic tradition." The new aesthetic tradition manifested itself in the form of affixing *do* ("way" or "path") to the names of martial and other arts. The use of *do* indicates that the activity in question is a means by which one can seek cultivation, enlightenment, or some other vague concept relating to self-actualization. By the end of the peaceful Edo Period (1603–1868), the movement of the warrior class away from immediately practical application of their skills and toward a more spiritual aim "reflects the social and political stability of the era and a growing public involvement with the martial arts." It was because of the incorporation of Zen and the martial arts in the modern period, then, that a descendent of immigrant parents like Oyama could become an influential force in the world of Japanese fighting arts. Likewise, the Zen emphasis on absolute focus strongly influenced first the conservative nationalist approach to masculinity and, after the war, that association of masculinity with absolute focus became a matter of individual pursuits, or *ikigai*.[15]

Oyama's own life illustrates this shift from a focus on the imperial system to the self. In his narrative version of history, ancient men "offered their lives willingly for the sakes of their lords. In the democratic society of today we must be willing to do the same thing for the people, but only as long as the people are saved from corruption."[16] That corruption can come in many forms, but two that he states explicitly are the "underworld … gambl[ing], and carous[ing] with women"[17] and "nuclear war, computerized fighting, and proxy wars."[18] The message that Oyama sent via his public character is powerfully reminiscent of the early strongmen and later costumed superheroes telling young Americans to drink their milk, take vitamins, and listen to their parents. He seems to have been aware of this wholesome message's appeal, even closing out his treatise by recognizing that "all young men want to be strong. Seeing what I could do made young Americans want to emulate my power."[19]

This story of transformation was depicted in a comic book and cartoon series about Oyama's life. The story goes that in his teenage years he joined the military out of love for his nation, underwent psychological trauma after losing the war, was imprisoned for fighting with American occupying soldiers, attained enlightenment after a lengthy period of solitary ascetic karate training in the mountains, and went on to prove the validity of his might by winning a number of fights and killing bulls with his bare hands. This would make for a truly incredible life story were it not a significant embellishment. One of Oyama's senior students, the Dutch karate and judo exponent Jon Bluming, was present during much of Oyama's formative period as an instructor and argues that "it wasn't a bull, it was an ox" that had been struck in the head with a hammer; the years of solitary mountain training took place "before some fight or some tournament in Kyoto," and that Oyama was there for only six weeks. In general, he contends, the extraordinary tales of Oyama's life are "absolute nonsense."[20]

This raises the question of why such a man, whose efforts were based around the physically verifiable exercise of karate, would bother to perpetuate his own legend. Oyama sought students and he seems to have realized that they would be attracted to a charismatic leader who embodied their notions of what a good, successful man should be. As Cox suggests of those who practice a different style of martial arts, "the point is not that men who study … seek to be ascetics, monks or modern-day Samurai.… [H]owever they are at least aware of and may be enchanted by these flattering images of themselves."[21] By embodying these images, Oyama found a way to attract like-minded followers who would, in turn, become more embodiments of these ideals. Monetary considerations aside, the success of Oyama's narrative shows that the reinvention of masculinity in modern Japan to include absolute dedication to one's *ikigai* while simultaneously fulfilling social responsibilities had mass appeal. His ability to attract foreign students through this narrative carries implications for the masculinity crisis taking place at the same time in North America and explains, in part, why Japanese martial arts were so appealing to Westerners in the decades following the war.

As Jon Bluming has made abundantly clear in every venue that will offer him a voice, the postwar Japanese martial arts community was unrivaled in its ability to hew myths and legends out of even the most mundane public figures. Oyama was a relatively simple man with a very straightforward goal: to popularize his brand of karate. The natural means for him to do so was the same as with other Japanese of this period and required that he exaggerate his own feats, which were then even further exaggerated by others. It was at this same time and through the 1960s that aikido's founder, Ueshiba, came into fullness as a superpowered figure and paragon of martial virtue (as interpreted by Western observers). Volumes have been written about Ueshiba's exploits in the *dojo* by his Western students from this period and observation has confirmed that each passing generation continues to further apotheosize his memory. Interestingly, the same has happened with the subsequent instructors of karate and aikido as figures like Shioda Gozo took up the mantles of their teachers. Shioda, a disciple of Ueshiba, is now credited with such extraordinary exploits as leaping over a moving vehicle and dodging bullets fired at close range. Folklore in the martial arts has, if anything, intensified over time.

The Barbarians Invade

By the time of the U.S. occupation, the Japanese had reoriented their behaviors, beliefs, and worldview sufficiently over the course of a century that several cultural commodities were not only demystified, but practically tailored to fit Western consumptive preferences. This can be seen from two fronts: auto-orientalization and a ready adoption of Western-style masculine imagery. In the years following World War II it became necessary for the Japanese to recast themselves as somehow different from the unified imperial engine into which their nation had been transformed by a fascist leadership. This was accomplished by campaigns to rediscover their own nation through an imagined foreign perspective and amounted to auto-orientalization. At the same time, the generation of men raised with a hyper-masculine set of beliefs and behaviors found that interfacing with young, recently victorious American servicemen was astonishingly easy thanks to a set of compatible values and interests.

In the world of post–Meiji Japan, it became necessary in the eyes of that nation's founding fathers to create a cohesive national identity for their people in order to avoid the negative effects seen in China. To accomplish this, a set of national characteristics would have to emerge that could be utilized to differentiate "Japaneseness" from other constellations of personality that form contemporaneous imagined communities. Functionally, this was done by locating unwanted social behaviors (including unionization of labor and individualism) as belonging to the "other," and more specifically "the West." The method proved highly successful, resulting in the nationalistic fervor outlined earlier, but also eliminating much public perception of heterogeneity within Japan. Despite the presence of indigenous non-ethnic Japanese (the Ainu), ethnically Japanese outcasts (the *burakumin*), and descendants of foreign immigrants (predominantly *zainichi* Koreans), the Japanese public came to view itself as decidedly homogenous, in direct contrast with the heterogeneous West.[22] In short, all that was favorable was defined as Japanese while those qualities deemed unseemly were identified as Western.

Such differentiation could only take place on a national and international scale through the cooperation of those acting as the cultural counterpoint. Americans, in particular, were useful to that end as they "have even a folklore about the Japanese which says that whatever we do they do the opposite…. [S]aying simply that these differences are so fantastic that it is impossible to understand such people."[23] Thus the Japanese, taking their cue from the American vision of their own culture, sought (whether consciously or unconsciously, though most likely a mixture of both given the degree to which militarization was the result of deliberate social engineering) to build a unified Japanese national identity that, in some ways, matched the expectations and assumptions of an American audience. This process occurred again after the end of World War II; however, it was necessary this time to satisfy both Japanese and American notions of Japaneseness. The American conceptualization of the Japanese was problematic in that it was not primarily based on actual encounters with the people in question, but rather had been cobbled together through the work of wartime scholars through the lens of Japanese-Americans and the few works of Japanese literature translated into English.[24] Likely the most influential example of this is the anthropologist Ruth Benedict's *The Chrysanthemum and the Sword* (1946).

Benedict was asked to undertake the creation of a comprehensive cultural profile of Japan with the aim of explaining the Japanese to Americans as it was assumed that: (1) it would be difficult to defeat an opponent with a non-European paradigm of warfighting and (2) occupation of the island nation would be significantly eased by having a knowledge of Japanese peculiarities. In modern terms, these assumptions would most probably be viewed as racist essentialism; however, as Benedict explains, the Pacific war marked the first time that large-scale conflict with a non-Western political entity fell on U.S. shoulders and the amount of psychological stress removed from American leadership by at least believing they held an advantage in the form of cultural knowledge would prove at least as meaningful as any tangible usage that her study may have seen.[25] The unintended consequence of the book's later publication for mass consumption was that it, more so than almost any other such material, formed the basis of American assumptions about Japan. Interestingly, it was soon translated and became a best-seller in Japan, where it was hotly debated over by nationalist scholars and liberal reform advocates as potentially demonstrating "weaknesses" to be found in the author's possibly correct assertions of "Japanese otherness."[26] In this way, Benedict's work was equally influential on the formation of postwar national identity within Japan as it was on general American assumptions about Japan.

The construction of this identity continued through the official U.S. occupation and well into the 1970s and 1980s (it may be argued that domestic Japanese quests for national identity continue *today*), when Japan National Railways teamed with other companies to encourage domestic tourism through a campaign called "Exotic Japan." Advertisements for the campaign depicted Japan as mysterious, decidedly Oriental, and showed native Japanese experiencing the wonders of their own culture, which apparently they had never investigated.[27] Exotic Japan and similar promotions demonstrate a case of self- or auto-orientalism in which traditions are invented and reinvented through the application of an outsider's perspective on one's own image. Re-creation of Japanese national identity was carried out in this way, in large part, because of the need to fit with American assumptions about the Japanese, as found in Benedict's work.

At the same time, specific elements of Japanese society went through shifts as a natural consequence of the occupation. Connell points out that cultures, having survived imperialist and colonial occupation, almost always adapt to Western concepts of masculinity by conforming to them in what he terms "perhaps the most important dynamic of gender in the contemporary world."[28] Japan was no exception, though the confluence of other global concerns appears to have worked this gender dynamic favorably for those who would commercialize masculine pursuits. In particular, American concerns over the Cold War made Japan appear quite favorable when compared with mainland Asian powers, like China, that went the way of

Communism. Treated with a degree of favoritism, Japan quickly became the window through which Americans interpreted the entirety of the continent. In this way Japan came to be seen as a friendlier and less threatening locale than the rest of Asia, in part because Japan, as Americans came to know it, was built with American assumptions in mind and in part because the Japanese did not pose a Communist threat.[29] This returns, then, to the case of karate, masculinity, and Mas Oyama.

Judo and Karate Become Manly Arts

Judo and karate were the first modern martial arts to receive mainstream attention outside of Japan. Servicemen of the World War II era had been taught "judo" of one variety or another as part of their combat training, Japanese-American enclaves on the West Coast and Chicago had organized judo clubs decades before the war, and Kano himself had shown such interest in internationalizing his art that he traveled extensively, sometimes as part of the International Olympic Committee and sometimes exclusively for his own purposes, including two trips to North America where he visited training groups, delivered lectures, and observed tournaments.[30] Even if it had not yet become an established sport within the YMCA or as a part of the Olympics, judo was at least commonly known throughout the Western world and even began to appear on the silver screen. In Japan, *Sugata Sanshiro* (1943), one of famed director Akira Kurosawa's earliest hits, was based on the life of Kano and dramatized the events of the 1886 police tournament between the Kodokan and a rival school. In the U.S., audiences saw what may have been the first appearance of judo in a major motion picture with *Blood on the Sun* (1945) starring James Cagney. Judo had become part of the American cultural landscape.

Karate, meanwhile, had only recently been popularized in Japan. Funakoshi had evidently been wise in choosing to focus on university-age men when promoting his art to the Japanese as those same men became political and cultural leaders during the postwar period. Among those who came of age at the zenith of domestic militarism was Oyama. In some ways, his life can be viewed as representative of many men his age: Just prior to and during the war, he felt powerful emotions of patriotism and love for his emperor; losing the war resulted in a lasting personal crisis as he felt directionless; the U.S. occupation initially brought hardships, but he eventually found that Americans were a steady consumer base for his version of the (invented) Japanese cultural legacy, in the form of karate.[31]

Karate, like all martial arts, carries with it certain social and cultural practices and beliefs. When Funakoshi adapted it to fit those of the Japanese, he demonstrated the plasticity of martial systems to retain (at least some of the) core physical practices while also drastically altering the state of their non-physical culture. One productive way to explain this phenomenon is in terms of "object of knowledge" versus "texture of knowledge." An object of knowledge can be more or less readily transferred between cultural groups because it consists of a coherent, packaged set of information. A given song, for instance, can later be transcribed and reproduced by others, even playing different instruments and without any prior understanding of the culture from which the song originates. A texture of knowledge, however, refers to cultural practices and beliefs of a greater complexity, which require a depth of exposure to properly absorb, and comprised of parts that may be altered in one way or another, forgotten, or that take on different meaning depending on both surroundings and practitioner.[32] If an individual song is an object of knowledge, then a genre of music is a texture of knowledge and its place in a larger cultural sphere will depend on any number of situational factors that affect its manifestation and interpretation.

In this case, karate was already employed as a tool intended for the masculinization of young men and for the purposes of expanding Japan's sphere of influence in Asia. Many of those who dedicated time and energy to studying the art before U.S. occupation held on to the beliefs with which they were enculturated thanks to the Okinawan system being retrofitted for appeal to Japan's controlling educational institutions, just as Kano had done with judo. Oyama, not surprisingly, saw no separation between those beliefs and the practice of karate, causing him to suggest that "the wandering adventurer is the ideal image for a man and that the patient, virtuous woman, waiting even until she is eighty and her head is crowned with white hair for the wandering adventurer to return, is the ideal image for a woman."[33] Although the continental adventurer image was, in point of fact, a creation of Japanese militarism, its connection with karate as a texture of knowledge was such that the two could not easily be split and Oyama continued to indoctrinate his own students with this conception of masculinity.

Although members of the occupying forces were probably familiar with judo to some extent prior to arriving in Japan, it was karate that came to be popularized by these men after returning to the U.S. One of the major reasons for this is undoubtedly something of a historical accident. MacArthur's General Headquarters was made aware of the use of martial arts as tools of breeding adamant public desire for expansionism, so one of the first orders issued upon seizing control of the country was a sweeping ban on the practice of Japanese fighting arts, including judo and kendo, as well as the more classical styles of *bujutsu*. Curiously, karate's status as a recent import—and therefore not yet fully incorporated into the school system—gave the occupiers sufficient cause to allow its practice for the three years (1945 to '48) when even the Kodokan was out of operation. The results were immediate and twofold. First, it became the only publically practiced martial art in Japan, so that even after the end of the ban it continued to be more prevalent than ever. Second, American soldiers and sailors who took an interest in Japanese fighting arts did not have to choose between styles.[34]

Karate was appealing to American men, too, for several reasons. Because Funakoshi's reforms were intended to gain favor with militarists, the art had taken on a militaristic flair that it never had in its original context on Okinawa. There were uniforms, ranks, set rituals, a defined curriculum, and paying of obeisance to the national flag. The Americans who chose to pursue karate would have recognized all of these as recently familiar due to their military service but, like Oyama and other Japanese instructors of his generation, would not have known that these elements were grafted onto the texture of knowledge. As Donohue argues, all of these attendant aspects are part and parcel of the power negotiation and identity-making that lies at the heart of modern Japanese martial arts.[35] Between the familiarity of surroundings and the appeal of messages like Oyama's supposedly traditional masculinity, karate was a natural fit for the captive audience of U.S. occupying servicemen.

In terms of pugilistic entertainment, American men in occupied Japan had come of age during the golden years of professional boxing, so karate's percussive methods, too, seemed familiar, but with sufficiently exotic components as to entice adventuresome interest. For example, Western boxing does not allow for kicking or use of the elbows as a striking tool, both of which are common in karate. Perhaps most important in this regard was the "sportification" of the art in the years leading up to the war. Funakoshi saw that, like judo, his system would lack a certain appeal for young men without some manner of competition. To resolve this, he invented a means of controlled sparring (*jiyu kumite*) that could be performed safely with minimal protective equipment (and often none at all) and translated well into a tournament structure, completing the process of modernization that translated the martial art of karate into a sport.[36] Already comfortable with the concept of boxing as a sport, American occupiers became a relatively common presence in karate dojo.

The years 1945 to 1948 proved to be crucial in the formation of Asian martial arts in Western culture. Krug explains this best: "The philosophic and esoteric practices of martial arts were generally not learned in the short time that Westerners spent among Asian cultures. Thus, what grew in ... Western cultures was ... the idea of karate as Westerners imagined it." Considered as a texture of knowledge, the martial arts require years—if not decades—to absorb due to their entrenchment within cultural complexes. On the other hand, an object of knowledge, such as a sport, can be acquired in short order to a minimum level of competence, and this was most certainly what young American men, on tours of duty lasting only a few years, saw in the sport, rather than the full cultural constellation of karate and other Asian martial arts.[37]

Return and Transformation

There were some Americans who, after a few years of dedicated practice, were awarded black belt grades by their Japanese instructors. In a Japanese context, while, of course, meaningful, the black belt typically designates one who has demonstrated an understanding of the basic corpus of a system's techniques. The first-degree of black belt, for instance, is referred to in Japanese as *shodan*, literally "first-initial step." That concept may not have translated well between cultures, however, and a number of returning veterans established their own martial arts academies and clubs in the U.S. It has been observed by well-established social scientists that, no matter the time or place of origin, all martial arts are ultimately subject to modification when propagated in a new setting, not only in terms of technical execution, but culturally and aesthetically due to differences in philosophic interpretation.[38]

Young people in Japan before the period of occupation took to karate and judo because they were either forced to do so by the educational and/or other governmental systems or because they saw in the practice of martial arts some means of developing meaning or personal power in their lives. Karate among university students, especially, carried a great deal of appeal since it was at once exotic and Japanese, held the respect of educators and military personnel alike, and could offer the kind of professional networking opportunities now associated with golf. The pursuit of karate at institutes of higher education was and continues to be serious business. That attitude contrasts rather sharply with the mindset of occupying servicemen, for whom it was a fun, interesting cultural pastime. Karate, for the soldier or sailor stationed in Japan, was a way to kill time, get some exercise, and have a bit of distraction from the dull task of overseeing a peaceful people. The mentality formed a uniquely American perspective in which karate (and later other martial disciplines) was seen as a suitable activity for recreation, but necessitated militaristic order; it was a hobby to which a few hours a week may be dedicated, but was also a rigid lifeway that employed rank, drills, and following the every command of an all-knowing superior. This was the two-minded approach of the men who returned home with what they knew of the Asian martial arts and can still be seen echoing in the confused, dichotomous messages in many present-day American martial arts schools: have fun, make friends, and get back in line.

It is widely accepted that the first professional (that is, for-profit) karate school in the mainland United States was founded in Arizona in 1946 by former Navy boxer Robert Trias. He claimed to have studied Okinawan karate under a Chinese janitorial worker and Buddhist missionary named Tung Gee Hsing, who also instructed Trias in the basics of Chinese "internal" martial arts and meditation. Trias called his style Shuri-ryu, after one of the major Okinawan schools that existed prior to Funakoshi's reforms. In 1948 he founded the United States Karate Association in order to license other schools and organize tournaments. Trias' interpretation of karate—and Japanese culture in general—is, at best, spurious. Although it will never be known how he actually acquired his martial arts training, it is apparent that he was a key figure in spreading the Orientalized pseudo-history, myths, and legends that continue in Western depictions of the arts. Most notable among these is his insistence that karate's history traces back to the Shaolin temple's connection with a mysterious Indian monk known as Bodhidharma, who, seeing that the monks of the temple were physically unable to meditate for long periods as a consequence of their sedentary lifestyle, devised a system of calisthenics that eventually became the Chinese martial arts which, in turn, were brought to Okinawa.[39] The Bodhidharma tale is still prevalent today in martial arts schools worldwide.

In terms of textural knowledge, it is interesting that Trias supposedly learned an Okinawan art from a Chinese man and yet, for reasons that will never be disclosed (Trias passed away in 1989), the vocabulary of Trias' Shuri-ryu is clearly reflective of karate as Funakoshi altered it for the Japanese. Even the *kata*—predetermined, dance-like patterns for practice—that he taught include versions of the new patterns that Funakoshi created for use in public education.[40] Trias carried forward another Western-created fiction about Asian martial arts in his teachings about *kata* that, like the

Bodhidharma legend, manages to persist despite historical data to the contrary. In this case, Trias asserted:

> Centuries ago the formal katas were conceived and developed by the masters as a system of prearranged techniques including the usage of personal weapons as well as the techniques for walking, stepping, pivoting, stances, and blocking. Since the formal katas lend themselves well to individual practice they should be considered as a Manual of Technique, and this is undoubtedly what the masters had in mind.[41]

This passage, more than simply claiming that karate's drill patterns carry some greater meaning in themselves, points to the central myth of Asian martial culture as invented in the Western world: Long ago, before recorded history, but still within cultural memory, there existed masters of the fighting arts who possessed extraordinary prowess now lost to the majority of people, but glimpses can still be had if one trains diligently and knows where to look.

We may best interpret this phenomenon by reinvigorating a Victorian social scientific process known as euhemerism. In a more modernized approach, what past researchers have termed "strong euhemerism" can be identified by three requirements: a clear delineation between the mundane and the fantastical or otherworldly; in which ordinary humans may not pass into control of the otherworld; except for some special individuals. Historically, euhemerism was concerned with literal apotheosis: Euhemerus himself supposedly proffered the rationalistic argument that gods of the Greek pantheon were simply exceptional humans, perhaps benevolent leaders, who, over some generations, came to be considered deities.[42] On a more abstract level, however, I would argue that this model of the concept applies well to situations in which an (at least partially) organized group comes to profess a belief in the extraordinary state of a prelapsarian past with regards to individual persons. For the first wave of Westerners bringing Asian martial arts to mainstream English-speaking audiences, such mythologizing as tales of the "masters" and Bodhidharma in particular amount to a nonreligious form of euhemerism.

The reason for such readiness to support unsubstantiated tales as those weaved by Trias and his generation may lie in a peculiarly American romantic image. Some have recognized the trends in American martial arts narratives as typically featuring the image of a "lone fighter."[43] Drawing on famed mythologist Joseph Campbell's work with the monomyth and the hero's journey, we can see a series of key characteristics that are nearly universal in the American warrior myth. The individual is somehow marginal to, but operates as a part of, society because, without some attachment to a community, the warrior's exploits lack meaning. The hero must be possessed of unusual skill or prowess, but reluctant to deploy it. He must be connected with the community on an emotional level without ever fully joining his fellows. The conflict by which he is defined is small and usually local, and the resolution must be somehow violent.[44]

The attraction of the Asian martial arts for the American psyche would appear to be their advertised ability to grant individual power, ensuring the autonomy needed for enacting the lone warrior myth. This is clear in Trias' pitch to attract new students, in which he described karate as "an expression of man's indomitable will to survive in the most direct, self-reliant manner possible, using only that which nature gave him, a mind and body, rigorously disciplined as an inseparable entity."[45] Attending classes is guaranteed to "give the student the physical training required to effectively handle himself offensively or defensively in any situation which may endanger his life or the lives of those dependent upon him."[46] Lest the potential student desire simply violence, however, it must be remembered that the "true master of karate-do has a sense of propriety and humility which will lead him to his own sense of honor."[47]

For such promoters of Asian martial arts, the mythos is established through such rhetoric as the above. Trias sets himself (and other teachers) in the role of the "true master," like those of the bygone age, who lives in a state of tranquil honor while commanding potentially devastating destructive skills, but which he will only—reluctantly—unleash as needed for the "lives of those dependent upon him." This perfectly conforms to Donohue's model, which is further complemented by the background narrative of mysterious origins for both the art itself and those previous masters who fit the mold of the lone fighter in the mythologizing process. Thomas Green, one of a few highly respected martial arts researchers, points to both the shadowy past and well-known patterns of mythic and folkloric narratives as requirements not simply for the lone fighter, who features heavily in martial arts folklore generally, but in particular for the founders and leading proponents of styles in which the stories are utilized to a number of practical ends, most notably as a means of legitimization for the system's efficacy as well as for one's own personal enactment of myth.[48]

With these features of the martial arts narrative in mind, the process by which Americans, particularly men, came to adopt Asian martial arts so readily from the 1940s and '50s appears cogently as a process that could have occurred anywhere in the world, but for which Americans were especially receptive given the cultural climate at the time and an already-strong predilection toward certain heroic symbolism. For a new karate student at Trias' school in 1946, then, the structure of the tale would have appeared in this manner: Long ago, before records were well kept, an Indian Buddhist monk came to a temple in China where the locals required instruction; to solve their problematic weakness, he taught them a near-magical sequence of movements that evolved over time into a system of combat; monk-like tranquility became entwined with combat skill and the art spread across East Asia, eventually reaching Okinawa, where it was mastered by extraordinary individuals; a mysterious Chinese man learned from said masters and passed his knowledge along to a young American sailor; the sailor, in an act of benevolence, opened a school to spread this knowledge to his people. In short, as Green states, the folk history "reflect[s] a desire of modern practitioners to establish credibility through association with a legendary past."[49]

Masculinity in Crisis Again

At the moment of America's move to join the war, professional boxing was at the height of its popularity. Before moving on to discuss the decline of boxing as a participant activity and the simultaneous rise of Asian martial arts from the 1950s to the 1990s, it is necessary to consider the state of American masculinity at the historical moment in which servicemen were returning from overseas. Here, too, Trias, himself having been a boxer, serves as an example of how many such individuals viewed the social scene for men at the time:

> [H]e is hampered from making any direct or spontaneous action, but must ever rely on an intellectual approach which weighs, sorts, and chooses and then finds that it has run into a brick wall and can go no farther. To overcome this limitation by letting the original mind make the decisions (on an intuitive basis) is alarming to the Occidental, because he does not trust himself beyond his conscious thought. He has never given himself to the type of introspective meditation practiced by Oriental philosophers and has missed a viewpoint of himself that is quite different from the ego-inspired approach.[50]

The vagueness of his criticism points to an undefined yet prevalent frustration with the social arrangement in which postwar men found themselves. It also demonstrates a rather drastic revision of history that eschews much of the Western humanistic tradition, including philosophy of all kinds, instead insisting that "the Occidental" is given wholly to scientific, quantitative thought, while "the Oriental" is more naturalistic, intuitive, and generally better at patterning a contemplative lifestyle. In order for Trias' approximation of Western philosophical thought to be true, one would have to ignore such introspective lineages as the Stoics. There is also the matter of the Theosophists, who were practicing a similar brand of orientalism far earlier than Trias. Anxiety about the shortcomings of "the Occidental" also appeared in the media, and point to the zeitgeist of his generation.

As Americans returned from the intensity of war, they found a homeland already concerned with the next great threat in the form of the nontraditional. Foremost among those ideas that threatened the "traditional" American lifestyle was Communism, which now represented all that which was not American, and the U.S. government began its campaigns against this political and social ideology (one that had conquered both China and Russia) from growing to a domestic threat. McCarthy and other anticommunists of the era saw such potential threats in all manner of groups and behaviors that failed to conform to a narrowly defined concept of American culture, including "racial integration, secularism, materialism, apathy, commercialism, conformity, youth rebellion, Jewish upward mobility, internationalism, and welfare statism."[51]

In 1949 Harvard historian Arthur Schlesinger's book *The Vital Center* received much public attention. This and several of his other works at once defended the liberal political traditional while also criticizing the degree to which its followers failed to express sufficient levels of individualism and masculinity. By 1958 his public calls for a more manly left wing grew popular enough that in his *Esquire* magazine article "The Crisis of American Masculinity" he decried the weakness of right-wing "organization men" who lacked independent wills and thoughts of their own, much like the automatons supposedly generated by Communist methodology. That same year, *Look* magazine ran a series based on the same theme, which were later collected and printed as a book, making evident the general concern that men in America had fallen victim to feminization by allowing an entire generation of boys to be raised by women while the men had been away at war and concentrating on their careers. To a lesser extent, though still meaningful, was the often implied and sometimes outright fear of the foreign. This was generally found in the form of rhetoric specifically focused on Communism. However the rise of foreigners went hand in hand with that of women in public social spheres, again pointing to the broader anxiety about non-traditionality.[52]

That the "organization man" was now considered weak and counter to productive masculinity is interesting in that it ran against to the prewar ideal of identity-affirming men's groups like the YMCA. Indeed, the YMCA had, for decades, referred to its members as "organization men."

The American middle class had shifted in a number of ways since the war, however, and anxieties from the turn of the century appear to have been somewhat warranted. Men no longer had time for leisure as they did during the 1920s and, coupled with the unacceptability of communal affirmation (lest one be labeled a Communist), sporting clubs like the YMCA saw drops in participation as men dedicated time and energy toward employment. To be seen by others as a practitioner of such frivolity as participating in a club for the playing of games was anathema to cultivating a manly image in the contemporary sense. Predictably, the drop in sporting behavior among middle-class men correlated with a rise in obesity and heart disease among that same group. The widely felt effects of this turn in social identity included the decline of boxing, the reprise of a masculinized consumerism of the body as seen in the pre-war years (accompanied by changes in the idealized form), and, most pertinent here, an intense consumptive drive to graft the Asian martial arts onto mainstream American culture.[53]

As men were spending more time at work in white-collar professions and American society grew less accepting of male camaraderie in sporting institutions due to both the conspicuous possession of leisure time and the public animosity toward organization men of all kinds, a new paradigm of masculinity was needed. Once again, some men found their solution by looking to the (imagined) past and abroad. One such consumeristic and past-oriented resolution came in the form of a mid-century update on the image "dandies," often referred to by the 1950s as "dudes" or "playboys." These were men for whom consumptive leisure activities were a display of masculinity not because of, but in open and direct opposition to the public rhetoric against non-productive pursuits. Members of the dude group made ostentatious shows of their choice not to work, thereby inverting the prevalent conservative push of McCarthyism and the anti-communists. The gender negotiation strategy was popular enough that *Playboy* magazine, launched in 1953, had over four million subscribers by the end of its first ten years. Other magazines of the time, including *Esquire*, *True*, and *Modern Man,* retooled to match the *Playboy* formula. Men were redefining consumerism in droves, and while it may have had a positive effect on their sense of masculinity, it most certainly was not working well for their physical health. Obesity and inactivity were on the rise. Those who embodied the man-of-leisure lifestyle may have enjoyed spectating at boxing matches, but they were unlikely to put in the amount of un-enjoyable time and work necessary to put on the gloves themselves.[54]

The middle-class man, increasingly identifying himself with Hugh Hefner and his set, responded to the obesity epidemic and social anxiety of American men being feminized by applying this new conception of masculine consumption toward dieting and weight loss. Where the previous generation turned to self-help magazines like *Strength and Fitness* and saw the body as a way to demonstrate the power of one's will, the postwar man of leisure followed a similar pattern of behavior, but with a greater emphasis on mail-order programs, doctor visits, and a vision of personal weight loss as a kind of combat in which food and the body were the enemies, professionals one's allies, and tales of suffering stood in for the glory of battle. In 1950, for instance, Elmer Wheeler, an advertising expert and salesman, published *Fat Boy's Book*, a personal account of his struggle to reduce adipose tissue. In it he recalls the toil and distress of starving at the dinner table. Serialized in newspapers, the book received a great deal of public attention. It was soon followed by a sequel, which does not speak well of Wheeler's success at maintaining a healthy state.[55]

Men like Wheeler exemplify how the social climate was changing drastically as a result of the postwar recovery. Urban dwellers became commuters as suburbs cropped up across the country. The G.I. Bill sent millions of former servicemen to universities, which allowed them to join the growing middle class and escape the world of manual labor. Silver (2008) points to this as having a directly negative impact on the popularity and quality of boxing in the U.S. While the middle-class man turned more toward a consumer style of conspicuous leisure and the economic class itself was growing larger due to new economic opportunities, the likelihood that a young man would seek his fortune by emulating Jack Dempsey and become a journeyman fighter continued to shrink. The decline in both spectators and competitors was palpable. In 1949 Madison Square Garden failed to gross more than $1,000,000 for boxing shows for the first time since before the war. As of 1952, the number of registered professional boxers had dropped by almost half what it was at the height of the sport. All over the country, YMCAs, once the breeding ground for future champions, began to remove amateur training and contests from their list of activities.[56]

Boxing was in decline, which proved to be as much a consequence of economic as social factors. American men were no longer comfortable seeking refuge in communal identity affirmation by engaging in club sports, the boxing gym included, nor were they seeking financial solvency through the fight game as education and other opportunities opened up less dangerous and uncertain pathways to monetary success. It may reasonably be suggested that the golden age of boxing ended on April 17, 1960, when a University of Wisconsin boxer named Charlie Mohr died as a result of injuries incurred during a sanctioned match at the university's gymnasium.

The National Collegiate Athletic Association responded by discontinuing its boxing program, effectively shutting down college boxing clubs in general and the last avenue of the middle-class prospect to be lured away from white-collar work and into the ring. Without talented and dedicated fighters to continue the tradition, the quality of boxing instruction went into decline. This naturally led to a drop in the number of spectators. This did not mark the end of combat sports in America, however, as television, movies, and comics presented new means of attracting a generation of participants alienated by the tumultuous 1960s and seeking a haven of physically expressive masculinity that wasn't threatened by feminism, anti-war politics, and the mundaneness of traditional America.[57]

The First Asian Martial Arts Boom

Young people coming of age in 1960s America were subject to a radically different social climate as compared with any domestic strife encountered by previous generations. The Korean War, essentially an extension and aftershock of World War II, had come and gone, and the U.S. was preparing to increase its involvement in the Vietnam conflict, which later proved to be extraordinarily unpopular with much of the general public. In addition to intensifying protests against the Vietnam situation, racial and gender inequality became issues of popular concern. In the midst of this volatile atmosphere, perceptions of traditional masculinity were transformed to associate it with violence, oppression, political conservatism, and xenophobia. Much of the backlash against notions of a traditional American masculinity were clearly drawn from the popular movement of feminism. This presents a complex case for negotiating one's male identity. On one hand, pre-war fashions of masculinity of the type associated with manual labor and neo-primitivism were unlikely to garner favor, but on the other, it would still be desirable for many or even most young men to have some identity to which they could cling during such uncertain social and political upheaval. If the *Playboy* lifestyle presented one option, there were most definitely others.[58]

In 1961, *Look* magazine's unusual article "Karate: Japan's Spectacular Art of Handmade Mayhem" drew national attention to an area of human activity that had previously only been seen in a few small regions within the U.S. where men like Robert Trias established their organizations. The extent to which the public was assumed to be knowledgeable about both martial arts and Asia in general can be gleaned from the article's contents.

Much of the space is taken up with an elaborate explanation of the history of karate, judo, and sumo. "There are probably a dozen distinct systems of Oriental hand-to-hand fighting, all of them allied," suggests Purdy; and then later: "Karate developed independently from jujitsu. Karate is the essence of violence—personal combat carried to an ultimate point." The author explains that karate, coming from this background of personal combat, "reject[s] the concept of fighting 'fair.' … [W]hile rules may improve a ball-and-stick game like baseball, they have no place in handling unprovoked physical assaults." Juxtaposing the no-rules karate with the most American of pastimes not only establishes the martial art as something different from conventional sports, but also strongly implies that it is something decidedly foreign, invoking, as Benedict pointed out almost twenty years earlier, that Americans frequently exoticize Japanese culture as precisely the inverse of America.[59]

The comparison between "Oriental" Japan and conventional America is carried to its ultimate conclusion at the end of the piece, wherein the author matches karate against boxing:

> Can a karateist beat a boxer? Of course—if he is not asked to fight by the boxer's rules. Usually, such contests are inconclusive because only the boxer can go all-out. No open fight between an expert karate or judo player and a boxer should last three minutes, no matter how good the boxer. This is not a disparagement of boxing. Boxing is a sport. Karate is not…. Open, all-out bouts obviously cannot be allowed.[60]

Karate was something altogether different from even its closest Western analog. Purdy stresses throughout the article that there are also meditative aspects to the art, and explains that "karate originated with a Buddhist monk," which may account for the fact that "it is designed to kill or maim, yet karate experts are nearly always mild, quiet men."[61] The implications are clear and echo those of Trias: Asian martial arts are better than Western ones because they are more physically powerful and will impart a state of inner peace to the practitioner. By Orientalizing the practice, it then renders participation into something wholly different from the traditionally masculine enterprise of boxing and, therefore, would be suitable for a young man interested in gaining power and identity without being subject to social discourse against his behavior.

Krug (2001) notes that new cultural practices do not integrate into Western "normality" until and unless they are accompanied by spatially defined multimedia that establish the existence of external authority. This happened with karate during the 1960s and with other martial arts over time. Magazines like *Look*, books by authors from Mas Oyama to Robert Trias, and major motion pictures including *You Only Live Twice* and *The*

Born Losers (both 1967) brought Asian martial arts—and especially karate—into the daily lexicon of popular culture. Soon instruction for these arts became a booming industry, generating a new market for the unique institution of martial arts schools, as well as learn-at-home books and magazines. Foreign instructors came from Japan, China, and elsewhere to take advantage of consumer demand. Less direct effects were also felt as Asian-American stars (most notably Bruce Lee) began to appear on screen, and the films grew more graphically violent during the 1970s as a new interpretation of masculinity was portrayed by muscular action heroes. As Krug highlights, though, none of this would occur without the normalization of Asian martial arts through books and articles penned by accepted experts in the field.[62] These experts were few, and although colorful characters appeared domestically in the United States, frequently passing themselves off as authorities, the core of professional specialists could be found among a small group of Westerners living in Asia (mostly Japan), including a circle of friends formed around Donn Draeger, Robert Smith, and Jon Bluming.

4

In Search of the Death Touch

Growing up as a kid, I wanted to be a ninja. In martial arts, even though I did Chinese kung fu, I always wanted to be this secret samurai or a ninja. There's something about ninjas that was very appealing to me as a kid. So of course, I was climbing a lot of trees and other things and getting up to mischief—good mischief.
—Ray Park, actor and stunt performer

I have some knowledge ... of *baritsu*, or the Japanese system of wrestling, which has more than once been very useful to me. I slipped through his grip, and he with a horrible scream kicked madly for a few seconds and clawed the air with both his hands. But for all his efforts he could not get his balance, and over he went.
—Sherlock Holmes in "The Adventure of the Empty House" (1903) by Sir Arthur Conan Doyle

The trifecta of Robert W. Smith, Donn F. Draeger, and Jon Bluming formed, for a time, the core of what became the most influential group of Western practitioners of Asian martial arts in the English-speaking world. Their collective work from the 1950s through the 1970s and '80s was central to the basis of Western martial arts folk culture, in particular with regards to the lexicon utilized even today, the nature of how performances are understood and evaluated by the group in terms of effectiveness, the availability and interpretation of the group's repertoires, and, perhaps most important, by establishing different modes of cultural preservation that resulted in radically different approaches to the subject matter by practitioners worldwide. These men can be juxtaposed against those selling their wares in the American domestic market without the scholarly rigor of works produced by the likes of Draeger and Smith. Such capitalistic figures include one of the most colorful figures in the history of American martial arts culture, John "Count Dante" Keehan.

   While the majority of pre-war practitioners were almost exclusively
Japanese- and Chinese-Americans living on the West Coast, there were
occasions on which people of other ethnic backgrounds ventured into their
clubs and training halls. Smith and Draeger were two of the first Anglo-
Americans to undertake the practice of judo. Their meeting at the Chicago
Judo Club via an introduction by the legendary Johnny Osako in 1948 or
1949 proved to be the start of a long and prolific partnership, resulting in
some of the first English-language treatments of the Asian martial arts as
a field of study. Unlike their counterparts for whom Japanese and Chinese
language and culture were still very much a part of daily life, the pair had
to introduce—sometimes explicitly, sometimes through happenstance—a
new lexicon through which Western martial artists could express their
thoughts on subjects for which there were few establish speech patterns in
English.

   In order to understand the monumental scope of their task, it is necessary to know who they were as people. Robert W. Smith (1926–2011) was
an astoundingly prolific author of martial arts books and articles that are
notably well-researched and with obvious attention paid to craftsmanship.
Raised in an Iowa orphanage until he joined the U.S. Marine Corps at sev-
enteen, Smith was known as a bookish child who developed a love for boxing and wrestling. Poetry and literature were other lifelong passions and,
in addition to his authorship in the fighting disciplines, he was a frequent
contributor to newspapers in the way of book reviews and criticism—particularly when there was an opportunity to reference G.K. Chesterton. On
one occasion, Smith was afforded an interview with legendary science fiction writer Ray Bradbury, which was recorded via audiotape.

   Smith leveraged the G.I. Bill to attend university after completing his
tour of duty, and received a graduate degree in history from the University
of Washington in 1953. He spent most of his professional career as a Central
Intelligence Agency analyst in Bethesda, Maryland. Before settling down
to family life in Bethesda, he spent three years (1959–1962) on assignment
in Taiwan. This allowed him to pursue an interest in the martial arts of
Asia on a much more intense scale. Although he did venture to Japan to
further his judo career and to investigate the martial arts scene in postwar
Tokyo, most of Smith's energy was focused on the various Chinese arts
available in Taiwan. The many teachers under whom he trained were outlined in *Chinese Boxing: Masters and Methods* (1974). One in particular
absorbed his attention so completely that Smith would eventually concen-
trate his time on practicing arts other than those of his youth. Zheng Manqing was and continues to be a much-storied exponent of *taiji*.

After returning home, Smith taught judo at his local YMCA for a few years before giving it up, due, most likely, to the shifting nature of competition judo in the U.S. and abroad following its introduction at the 1964 Tokyo Olympics. It is widely bemoaned by more traditional judo adherents that the past few decades have caused the community to center itself squarely on the sportive elements to the detriment of moral or philosophical development in its participants. Smith also abandoned boxing, an art of which he held an encyclopedic knowledge; he had even trained amateur fighters. In this case, though, Smith's opposition was stauncher and rooted in concern for physical health. With his friend and neurologist, Dr. Andrew Guterman, he wrote the sports medicine journal article "Neurological Sequelae of Boxing," in which they explain the physiological and subsequent psychological effects of repeated minor head trauma compounded over years of engaging in the sport. Worried that boxing does more harm than good, Smith ended his involvement and was somewhat outspoken on the matter. His martial arts activity in the U.S. was constructed around a small group of students in *taiji*, *bagua*, and *xing-yi*, and a large, free *taiji* class that he taught every weekend, rarely ever missing a session.

Smith's good friend and frequent collaborator, Donn F. Draeger (1922–1982), is often seen as a somewhat shadowy figure in the history of Asian martial arts scholarship. Born in Milwaukee, Wisconsin, Draeger began his martial arts career as a child, purportedly studying a school of *jujutsu*. There are no details on which style or lineage he studied, a particularly troublesome point, historically, as the art was quite rare in the U.S. at that time. He began to train in judo sometime around age ten, and continued to participate in the judo community for the rest of his life. He joined the Marine Corps and served as an officer in various locations in North America and the Pacific from 1943 until retiring in 1956. He attended Georgetown University and then Sophia University in Japan. Having maintained a strong interest in East Asia and the fighting disciplines, Draeger chose to make Tokyo and, later, Narita his base of operations.

During most of the 1960s, Draeger rented a house in the Ichigaya section of Tokyo, where he lived with a rotating crew of other non-Japanese martial artists, including luminaries Doug Rogers (the Canadian who won a silver medal in judo at the 1964 Olympics) and James Bregman (the American who took bronze at the same games) in addition to Smith and Bluming. The members of this household were an adventurous lot, often taking the time to investigate different martial arts on offer in the cosmopolitan space of postwar Tokyo. One character frequently mentioned in

Draeger's correspondence is Wang Shujin, a Chinese sometimes-expatriate who lived in Japan off and on as finances allowed. Wang taught *taiji*, *xing-yi*, and *bagua*, like Smith, and was something of an eccentric with regards to his physical abilities. As will be discussed below, he was especially famous for the ability to absorb blows with his prodigious gut. This was also a time of innovation within the Japanese martial arts, and those staying in the house were exposed to new teachers and methods that were just coming into public notice after the haze of American occupation.

Draeger, perhaps more so than any other martial arts scholar of his time, contributed virtually all of his resources to the study and dissemination of the Asian combative disciplines. He wrote articles for the popular magazines *Strength and Fitness* and *Black Belt*, which launched in 1961. In the English-speaking world, the entire realm of Asian martial arts was a new frontier that gripped the attention of young men. Draeger capitalized on this to some extent, writing pieces on weight training for judo and co-authoring the multi-volume series *Practical Karate: An Everyman's Guide to Self-Defense* (1963) with famed Japan Karate Association founding member Nakayama Masatoshi. He and Smith came together as a writing and research team, in large part because they formed complementary opposites. A lifelong lover of the English language, Smith was very accomplished in writing as a craft and prized intelligent, well-placed humor. Draeger wrote in a brusque, straightforward way that left a great deal to be desired in terms of readability. Together, they composed works that continue to be among the best in the genre.

Like Smith, Draeger eventually grew weary of competition judo and even kendo, turning instead to the classical Japanese martial arts that were nearly wiped out in the course of the American occupation and dismantling of the Butokukai. Whenever possible, he also ventured to Southeast Asia in the interest of field work. He spent some months each year traveling to different remote locations and attempting to learn the local styles of fighting, which he would then record as thoroughly as possible so that future articles could include his findings. He also visited Hawaii, where he harbored dreams of opening a center for the study of martial culture. One of his field trips proved disastrous: He came down with dysentery in Sumatra in 1979. After recovering somewhat, his body began to deteriorate and he eventually sought treatment at Tripler Army Medical Center in Hawaii. He passed away in 1982 from cancer, many of his projects still underway. Like Smith, Draeger's contributions to the martial arts in America are legion, even accounting for much of the language encountered by those who venture into these practices today. It is telling of the camaraderie between the two that Smith tirelessly continued efforts to have Draeger receive the best possible care until the time of his friend's passing.

Toelken (1996) notes that, in many cases, a group's folk speech is the only way to appreciate and express a style of performance. One issue during the creation of a folk group, then, is establishing a new form or mode of speech for the purposes of transmitting knowledge and communicating aesthetic values where no concept of such values previously existed. The new folk speech had to be constructed and molded and over time this took place through a bricolage of translations, transliterations, and neologisms.[1] One relevant example is their editorial debate over the term "Chinese boxing." Smith had long used the term to reference Chinese unarmed martial arts in general; however Draeger was vehemently opposed.

During their negotiation over articles in Draeger's ill-fated magazine project *Martial Arts International,* the subject of editorial changes came up. Smith was apparently less than amenable, and Draeger responded, "As for leaving your work stand as is … of course…. But we do have some house rules." Draeger's group, operating primarily in Tokyo, had intentionally chosen to "not normally use the expression 'Chinese boxing'" as they considered it to be "an old, misused, wornout [sic], and improper term for something that already has its own proper name." Legitimacy, in Draeger's view, was in hewing as closely as possible to the culture from which a martial art originated. "No self-respecting Chinese ever refers to wu shu as 'Chinese boxing,'" he argued, "which is a British phrase."[2]

A decade prior, in his seminal *Secrets of Shaolin Temple Boxing* (1964), Smith had already established his desire to use the term "boxing" in English-language discourse about *ch'uan fa* given that ch'uan is the Chinese character for fist.[3] Despite as a youth having been a boxer and boxing trainer himself, Smith does not appear to have felt that the word carried any special weight or implication aside from pugilism in general and so the use of it to connote any other style within the confines of the English language was acceptable. Draeger disagreed with some fervor, continuing the argument in a follow-up letter, this time suggesting that legitimacy relies not only on remaining close to the mother tongue's usage of a term, but to professional practitioners' official usage of said term:

> The term "boxing" is simply not used by pros. We will follow the pro view. The ideograms for ch'uan-fa in Chinese mean the same when read in Japanese, and do not include the word or idea of "boxing!" We prefer "sparring arts" to "boxing," tho [sic] no ch'uan-fa, in its fullest sense, is entirely made up of sparring techniques. Likewise we decry use of "fencing" for Japanese swordsmanship, "school" for ryu, etc. We will go pro route and try to educate some, re-educate others.[4]

"Boxing" clearly held different connotations for Draeger than it did for Smith, as did the cultural clash between the British and Chinese referenced as sufficient cause to avoid the term in publication.

At the root of this issue was an even more complex negotiation between two different approaches to interpreting Asian martial arts for Western audiences. Draeger, a former Marine, was primarily interested in issues of efficacy in the fighting arts and had little patience for those styles and exponents that failed to meet his expectations. For instance, he saw the Chinese art of energy cultivation, *chi gong*, as nothing more than stage magic: "These Chinese are fantastic with their ch'i kung garbage.... I've yet to see one demo that isn't involved with circus tricks ... all crap."[5]

For Draeger the use of theatricality in martial arts demonstrations was both unnecessary and undesirable. He was searching for the most effective means of meeting particular combative requirements in all different social and cultural situations, as indicated by a somewhat oblique reference in a 1968 letter: "Among mainland Chinese here [Java], kuntao places t'aichi lower on the combative scale than what you have focused on in your work. I'll elaborate on this later."[6] With such specific emphasis on systematic fighting rather than generally performing, he praised only one demonstration during his 1973 trip to Malaysia, noting that they were "indifferent to what audience likes or wants, and goes about business of training."[7]

Smith's views of legitimacy and successful performance within the martial arts were somewhat more complex. Although he sometimes referred to sheer fighting prowess as being desirable, he also clearly supported other goals of less combat-oriented activities, which drew strong contrast between himself and Draeger. Smith's willingness to explore and embrace the alternative roles of the martial arts has at least some origin in the end of his

Draeger in Japan (Robert W. Smith Collection at Cushing Library, Texas A&M University).

period as an amateur boxer and boxing trainer. Despite having been an avid fan of prizefights in his youth, Smith's later education on its long-term health effects led him to give up the sport entirely in the 1950s, and to work toward having it banned. In his memoir he writes that "all boxing should be banned ... too brutal for civilized societies.... This sterile intentionality is what stamps this remnant of primitive savagery as unfit for human beings."[8]

By Smith's own admission, there was an element of bias in each side of the debate over Chinese martial arts, and the use of "boxing" was simply an indicator of a greater rift between the two. Smith said, "I believed that the men and systems he showcased were inferior to those I studied under in Taiwan. I had visited the other areas [that is, mainland China] and met their leading teachers and found them lacking."[9] For Draeger's part, it was more a matter of falsifiability, even where Smith's primary teacher, Zheng Manqing, was concerned. By July 1974 the two were in the heat of their differences with Smith advocating for the Taiwanese martial artists and Draeger losing interest in investigating them, especially *taiji*, which Draeger saw as lacking any real-world application. Wrote Draeger, "You seem to have lost your position of objectivity Bob ... and with it your sense of realism. Cheng Man ching a fighter???? [sic] A scuffler, no doubt, who isn't, but a real fighter ... hardly ... more literati."[10]

Draeger later offers, at least somewhat tongue-in-cheek, to introduce Zheng to a lucrative business opportunity training professional sumo wrestlers: "Pro sumo assn. [sic] tells me that they would pay all expenses, etc. to have man like Cheng show them how to remove opponent from ring."[11] Smith continued to counter that Draeger simply didn't understand Chinese street culture well enough to locate the most skilled martial artists as he had in Japan. In addition, he claims in his memoir that Draeger had developed a prejudice against the Chinese due to his service in the Korean War which was exacerbated by spending so much time with the Japanese.[12] At the same time, the Chinese fighters with whom Draeger was in regular contact were unimpressed with Zheng himself or *taiji* in general, "Nobody here [Malaysia] has illusions about tai-chi being useful as a sole system in combat of any kind.... [T]his confers [sic] what Wang [Shujin, a mutual friend and teacher of Chinese martial arts] always said and taught.... [N]obody thinks [Zheng] is all that good come a good punch up."[13]

The reference to Wang Shujin is significant. Wang spent much of his adult life in Tokyo, where he became a regular at the house in which Draeger and a rotating group of foreign martial artists lived (it was walking distance from the Kodokan Institute and several other training centers).

Draeger, ever on the lookout for opportunities, was intrigued by Wang's ability to withstand blows to the stomach seemingly without injury. In a letter to Smith, Ellis Amdur explains that "Wang set out to teach him Pa Kua [sic], but for two years simply had him walking around a tree in Meiji shrine, and he would come by, look at the trench being scuffed in the dirt and say 'not deep enough.'"[14] This may have been frustrating enough for a talented athlete and fighter like Draeger; however, the final straw with his training was likely "at Donn's house one day, Wang said, 'The trouble with you is you have no control over your body' and he picked up an iron meteorite Donn was using for a paperweight, and … held it out at arms [sic] length, immovable."[15]

Draeger's interactions with Wang colored his vision of the Chinese "soft" or "internal" arts as consisting of time-intensive, non-combative practices that ultimately yielded few meaningful results. He also respected Wang's abilities but was not in awe of them or the Chinese arts in general. Defensive of his teacher and confident in what he'd experienced of the internal martial arts, Smith eventually proposed a solution to the rift: Draeger, in his frequent travels, was welcome to visit Taiwan and "test" Zheng's abilities for himself. Draeger was not amenable, insisting that "'testing' and fighting are completely different…. It's not for me, though Jon Bluming, the Dutch animal, might consider it now as he has in the past. Short of a fight to do somebody, or myself in, I am not equipped to test anybody."[16]

It remains unclear what, precisely, Draeger meant by the final portion of this comment—given that he was then fifty-six, and two years prior had admitted to Smith, "[A]s I look on my multitude of injuries, I see them all stemming from my association with judo. I don't want to batter myself anymore…. I have better things to do now."[17] This seems rather sudden since as recently as 1967 he was still "testing" others; on his trip to Singapore that year Draeger recounts investigating the world of silat via "my method—combat vs. one of their experts. To shorten the story—I flattened him with osoto-gake makikomi; only I got up!"[18] He had also, however, given up on competition roughly around the time of his 1974 trip to Malaysia. In a letter to Smith some years later, Pat Harrington, another foreign judo luminary in Tokyo in the storied days of Draeger's Ichigaya house, comments, "[N]obody tried harder than Donn, but they still would not accept the advice of a foreigner. Yes, it broke his heart, and he then put all of his energy into other martial arts … and most of his time into researching and writing books."[19]

Thus the seemingly innocuous statement that he wasn't "equipped" to test others could be a reference to the unpleasantness of political entanglements that he preferred to avoid, being an avid researcher and not a politician. Draeger had another means by which to test his ideas, one that also provided a buffer between himself and organizational fallouts: Jon Bluming. Bluming, from Holland, was younger than Smith and Draeger during their years of active training and research in Asia and possessed certain physical attributes that allowed him a degree of leniency in questioning the efficacy of another's fighting method. Specifically, Bluming claims that at the time he weighed an intimidating 102 kilograms (224.9 pounds) and regularly trounced the finest judo experts at the Kodokan Judo Institute, including several world champions.[20]

In personal communication, Bluming confirmed that he had met Smith and Draeger at a time when both were most active in judo practice at Kano's reopened Kodokan Institute, but that Smith was, even at that time, much more interested in Chinese martial arts than his judo studies. He further characterized Draeger's thoughts on the matter as, at best, begrudgingly accepting of the state into which he felt Chinese martial arts had fallen in recent decades, apparently having believed that there was a time when styles such as *taiji* and Shaolin were truly effective combat methods against resisting opponents, but that this was no longer the case. In keeping with his tendency to illustrate points with blunt and evocative language, Bluming informed me that he and Draeger shared the same sentiments, but only Bluming "told Bob [Smith] that I never met a Taichi [sic] champ who could beat my Granny when she had an umbrella in her hands."[21]

Born in Amsterdam in 1933, Bluming joined the Dutch Marines at age sixteen. When the Korean War broke out in 1950, he volunteered to go and saw combat, and was injured multiple times. While hospitalized in Tokyo, he was first exposed to judo. He returned to Holland, trained intensely, and returned to Japan for more long-term study in 1959. He met with Draeger and the others, took up multiple styles, and, after crossing paths with Masutatsu Oyama, became a devotee of the kyokushin style of karate in addition to his primary judo studies. Rough-and-tumble by nature, Bluming combined these experiences to form a training system of his own, covering both grappling and striking skills, in a move predictive of what would come to be called "mixed martial arts."

While Smith and Draeger were committed to maintaining mostly congenial relations with other martial artists and researchers, Bluming was interested in personally verifying the effectiveness of any given method, theory, and individual and did so seemingly without regard to political (or

Jon "The Dutch Animal" Bluming at the Kodokan Institute (Robert W. Smith Collection at Cushing Library, Texas A&M University).

sometimes legal) consequences. Smith shares the story of the ever-upfront Bluming and himself being approached by a "strapping 200-pound Korean carrying an umbrella" who attempted to sell them pornographic magazines. He recalls that Bluming "seized the man's umbrella and chased him down the street beating him about the head. I didn't see him again until later in the day. His first words: 'Bob, do you want an umbrella?'"[22]

Draeger, beleaguered with cross-cultural issues as both an expert and a foreigner in a Japanese institution, saw in Bluming the opportunity to prove at least some of his more contested points. During the early days of the Ichigaya house (around 1958), Bluming traveled from Holland to Japan to practice judo at the Kodokan and soon began working with Draeger and company: "Draeger said, 'Look, I am trying to prove a point that weight training and judo, if you do that, you become a better judoka. So I want you in the team to prove that point.'" The experiment was successful and the already impressive Bluming claimed to have put on twenty kilograms of muscle within the same year.[23]

Draeger's triumph in the weight training experiment led him to consider Bluming as a litmus test against which to compare anyone laying claim to superhuman abilities or unverified levels of achievement in the fighting arts. In particular, the matter of Wang Shujin remained suspect in

Draeger's mind. Indeed, it wasn't until the mid–1970s that his opinion on the matter of Chinese internal martial arts like *taiji* came to rest squarely in the critical camp. In a letter to Smith he references his time in the Marine Corps during the Korean War:

> Chinese in general lack guts such as compared to Thai or Japanese fighters. The history books are filled with evidence of the general lack of Chinese fighting ability when they are faced with real fighting men.... I know from Korea when my company knocked hell out of 4 Chinese divisions.... Milling mobs and masses, yes, but fighters ... I have not seen any.[24]

Draeger's wartime experience gave him a distinct prejudice against Chinese, which, as a passionate expert on East Asian martial arts and prolific writer on the topic, was an issue that continued to trouble him throughout his career. This may explain why, despite insisting that he personally make all contributions to the field regarding Japan and a myriad of Southeast Asian culture groups (which caused him to be constantly traveling and drained what little funds he had), he was quite comfortable asking Smith to handle Chinese martial arts in their joint publications. This personal struggle seems to have fueled his interest in Wang, eventually leading him to bring the Chinese man together with Bluming for a "test."

Wang was known for his apparently indestructible belly. Possessed of a prodigious waistline, he would assume a *taiji* posture and invite anyone to strike at his abdomen, simply absorbing the blow no matter how large or powerful the aggressor. Draeger saw this as a parlor trick of some sort and resolved to test the durability of the man's gut. Bluming recalls that he was invited to meet Wang at a private training hall where few could be witness to the spectacle. Because of the somewhat secretive nature of this meeting, a number of rumors have been generated over the years with all manner of variations on the basic idea that Wang and Bluming had an all-out fight. Bluming insists that this was not the case, explaining that, at first, Wang took his usual stance and allowed Bluming to punch him in the stomach. The Dutchman did so, with predictable results. At that time Bluming was focused much more on judo than karate, however, and they agreed that testing the European's grip would be a better means of judging Wang's powers. Gripping Wang's shoulders (he was not wearing a judo uniform), Bluming was surprised when the *taiji* expert shot his belly forward, checking Bluming so hard that he was thrown "meters away." There ended the meeting, with Bluming and Draeger walking away unconvinced that Wang would be of much use in a street altercation. "I did not at the time and still dont [sic] think much of their style," comments Bluming. "[H]e died Young and FAT [sic]."[25]

The Chinese were not the only group with whom Draeger and other Westerners then in Asia encountered racial tensions. Bluming also knew of the political issues at work during Draeger's time with the Kodokan as he insisted that "they did very dirty things to foreigners.... Draeger was a better teacher than anybody else there. He was a better kata man than anybody else."[26] In spite of these issues with the Japanese and others within the foreign martial arts community, Bluming remained anything but timid in his career of challenging and testing others. This did not escape the observant Smith, who acknowledges that "over the years, there have been rumors and gossip about Bluming's so-called misconduct on and off the mat. He was a fierce competitor ... giving no quarter to anyone."[27] Despite any number of personal misgivings, it was more or less universally understood at the time that Bluming was nearly unbeatable in a fair match of any kind. He was also not afraid to issue personal challenges. Another successful Dutch judo competitor of the 1960s, Anton Geesink, quickly rose through international competition toward the end of Bluming's main activity in judo; the press often made them out to be rivals, although the narrative concocted by journalists was, according to Bluming, not entirely accurate given that he issued seven requests for a private match with Geesink via registered letters (that is, said Bluming, "he has to sign for it. So his signature is on the paper, he can never say he didn't get the letter") with the sole intention of proving who was the stronger judo player.[28]

Bluming's interests were primarily vested in fighting itself. As time went on—and especially after Draeger's passing—he spent more time focusing on Mas Oyama's kyokushin karate and a system of Bluming's own invention that he calls simply "free-fighting," something akin to contemporary mixed martial arts in which both percussive and wrestling techniques are permitted. Such disinterest in the narrative surrounding an event and the greater spectacle of the performance may serve to explain at least some of Bluming's and, to a lesser extent, Draeger's political quandaries.

Regarding further cross-cultural frustrations, Bluming complained, "[T]he Japanese are great at manufacturing legends. When I hear the stories they tell about me from the old days I'm really amazed that they are so naïve to believe it."[29] Here "legend" is indeed the correct term for such tales. His karate instructor, Oyama, became the embodiment of the very manufactured narratives that Bluming despised. There are several stories surrounding Oyama, but one example serves to prove Bluming's point. As one Internet site dedicated to kyokushin karate explains:

> In 1950, Sosai (the founder) Mas Oyama started testing (and demonstrating) his power by fighting bulls. In all, he fought 52 bulls, three of which were killed instantly,

and 49 had their horns taken off with knife hand blows. That it is not to say that it was all that easy for him.... In 1957, at the age of 34, he was nearly killed in Mexico when a bull got some of his own back and gored him. Oyama somehow managed to pull the bull off and break off his horn.[30]

Oyama's bull stories are common fair in karate circles; Bluming's frustration with them stemmed from having been so close to the source that his information, if not more accurate, was certainly more believable. "It wasn't a bull, it was an ox," he insists. "[One of Oyama's students] comes along beforehand and hits him on the horn so the horn is loose, and then Oyama comes in there and makes a lot of noise ... and the horn comes off." The rest of the Dutchman's version follows a similarly unimpressive vein as he reveals that Oyama "never killed a bull. That's absolute nonsense."[31]

As with all communities, legend narratives tend to propagate among martial artists. This forms a substantial portion of most every training group's social identity and invented history. Bluming, in his ceaseless search for the strongest fighters, not only failed to recognize this element of the culture with which he had surrounded himself in the 1960s, but from the beginning seems to have despised that it makes up such a meaningful part of the social milieu. A trope of Japanese fiction that especially bothered Bluming is the protagonist who takes to solitary ascetic practice in the mountains in a neo-Taoist search for greater power, enlightenment, or some other missing portion of the success formula before returning to society with revealed knowledge or ability. Oyama utilized this trope to great effect; the stories of his solitary training in the wilderness claim anywhere from eighteen months to three years of daily feats that would perhaps hospitalize a lesser man, including toughening his knuckles with rocks and punching trees until they died.[32]

In his 1998 interview Bluming insisted on telling a more believable account of Oyama's asceticism: "When I came to his dojo the first time the old man told me that before some fight or some tournament in Kyoto he went to the mountain and stayed there six weeks for training, hitting a tree so many hundred times a day, training hard and doing Zen meditation." He went on to note that, by the time he returned to the Netherlands, Oyama's followers were claiming much more extraordinary occurrences, even resulting in the publication of graphic novels, films, and a cartoon series based on the legendary version of the man's life. Even Bluming was unable to escape the rumor mill that turned out these narratives: He found himself playing a supporting role (branded "the Dutch Animal"), he and his teacher were said to have "really went to the yakuza ... and knocked them all out and so on. Unbelievable!"[33]

Bluming argues that the fantastic martial arts stories that came to be commonplace among generations of Westerners have roots in the Asian cultures from which the arts themselves originate, stating, in his singular way, "Chinese and Japanese are great storie [sic] tellers and legends builders and when you check tham [sic] you will find mostly BULL shit." Oyama was perhaps more prolific at commercializing the fantastic stories than anyone, a matter at which Bluming continues to balk even decades after their parting:

> Oyama was a great teacher and shared the stories about him with a smile, but never denied them. He was a perfect example, well-built and he used the stories to his advantage. But in the [S]eventies he really overdid it by not letting people stand on his shadow and things like that. That's when I stopped…. But I am sure when he had to fight, he was a terrific fighter and not many people could beat him.[34]

Bluming, once offended by the tales spread about him and his teacher, has come to accept the transmission of myths and legends as a necessary part of the fighting arts regardless of location. "I thought it was very funny and hearing all the stories thrue [sic] many years its like part of Budo and Wushu they cannot apparently [sic] get without it," he notes with a more congenial frame of mind than the Bluming of fifty years prior may have had. Just the same, "many idiots still believe it."[35]

The most confrontational member of Smith and Draeger's circle was judgmental of more than just the Japanese public's aggrandizement. His general policy toward other martial artists was: "I respect anybody, as long as he doesn't say, when I see that it is bullshit, he says it is terrific. Because then I challenge him." His judgments—as well as his willingness to express them—were clear and simple, as when asked his thoughts on being in Tokyo during the final active years of aikido founder Morihei Ueshiba: "Aikido is a kind of phony dance for girls and queers. It's nothing to do with fighting. But—some of the techniques in aikido are good, you should learn some of them."[36]

Although Bluming faulted the Japanese for their tendency to stretch the fabric of history, the 1960s and '70s were a time of similar tale-spinning in the West. Following the 1967 release of the James Bond film *You Only Live Twice*, a media blitz surrounding the Japanese fighting arts included interviews with Draeger, who did some choreography and stunt double work during the Japan unit's production. These often sensationalized his life much in the same way that the Japanese public morphed the exploits of Bluming and Oyama. One article, "Donn Draeger: Man with the Deadliest Hands in the World," refers to his ability to "take the loudmouth and bend him into a pretzel, break every bone in his body or reduce him to a lump of lifeless flesh with a single sweep of his hand," claims that his hands are "so lethal they are outlawed by the courts," and ironically recognizes that "a lot of poppycock has found its way onto the printed page."[37]

In such surroundings, with Draeger (and Oyama, as well) hoping to prove his value to the Japanese through the vessel of the physically gifted

DONN DRAEGER
MAN WITH THE
DEADLIEST
HANDS
IN THE
WORLD

The first non-Japanese ever asked to fight at the famed Kodokan combat academy, Draeger upset hosts, received r nition as No. 1 and stayed to teach.

by JOHN GODFREY

WOULD YOU believe that if a professional boxer hits you with his fists during an argument he can be charged by the police for the criminal act of "assault with a *deadly* weapon?"

Would you further believe that if a Karate or Judo instructor gets it into his head to tangle with you – even if he only means to "mess you up a little" – he will be guilty in the eyes of the law of "aggravated assault with intent to kill?"

And lastly, would you believe that if a guy's been trained to kill in 36 different ways – *all of them with just his hands* – he's a good type to steer clear of?

Well, if you believe those three things you've got a pretty good idea of what it's like to be Donn Draeger, the man who is widely reputed to have the world's most deadly hands.

Forty years old and an ex-Marine, Milwaukee-born Draeger has devoted his life to learning (and teaching) the 2,000-year-old fighting arts of Karate, Judo, Jiu Jitsu, Kung Fu, Savate, Yawara, Kendo, Aikido and Ate-Waza to name just a few. All of them involve killing with hands. And Donn Draeger is an expert in every one.

"That means Donn has to 'walk softly' because he sure as hell carries one big stick," a friend of the former Marine Corps major (Continued on page 68)

Photo accompanying a promotional article about Draeger for *You Only Live Twice.*

Bluming while also vigorously studying and documenting the martial culture around them and, at the same time, realizing that Western popular culture and magazines had embraced unrealistic notions of their activities, the trifecta came to a decision: If one couldn't correct the situation through upfront presentation and frank discussion, it would at least be possible to enjoy some mockery of the newly popular Asian martial arts community in the West as it emerged. With Bluming's power, Draeger's experience, and Smith's keen wit, they created a fictional representation of their real-life conglomerate: the Bruce Wayne-esque John F. Gilbey.

"Gilbey was a joke, an exaggeration, a fantasy," Smith admits in his memoir. "He had money, time, and amazing skill in everything. We were sure that readers would be smart enough to realize this. We were wrong."[38] The original intention was to lampoon the legends of superpowered fighting men by having Gilbey's adventures be so over-the-top that those with some sense of reality would understand the joke. A great deal of these fictions are based on actual events that were made legendary, such as Bluming's meeting with Wang. In *The Way of a Warrior*, for instance, Gilbey recounts his efforts to learn the secret Kurdish art of Fiz-les-loo by traveling throughout the Middle East, eventually meeting a master of the system, testing his abilities, and, in what was clearly intended as a punchline, "after a week's hiatus I had walked away from hitting myself in someone else's groin."[39]

Despite such a concerted effort to point out the absurdities of some modern legends of the fighting arts, many readers simply accepted that men such as Gilbey existed. This unintentionally served as an experiment in the spread of information among a community and was perhaps the turning point in the three men's approaches to studying and preserving different aspects of the fighting arts and their attendant cultures. Draeger all but gave up on the modern Japanese arts, dedicating more time to classical systems and his forays into Southeast Asia. Bluming returned to the Netherlands and set about establishing an international branch of Oyama's Kyokushin organization while also teaching his own "free-fight" or "all-in" method. Smith raised a family, earned a graduate degree in Asian studies, and took a job with the CIA in Taiwan. During the course of his travels, Smith never stopped training, even managing to locate a judo club in Taiwan. His experiences with the man who became his teacher, however, were sufficiently influential that he spent more and more time concentrating on the internal styles and taught a repertoire of three Chinese martial arts to a small group of followers, in addition to an enormous group of *taiji* students at his free weekly classes.

Upon his return to the Netherlands, Bluming became the head of his own judo and karate organization. He eventually ran into myriad political roadblocks:

> When I came back to Holland ... I was supposed to participate in the world champ [sic] judo in Paris. But because of hate and bickering ... they really screwed me and in the end I was put on a side track and I stopped competing and instead became a teacher. [I]n 1990 I founded the Kyokushin Budokai.[40]

As Bluming made the transition back to his homeland during the 1960s and '70s he fell out of touch with Smith and Draeger, even stating in his first letter to Smith in over two decades, "I heard years ago that you passed away, so you old rascal welcome back."[41] Bluming was soon preoccupied with his own dealings in Europe, spending less time in Japan and eventually losing nearly all contact even with his teacher, Oyama.

Meanwhile, Smith and Draeger continued their cooperative efforts, publishing the first edition of *Asian Fighting Arts* in 1969. This was an achievement for the pair as writing had begun at least six years prior—a 1963 letter has Draeger complaining about the Charles Tuttle Company, the intended publisher, mistreating its authors and "fudging my royalty statement"—and was arranged primarily through the mail while the two were mobile, Smith moving to Washington, Taiwan, and Maryland and Draeger frequently conducting field work in Malaysia and elsewhere.[42] By 1972 Draeger was planning a magazine of his own with heavy contributions and editorial support from Smith. This seems to have been inspired by Draeger's contacts at the University of Hawaii's East West Center and he even had the support of the director "for academic study of world martial culture."[43]

The initial foray into the world of institutional academics set off a spark that laid Draeger's later plans, which grew more ambitious in both the publishing and academic realms. Smith's involvement with the projects lessened as Draeger put a new team together. Although his June 1972 news of the magazine plans included the use of Smith's "name on masthead, and give you what scope you feel is necessary or can do," by November of that year Draeger's expectations of his friend's assistance had fallen to "any good article, that is thought provoking will be gladly accepted."[44]

Draeger's efforts to document the fighting arts in an organized and at least quasi-official fashion became a career goal. He also realized that his aging body could not continue in the lifestyle he had chosen for the past several years. A trip to Hawaii to give guest lectures on his experiences with martial culture solidified this reality and he became determined to settle in Kona: "I've ambled around this ... earth, and insofar as the U.S.

is concerned, if one must live somewhere, for me it is Kona." His plan was relatively simple, if not easily accomplished: "to build international martial culture research center, and to tie close to U of H on such study. We will be teaching local police and civilian units on various arts." His plan was to continue living in Asia for half the year and Hawaii the other. For Draeger, the plan to preserve and spread the fighting arts (as well as to live comfortably) necessitated institutionalization and organized study.[45]

His focus on institutionalization was no more clear than in his (re)invention of hoplology, the study of the science and mechanics of human combative behavior and a term lifted from Sir Richard F. Burton's work in the nineteenth century. This study would be the basis of Draeger's dream to build a martial culture center and, as the 1980s began, the plans seemed to be coming together. He wrote to one of his primary supporters in the endeavor, "While I am here [Hawaii] I will attend to the legal matters which will make the Center a tax-exempt non-profit corporation, an educational institution."[46]

Draeger passed away in 1982 after several months of hospitalization. By the time of his passing, the magazine project he had initially planned with Smith was transformed into *Hoplos*, the newsletter of his International Hoplology Research Center, the term that he planned to apply to the martial culture establishment at the University of Hawaii. Unfortunately for those vested in the development of the Center, only a small cadre of Draeger's associates would carry on his hoplology, continuing to publish *Hoplos* at irregular intervals, but abandoning the Hawaii connection entirely. Despite his best efforts to avoid the kind of political intrigue with which he and Bluming wrestled on a daily basis in their training and competition lives, the hoplology group fell to the same sorts of squabbles following Draeger's death. Regarding the scholarly work of Geoff Wilcher, Chris Bates, a member of Draeger's circle and one of Wilcher's martial arts students, explained that Draeger "decided when near death that he wanted Geoff to take over as research director for the IHRC. This was not to be. Phil [Relnick] killed it as soon as Donn died and when the dust settled it was 'Geoff who?'"[47] The IHRC became the International Hoplology Society under the direction of Hunter Armstrong. Now based out of Sedona, Arizona, the IHS continues to produce and republish material, primarily through *Hoplos*, with a much more evolutionary-biological component than much of Draeger's own work.

Robert W. Smith, meanwhile, embraced the Chinese "internal" martial arts that he studied in Taiwan from 1959 to 1962 and then for the rest of his life. His approach to these arts is complex. In *Comprehensive Asian*

Fighting Arts he suggests that "solo form work is a useful exercise…. But the solo exercise is not fighting [and therefore] in the end in fighting we must come to scratch with an actual antagonist…. It little behooves … never to try conclusions with a living man."[48] In *Martial Musings*, however, he is very clear that "the main thing I wanted to elicit from [Zheng Manqing] was simply: what can *taiji* do for character?"[49]

Smith's focus on the reality of combative engagements in the earlier work may be an accurate reflection of his experience at the time, given a strong background in amateur boxing and judo and having first encountered such training while serving in the military. While in Japan he spent a great deal of time with Draeger and Bluming, whose single-minded concern for effective violence is apparent. Smith's time in Taiwan—and especially with Zheng Manqing—seems the likely catalyst for his shift toward the artistic and sentimental aspects of martial study. It is important to note here that focus is given to Smith's artistic leanings rather than his interest in combative effectiveness. This is intentional, though not to downplay Smith's ability in the physical realm: It has been noted by many who trained with him that the man was able to apply his art to great effect even later in life. Smith's aesthetic interests are highlighted here because they introduced a new and more sophisticated realm of the Asian martial arts to the American public that isn't found in the work of most other luminaries of his generation.

His efforts to preserve the art of Zheng through both documentation and teaching would have been hampered by a purely empirical method as Zheng was, at least in Smith's eyes, "the multifaceted savant, the 'Master of Five Excellences,' famed as a painter, calligrapher, poet, medical doctor, and *taiji* genius."[50] Here it is plainly visible why Smith and Draeger disagreed over Zheng; Smith had found a teacher who captured his attention and, possibly, imagination while his friends from the old Ichigaya house were traveling the world, "testing" fighters and systems. Draeger spoke broadly with exponents of many systems, some of whom were unimpressed with Zheng, while Smith undertook deep study with a small group of Zheng's acquaintances who held the teacher in high regard. For Draeger, preservation of the fighting arts was systematic and essentially scientific; for Smith it was more artistic, conceptual, and emotionally experiential. This is a comparative statement; to be sure, Draeger had his own emotional ties (as with his sword teacher, Otake Risuke) and Smith was not shy in reporting about the physical abilities of his teacher and fellow *taiji* practitioners.

Another *taiji* pupil, John Lad, illustrated the sort of mindset necessary to learn their style:

In a sense, it does not really matter what [Zheng] knew or didn't know about science. His conviction that T'ai Chi Ch'uan could and should survive in the modern world, and even be communicated to and developed by people who are relatively innocent of traditional Chinese concepts and values, was evident in his teaching efforts. It was obviously the result not of a scientific analysis, but of his own understanding of the depth of the practice itself.[51]

Smith had joined what may be considered a more traditional model of pedagogy and preservation within the Chinese martial arts than Draeger and Bluming found in their experiences (with the possible exception of Draeger's dedication to his classical bujutsu teacher and mentor, Otake Risuke). The result was a non-institutional, highly personalized method of instruction that Smith passed on to his own students, only granting teaching permission to those who mastered the full repertoire of the genre. This contrasts strongly with Draeger's notion that the fighting arts can be dissected, analyzed, and passed on through institutional orchestration. Concludes John Lad in his letter, "[Use of] scientific terms and formulas only serves to obscure the teaching concerning T'ai Chi Ch'uan that Prof. Cheng was no doubt trying to communicate."

The three men, especially in their respective later years (Bluming, the youngest, is still active as of this writing), grew more interested in the preservation of the various arts with which they had experience. Bluming formed his own organization to teach judo, kyokushin karate, and his method of mixed martial arts. Draeger had planned to open a research center in Hawaii and already had a team of researchers prepared to staff it. Smith, a dedicated family man, taught local students in *taiji*, *bagua*, and *xing-yi*, fostering personal relationships with each individual while working full time for the CIA.[52]

It could be argued that Smith's approach to continuing the line of his adopted community (that is, the collective of students following the lineage of Zheng) was not only more traditional, but more effective in the long term than institutionalization. Toelken notes that repertoires of performance are rarely confined to a single genre and, indeed, tend to integrate several at once, particularly where preservation of the performance style is concerned.[53] Smith's repertoire included not only the three physical arts he studied in Taiwan, but also a litany of jokes, anecdotes, riddles, and printed material. What might be termed his "legitimate" information was passed to others through these media, particularly among his private students, but so was another, "illegitimate" lineage through the person of John F. Gilbey, the unreliable narrator who perpetuates unbelievable tales amalgamated from Smith, Draeger, and Bluming's accumulated knowledge of legends and humor.

EX-MARINE BRAWLER

They swing like hatchets on muscle-corded arms, ready at an instant to take apart any guy dumb enough to try with a combination of Leatherneck reflexes and Oriental training, hands so lethal they are outlawed by the courts.

Even Draeger could not escape the media's sensationalism.

Two other important personalities who deserve mention, but have been largely forgotten in recent decades, are pioneer American martial artists Bruce Tegner and Victor Moore. A Chicago native, Tegner was born in 1929 to parents who, quite ahead of their time, were devoted martial artists. Tegner's introduction to judo and karate came before even he could remember and he enjoyed the benefits of being raised in a particular sport;

that is, he achieved advanced competency well before most Americans had even heard of the styles he studied. Like Smith, Tegner wrote prolifically on the martial arts and, also like Smith, was a stalwart realist, maintaining that anyone could competently defend himself against an assailant and many of his publications were aimed at that particular need. Tegner's instruction books sold well and featured detailed photographs of himself and assistants performing techniques from karate and judo, but also stick fighting, aikido, *taiji*, and even savate. Tegner's catalogue of styles and experience made him quite unusual among early American martial artists, especially given that he remained mostly in the U.S., unlike the other pioneers of the field. He is also unique for developing his own proprietary self-defense system combining karate, judo, and jujitsu, which he called "jukado." Setting up shop in Hollywood, Tegner helped to choreograph fight scenes in films as well as operating an academy. Perhaps his most notable entertainment feature was *The Manchurian Candidate* (1962), when he was given the chance to train Frank Sinatra. Like Draeger, Tegner passed away at an early age in 1985. His message that there is nothing mystical or exotic about the martial arts was almost certainly before its time. Had he and Draeger lived to see the fruition of the martial arts research facility in Hawaii, it is almost certain that Tegner would have had tenure there, continuing to promote the idea that one need not go to great expense or distant travel to study a fighting discipline.

Born in Cincinnati in 1943, Victor Moore was among Robert Trias' first students. He remained loyal to the Trias system for his entire career, continuing to teach the Shuri-ryu method at his own school in North Carolina. Moore is most often cited for two important factors, neither intentional: He competed or otherwise interacted with nearly every famous American martial artist of the 1960s and 1970s and he is African-American. It may have been the international flavor of early American martial arts and the exoticism of Asian cultural trappings that allowed a man of color to be successful in an otherwise white-dominated field in the 1960s, but whatever the reason, Moore achieved accolades at the highest levels of competition against the likes of Joe Lewis and Chuck Norris. His greatest claim to fame: Moore was on stage at the 1967 International Karate Tournament in Long Beach, California, as Bruce Lee's demonstration partner. Moore's imposing size and musculature made for an amusing juxtaposition to Lee, whose performance of various tricks like the "one-inch punch" is still discussed with reverence in some circles. Beyond simply having been present for a number of great moments in martial arts history, Moore was accomplished in his own right and warrants mention in any studies of

African-American martial artists. Another of Trias' students proved much more commercially successful, however, and it is to his story that we turn next.

Deadliest Man Alive

Gilbey, the unreliable narrator and obvious joke that proved not-so-obvious to English-speakers in the Western world, may have succeeded because the character so accurately portrayed the fantastical figures he was intended to lampoon, thereby blurring the line between real people with extraordinary stories and the purely fictional. Although the individuals willing to undergo the rigors of training and living abroad for years at a time formed a basically cohesive community with an understood camaraderie, the domestic community of Asian martial arts practitioners in the U.S. during the 1960s and '70s was of a much more questionable nature as far as historical legitimacy and commercialism are concerned.

Almost certainly the most colorful figure in the world of American martial arts during this time was a man name John Keehan. Keehan's background is uncertain but his role in the popular mythos of the time is unrivaled. The child of a well-off Chicago couple (his father was a physician who moonlighted in banking), Keehan was born in 1939 and attended the famed Mount Carmel High School, which has also produced a Who's Who of professional athletes, artists, actors, and scholars, including novelist James Farrell and basketball coach-turned-commentator Craig Robinson, the elder brother of First Lady Michelle Obama. At some point in his formative years, Keehan broke with the milieu established by his parents and took a keen interest in the fighting arts. He engaged in some scholastic wrestling and boxed at the 63rd Street Gym. It has been claimed by some that he trained at the Chicago Judo Club, but there is little evidence that he made much of an impression on the membership.

Keehan joined the Marine Corps as a reservist, but was soon discharged. He then signed up with the U.S. Army and served a single tour of duty, although it is still disputed if it involved a stint in Asia. Dante and his followers would later claim that he capitalized on the opportunity of venturing to the mysterious East by locating and apprenticing under various masters of the martial arts. The names, titles, locations, and expertise of these supposed masters changed so frequently that it is virtually impossible to track them in any sort of coherent fashion. It seems that Keehan's strategy in this regard was to overwhelm potential customers-students with his list of qualifications such that no further questions would be asked. It is also likely that, given the early period in American martial arts history during which he operated, the names of various martial disciplines would have been wholly unknown to the public anyway.

In the late 1950s and early 1960s, Keehan made a number of trips across the country to visit the karate school of Robert Trias. Under Trias, he was awarded a black belt and made region director of his teacher's United States Karate Association (USKA), a group that still exists, is highly active and boasts an astoundingly large membership. With Trias' blessing, he organized Chicago-area karate tournaments, some of which he billed as full-contact affairs without actually defining the phrase's meaning. Some informal sources indicate that, upon arrival, the parties would be informed that events were either changed or canceled by the authorities due to the inherent danger to participants. Yet again, these claims cannot be substantiated, but using such extraordinary tactics to garner public attention would not have been out of character for a man who billed himself as possessing a "death touch."

Following a less than amicable split with Trias, Keehan's martial arts career took a fascinating direction. He is now best-known for a series of advertisements that appeared in graphic novels and magazines aimed at young men, much like the muscle-building advertisements that began to crop up in such publications during the early part of the twentieth century. Keehan, though, was not selling a system of weight gain, but rather promised to impart "secret fighting arts" as won through hard training in death matches around the world by the "Deadliest Man Alive." The product was a short pamphlet containing photographs of Keehan and students executing eye gouges and groin strikes of various kinds, stressing the danger of unleashing these "dim mak" or "death touch" techniques on live subjects.[54]

Draeger hated these publications. *Black Belt* magazine, which once contracted him to pen a series of articles about competitive judo, was especially offensive in his eyes for printing articles without fact-checking or even considering the qualifications of the authors:

> *Black Belt* gets nothing from me ... only criticism. I'm on them now for series planned on Japanese Budo which includes article on Jodo which some Kendo teacher is writing. Jodo federation here tells me that this man is not qualified in Jodo and has no knowledge of what he writes. Hope to get [*Black Belt*] to realize that this type of crap always hurts them and to go directly to source for info.[55]

Despite obvious problems with the quality of information presented in these popular publications, they continued to sell well thanks in part to the fodder they presented for self-mythologizing among young men seeking personal power by making public experts available and thereby normalizing the practice of Asian martial arts in America.

Keehan was the polar opposite of Draeger and Smith in most ways, so it is interesting to note how they came from similar backgrounds. Keehan's first exposure to Asian fighting arts was probably during his time spent with Johnny Osako in the late 1950s or early 1960s at the Chicago Judo Club, the same club where Smith and Draeger met. Another of Keehan's instructors during the 1960s was Robert Trias, the promotional rival of Mas Oyama and founder of the first national karate organization in the U.S. Like Smith and Draeger, Keehan was also a Marine and later joined the army during the Korean War, although his deployment overseas is disputed.[56]

There the similarities end, however, as Keehan was much more interested in making money by furthering his spurious claims than spreading the most accurate and reliable information possible in order to educate the public. Keehan enjoyed building his own legend, even changing his name in 1967 to render his public persona more amenable to aggrandizement. From that year until his death, he became Count Juan Raphael Dante. He claimed that the royal title was legitimate and, according to those who knew him, this is almost certainly the case, although not, as he asserted, by inheritance from his mother's Spanish ancestors, but rather through a significant check written to an office in the Spanish government.[57]

According to Keehan, Count Dante was a globe-hopping playboy who spent his time ferreting out martial arts masters in the exotic "Far East," learning their secrets and winning personal glory and inner peace by engaging in death matches. The character sounds suspiciously like Gilbey, and it is quite likely that some portion of Smith's creation was aimed straight at mocking the absurdity of Dante's masquerade. In reality, Dante's qualifications in judo, karate, and some systems of his own design appear to be legitimate, if substantially inflated. However, his alleged personal tutelage from aikido founder Morihei Ueshiba in 1964, mastery of *taiji* and other Chinese martial arts, and participation in underground no-holds-barred fights in Thailand are unsupported by evidence. What is certain is that Count Dante owned a chain of karate schools, sold used cars, was a licensed hairdresser who worked for *Playboy*, operated pornography stores in Chicago, and unsuccessfully attempted to launch his own brand of Count Dante cigarettes. If not a master of martial arts, Dante was at least a master of business promotion.[58]

Dante famously claimed membership in something called the Black Dragon Fighting Society. The name is evidently taken from one of the militant nationalist organizations operating in Japan before and during World War II with the stated goal of ousting foreign powers from Japan and Manchuria. According to Dante, the occult group was an invitation-only, anonymous (except for himself, apparently) society for the preservation and dissemination of Asian martial arts. In order to accomplish this, the Society was supposed to have held tournaments around the world in which exponents of the different styles would face each other in one-on-one combat without rules. It was in these tournaments that Dante is alleged to have killed two men with his bare hands. In reality, the Japanese Kokuryukai (literally, "Black Dragon Society") was named for the Amur ("Black Dragon" in Japanese) River that marked the boundary between Japanese-controlled and independent areas of China, campaigned for Japanese political and military sovereignty over East Asia, and, as far as any inquiry has revealed, had no involvement with secret death matches.[59]

In a perplexing case of life imitating lies imitating art, the Black Dragon Fighting Society has gone on to become a real organization—of sorts. What began as an apparent marketing ploy based on an appropriated name from the annals of World War II went on to garner a sundry membership of other questionable figures in the mold of Count Dante. Perhaps the best known are Ashida Kim and Frank Dux. Kim's name is often the initial indication that his offerings may be dubious. The combination of a Japanese given name and Korean surname is quite unusual. The author of a catalog of books on the subject of ninja skills, Kim's career has been long and seemingly profitable given the prevalence of his titles on bookstore shelves. His offerings have changed little over time, with such promising titles as *Ninja Hands of Death* (1985), *Ninja Mind Control* (2000), *The Invisible Fist: Secret Ninja Methods of Vanishing Without a Trace* (2002), and, apparently having abandoned all semblance of mystique, *How to Become a Ninja* (2003). All other matters aside, Kim has done a remarkable job of keeping his true identity a secret. Many who have attempted to uncover further information point out that checks for his wares are not to be made out to Ashida Kim or the Black Dragon Fighting Society, but instead to one Radford Davis. As for the techniques, effective though they may be, none of the instructions in his how-to guides resemble historically legitimate Japanese martial arts.

Kim is known as the leader of the current American incarnation of Dante's Black Dragon Fighting Society (there are others in other nations that have no discernable connection). Another high-ranking member, Frank Dux, is most popular thanks to the box office success of a film supposedly based on his life's story, *Bloodsport* (1988), starring Jean-Claude Van Damme

Advertisement for Count Dante (Black Dragon Fighting Society 1968).

as Dux. Unlike Kim, Dux has followed the Count Dante school of self-aggrandizement by claiming an extraordinary military history that, just like Dante, gave him the opportunity to study martial arts under fantastic masters in the mysterious East and to fight in Southeast Asian matches to the death. Dramatized in the film, Dux claims to have received secret ninja training from a Japanese teacher named Senzo Tanaka, who eventually declared him successor to the art. The outlandish story presented in the film—and, for that matter, the slightly less outrageous story told by the man himself—cannot stand scrutiny. In what may be one of the more well-concealed winks in such advertising exploits, Dux referred to his no-holds-barred matches as the *kumite*, a common word in karate circles that simply refers to free sparring, typically with safety gear.

It is clear that such a man as Count Dante, with his flamboyant, provocative personality and memorable public image, was fertile ground for creating myths and legends about an imagined Asia, home to elusive masters of esoteric fighting arts. The narratives formed the basis for popular culture of the 1970s through the 1990s as films and television latched onto the desires and whims of a generation of young men in search of a new means to express masculinity in a nation where their notions of traditionalism were no longer suitable to the social climate conceived in the wake of the Civil Rights movement, the Cold War, and the rise of feminism. Fantasies of the hyper-masculine became fundamental to the new masculinity and the exotic East proved a useful imaginary space in which to enact it. Men like Draeger, Bluming, Smith, and Keehan served vital roles, bringing attention to the Asian martial arts in American culture during this period, as well as making the practice and depiction of these arts a part of the "normal" texture of knowledge in the process.

5

Bigger Muscles, Mutant Turtles and Cage-Fighting Philosophers

The techniques of kata have their limits and were never intended to be used against an opponent in an arena or on a battlefield.
—Motobu Choki

When I was in school, martial arts made you a dork, and I became self-conscious that I was too masculine. I was a 16-year-old girl with ringworm and cauliflower ears. People made fun of my arms and called me "Miss Man." It wasn't until I got older that I realized: These people are idiots. I'm fabulous.
—Ronda Rousey

A sudden boom in the popularity of Asian fighting arts, both as an object of spectatorship and participation, came about during the 1970s. Due to the work of pioneers Robert Smith and Donn Draeger, it was spurred on by the ubiquity of karate, kung fu, and other styles in films, television, and other media. The Americanization of these foreign arts can be seen in their manifestation through actors who, with the exception of breakout stars like Bruce Lee and Jackie Chan—who were far more successful overseas than in North America—were overwhelmingly Western and conformed to a new male body ideal, more aggressive and muscular than ever before in American history. Through the 1980s and 1990s media portrayal of ideal masculine traits became more extreme, reflecting a male preference for intensive sexual division in reaction to social pressures against perceived traditional Western male identity traits. During the 1990s and early 2000s this tension came to a head in the form of (predominantly white middle-class) male backlash against those social norms adopted in the 1970s. In particular, interpersonal violence as a refuge of personal expression and bonding was adopted as a focal point for sense-making. The multimedia franchise *Fight Club* and the rise of rationalistic mixed martial arts contests are strong indicators of how widespread this sentiment had become. Analysis of the social climate both generated by and reflected in the media, when paired with interviews within the martial arts community, indicate the ways in which American interpretations of Asian martial disciplines have changed in recent years. This progression could provide social tools for negotiating identity, frustrations, and other anxieties in a culture that has also changed drastically since the introduction of martial arts into the mainstream in the 1940s.

1970s and 1980s

By the end of the 1960s, American attitudes toward Japan had gone from the pre-war indifference and ignorance, through a period of postwar fondness, to a level of respect for the nation's achievements in rebuilding itself. A survey of American businessmen published in the January 1970 issue of *The Journal of Marketing* found that Americans had developed a high opinion of Japanese-made products, and that this esteem correlated with positive assumptions about the character of the country and, by extension, the Japanese people themselves. Indeed, this extended so far that "U.S. businessmen rated Japanese products much higher than Japanese businessmen rated their own products."[1] Karate and other Japanese martial arts were also subject to this turn. The work of Smith, Draeger, and the other expatriate experts was in full service by the 1970s as a gateway for Americans to appropriate Asian martial arts for their own ends. While Bruce Lee depicted Chinese martial arts as ethnically based social tools in films like 1972's *The Chinese Connection* (in which Lee's character fights members of an oppressive Japanese martial arts school in 1910s Shanghai), the Japanese martial arts were adopted by Westerners more readily for their own ends, with James Bond studying the mythical art of *ninjutsu* in 1967's *You Only Live Twice*. Likewise, Asian and Asian-American actors were exceptions even in martial arts media; the critically acclaimed series *Kung Fu* (1972–1975), which featured a bevy of Asian-American actors, still starred the Caucasian actor David Carradine as the wandering Shaolin monk, Kwai Chang Caine.

The premises of *You Only Live Twice* and *Kung Fu* are important in that they both rely heavily on notions of invented tradition. James Bond's liaison with a colony of ninja foreshadows the later American fascination with mysterious warriors who hide in the shadows. In reality, the historical people who would later be associated with the term "ninja" were nothing more than run-of-the-mill espionage and reconnaissance specialists. A frequently referenced analog would be the American CIA, with equally dull implications, such as analyzing economic data and tracking the demographics of various regions. As for *Kung Fu*, the series revolves around a former monk of China's Shaolin Temple. While the temple itself has existed for centuries, there is no indication that it was primarily focused on the development of invincible warriors who dispense fortune cookie wisdom in the search for inner peace. Rather, while there have been martial monks at the temple throughout several periods of history, it was only in the past few decades that the Chinese government has seen fit to build up the temple complex and fund large numbers of "monks" to spend their days practicing fighting arts. The primary purpose of the temple in recent times has been as a propaganda machine, the monks being sent out to all corners of the globe to perform for audiences and spread Chinese soft power.

The inclusion of ethnically Asian cast members in forms of popular media is indicative of a common strategy employed during this period in the American negotiation of identity. It has been pointed out for some time that all manner of alternative identities turned to an imagined and ubiquitous "East" for means of escaping the mundane along with those elements of domestic social crisis that proved frustrating. Shortly after World War II, the Beat Generation writers and artists found solace in Zen Buddhism. During the 1960s, the hippies followed suit by escaping into varieties of mysticism, Indian and Tibetan meditation, and yoga.[2] These countercultures were chiefly the product of disdain for the postwar consumerist culture of middle-class America. This consumerism was driven by the rise of major corporations which, in the opinion of the counterculture movement, were exploitative of weaker foreign economies in the third world. By fleeing to products of those same foreign locales, counterculture members were at once rejecting hegemonic American consumer identity and exploiting the very foreign cultures in question through exotification and commoditization.[3] The hippie movement especially relied on the notion that exotic cultures from India to Japan to Native America were somehow more pure or contained greater depth of meaning than hegemonic American culture because of their primitive status. In essence, fleeing from American corporatization led them to be exploitative by other means.[4] Such a longing for a return to a supposedly simpler state that has been lost in the U.S. was nearly identical to the neo-primitivism of Theodore Roosevelt and the other early twentieth century commentators on that period's male anxiety.

During the 1970s, such elements of the counterculture movements became, ironically, mainstream with Bruce Lee and David Carradine issuing Zen-inspired nuggets of wisdom between commercial breaks. It was in this milieu that a new interpretation of masculinity took hold of many young men and became hegemonic. The new masculinity, as expressed in popular media, was decidedly muscular, unapologetic for its treatment of women, and clearly in response to the rise of the feminist movement within historically male-dominated realms like the university.[5] If uniquely male power could not be had in the workplace or the university due to the general move toward equal opportunity and the postwar trend away from manual labor, then it was perhaps inevitable that a primitivistic, physical, and decidedly violent fashion of the ideal male would come about. Clint Eastwood's films achieved box office success as his antiheroes exacted justice and violated modern social norms in *Dirty Harry* (1971) and *Magnum Force* (1973). Eastwood tended to play characters situated on the social periphery, often outlaws in westerns or law-breaking detectives. These characters would, inevitably, save the day while carrying out unnecessary destruction, objectifying women, and generally expressing a near-primal level of behavior that pulled back the veneer of civil society.

If Eastwood's characters implied a fantasy of primitivism, the implication was eschewed in favor of blatant messaging in the embodiment of American male frustration in *Rocky* (1976). Sylvester Stallone's down-and-out boxing fairy tale struck a chord with young men and rocketed the actor to global fame. While Stallone's larger, more muscular build separated him from other movie stars and rendered him iconic for the new generation of young men in the post–Vietnam era, it wasn't until the 1980s that the new male body ideal became fully hegemonic. The year 1982 saw the release of two major films that demonstrated the extent to which body preferences had changed in U.S. culture over the course of three decades. Stallone's *Rambo* (1982) featured a hyper-violent Vietnam veteran, unable to cope with the artificial niceties of American culture, who established himself as an entrepreneurial force of destruction that does not require much interpretation to understand as social commentary. That same year another hit film, *Conan the Barbarian*, starred bodybuilder-turned-actor Arnold Schwarzenegger as Robert E. Howard's 1930s pulp magazine hero. *Conan* was literally looking to the past for inspiration as it displayed a model of behavior, like *Dirty Harry*, that intentionally violated discourses of feminism and modern social behavior. These characters had in common that they displayed impressively muscular physiques, clearly the result of hard work and self-discipline, which also enabled them to most effectively carry out the extreme violence needed to negotiate their situations. It is evident, then, that the new masculinity of the 1970s and 1980s idealized a man who "learns to master his frail body, to make it submit absolutely and repeatedly to the cruelty of his will."[6]

These films may have provided a fantastical release from the disconcerting arrangement of missing male-exclusive power in daily life, but lacked any semblance of reality. One could no more realistically assume the physical dimensions of a world-class bodybuilder than he could carry a broadsword to the office or fight for the heavyweight title. The Asian martial arts, however, had become fully assimilated into American popular culture by this time and offered a suitable outlet for power fantasies, along with other attractive benefits. Looking to writings of Trias and Oyama, the imagined exotic "East" could serve as a psycho-social space within which a physically powerful male identity could exist alongside emotional stability, personal autonomous competence, and fantasies of near-supernatural experience while also providing a supportive group setting for these beliefs and practices without having to worry about several decades of cultural baggage from prior generations of American exposure. Continuing with the analysis of this transformation as seen in film media, the 1980s Asian martial arts boom brought with it some of the nation's most popular movies of that decade: *The Octagon* (1980), *Missing in Action* (1984), *The Karate Kid* (1984), *American Ninja* (1985), and *Bloodsport* (1988), all of which spawned numerous sequels. In a cyclical pattern of supply-and-demand, the popularity of the martial arts entertainment genre drove enrollment in academies, which then drove demand for consumables. By the end of the 1980s, the martial arts craze was in full bloom in the U.S.

A May 1986 *New Yorker* article by Mark Singer demonstrates how far American commoditization was able to take Asian martial arts as an object of cultural knowledge. It concerned what was most likely the nation's (perhaps the world's) first karate-themed, child's birthday party, held at an academy, and designed and operated by professional instructors. Tokey Hill and Howard Frydman produced the concept in their Queens, New York, dojo to mitigate financial troubles. According to Singer, "For the basic fee—$100—you get a 30-minute karate class for the entire party, plus 15 minutes of professional kicking, punching, blocking, and board-breaking," which, for an additional fee, included, "a ninja to come out and terrify the guests with one of the magnificent steel-and-chrome ninja swords that you see advertised in martial-arts magazines." All of this was followed with pizza and ice cream.[7] Comparing this incarnation of karate with Oyama's, it is apparent that mainstream popularity, while financially lucrative, caused public perception of Asian fighting arts to travel from a deadly-serious, hyper-masculine endeavor to the stuff of children's entertainment. The relationship between boys and men seeking to establish a masculine identity, however, was not damaged by this change so much as it was led to intensification during the 1990s.

1990s

It has been established at this point that the nature of Western masculinity has historically been associated with issues of power and control. As the social makeup altered drastically during the twentieth century, certain types of victimization were selected by scholars and activists as especially abhorrent examples of men's abuse of power, including homophobia, misogyny, and violence.[8] As Boon (2003) points out, the fact that violence in general has been identified as a universal negative is both unfair and unrealistic. He cites the example of airline passengers who carried out violence against hijackers, preventing mass fatalities. In this case, as in any situation where one is forced to protect others in the interest of a greater good, a radical sense of pacifism is necessary in order to justify inaction in the face of imminent threats to the safety of loved ones. Certainly, then, violence cannot be written off as wholly bad, but instead should be viewed as a tool that can serve any number of functions.

In that vein, it would seem that one of those functions is a reassertion of a sense of control and masculinity. The wildly successful novel *Fight Club* (1996) and its film adaptation of the same title (1999) serve as a prime illustration of this potential use for violence. One of the central characters, Tyler Durden, sets off on a quest to carry out his aggressive intentions against a culture "which has caged men within bars of denial and shame."[9] By destroying that which he finds oppressive, Durden intends to free himself and other men from the bonds of a cultural norm into which they cannot comfortably fit. If violence is, in fact, a part of human male biology—or at least a part of the deep history and psychology of the cultural tradition in which they are raised—it makes sense for the surrounding culture to allow some outlet for that expression lest, as occurs in *Fight Club*, the violent side of the psyche lashes out from repression.

With this in mind, the 1980s boom in Asian martial arts media makes sense from a social standpoint, but leads to questions of authenticity and validity with regards to their consideration as a pursuit for the establishment of masculine identity when instructors offer karate-themed birthday parties, when bucolic children's television is taken up with images of mutated ninja amphibians in the same cultural space as instructors claiming to impart inner peace alongside deadly combat training. These represent two separate spheres of exotification in terms of Asian martial arts in America. In one, cultural elements from Japan, China, and Korea carry the cache of harmless fantasy, with the martial arts being seen as no more threatening or real than other children's make-believe games. Jones (2002) makes the argument that play-fighting and imagined violence form a necessary and ubiquitous part of a healthy childhood, so the specific manifestation in question (ninja mutants, for instance) is more or less incidental.[10] In the other sphere, the exotification is aimed at a more serious (if not more fantastical) application as a more meaningful level of interaction with the cultural knowledge and community are sought. In this case, an example would be adults who carry a sense of identity as "fighter" or "martial artist" with them in daily life, choosing and justifying action based on abstract notions learned from the martial arts practice community.

Far from being rigidly divided, these two spheres interact. An example of this would be the fantasy of 1984's *The Karate Kid*, which plays off of the idea of the mysterious, exotic mentor to a troubled American youth. The image of the film's mentor figure, Mr. Miyagi, is an obvious utilization of Campbell's monomyth concept in which the hero seeks out a marginal member of society—often an older male—to acquire the skills needed in order to then successfully navigate his adventure.[11] Mr. Miyagi, a Japanese-American who lives on the edge of town and speaks in a stilted manner, is the ideal form for the mentor and teaches the protagonist to both physically defeat his opponents and spiritually master himself. This became the template for Asian martial arts teachers in the U.S., coloring the perceptions and expectations of real-life participants as well as being copied whole cloth by successive films. *Teenage Mutant Ninja Turtles* (1990), *Sidekicks* (1992), and *3 Ninjas* (1992) all feature elderly Asian martial arts masters who mentor troubled teenagers as they solve both physical and spiritual dilemmas.

Ninja Turtles, in particular, is a fascinating look at how far American popular culture's orientalist discourse was able to carry the fighting disciplines. The main characters are four pet shop turtles and a rat transformed into quasi-humans through exposure to industrial waste in the sewers of New York. They learn the martial skills of the imaginary ninja and use their training to combat crime. Elements of Japanese culture are blended with slapstick comedy and both the humorous and action-oriented portions of the franchise are obvious lampoons of American orientalism. By having the characters possess such extraordinary abilities and being rather obvious about the absolute impossibility of the whole enterprise, the franchise makes a significant—if undervalued—commentary on how Americans were grasping for sources of legitimacy at the time, willing to buy into nearly every fantastical notion of power that presented itself, no matter how obviously mistaken in the greater reality of history and culture. It would have been difficult for an adult consumer to fail to see the statement being made that martial artists cannot truly eat their cake and have it; fighting arts media could either be aimed at children or serious adults, but not both at the same time and in the same way.

By 1993, however, the desire to separate spheres became more prevalent. Perhaps spurred on by films like *Bloodsport* (1988), in which "full-contact" fighting tournaments offered a proving ground to determine the most powerful system of fighting arts, an untapped market for mixed style combat sports was identified by a synergy of foreign and domestic interests, resulting in the first nationally televised, state-sanctioned mixed martial arts (MMA) contest, *The Ultimate Fighting Championship*. Held in Boulder, Colorado, the tournament featured exponents of popular styles (including karate and boxing) and served, essentially, as a commercial for a brand of martial arts taught by immigrants from Brazil, known as Brazilian jiu-jitsu. In order to understand this odd amalgam of terms, it is necessary to give a brief account of how it came to be as, in the present day, Brazilian jiu-jitsu is not only widely practiced, but comprises a central part of the contemporary MMA movement.

The Rise of MMA

The men who left Japan to introduce Kodokan judo to the world were tasked not only with demonstrating the system, but, as they learned, proving its efficacy. Many of them opted to follow a century-old method of accepting challenges with local "champions" (often boxers and wrestlers of less-than-global standing), frequently with special rules, and tended to find themselves victorious.[12] One such luminary, Mitsuyo Maeda, traveled extensively through North America and Europe, and ultimately settled in Brazil. He encountered financial troubles along the way and took to participating in paid exhibition matches and professional wrestling, both of which were forbidden by the Kodokan.[13] Around 1920 Maeda took a job with a traveling circus that also featured a boxer managed by Gastao Gracie, a Brazilian national of Scottish heritage. Gracie's oldest son Carlos learned judo from Maeda, opening his own academy in Rio de Janeiro five years later; he called it "Gracie jiu-jitsu."[14] This proved to be of monumental importance to the American martial arts scene.

Much has been made of the Gracie style of judo/jiu-jitsu. The use of "jiu-jitsu" likely derives from Maeda, who, having left Japan in the early days of Kano's school, was still used to referring to his art as such rather than as "judo," which was only utilized later in the century as the primary name for the system. Of special interest to many who see Gracie jiu-jitsu and judo side by side today is that judo fighters tend to prefer standing and throwing techniques while jiu-jitsu exponents spend most of their time horizontal, wrestling with their opponents in a snakelike fashion. While the full catalog of techniques for each art is represented in the other, the divergence is relatively recent, as video from early judo tournaments in Japan can substantiate. It is possible that the Gracie preference for ground techniques stems from Maeda, as well. During the period when he initially left Japan, judo was becoming more popular in schools and, as a result, tournaments were held with some frequency. Preparing for a tournament in any sport necessarily entails practicing those skills that will lead to victory, and in the case of grappling, that means spending a great many training sessions on the ground given the rarity of clean, technically perfect throws. Competition judo rewards only highly expert throws, so forcing an opponent to surrender via choke or joint manipulation is statistically the better option. If this were the mode of preparation in Japan in the 1910s, it is conceivable that Maeda was most well-versed in ground tactics and, therefore, the Gracie style simply followed suit.

Decades later, Carlos' brother Helio, who had performed as a wrestler with the circus, trained his children in the Gracie method of judo. One of them, Rorion, traveled to the U.S. in 1979 and discovered that films and television, along with soldiers who had served in the Pacific Theater during World War II, fueled a martial arts craze among the public. Rorion began teaching his family's style, but with limited success until 1993 when he introduced the idea of the *Ultimate Fighting Championship* (UFC) to cable television. It was based in large part on Helio's days as a performer in Brazil; the octagonal ring was surrounded by a chain-link fence, and exponents of different styles (karate, kung fu, etc.) were chosen to participate. As might be expected, one of Rorion's brothers competed and won with little difficulty, crediting the achievement to their family's technical innovations. More objectively, the participants were less-than-topnotch examples of their respective disciplines with at least one admitting during the course of the broadcast that he was out of shape. Another, Ken Shamrock, was a well-known professional wrestler in Japan and had only recently begun to train for real, unscripted fights.[15] It is especially telling that members and alternates of the Olympic judo team were not convinced (and perhaps not even invited) to participate in the early days of the UFC when the Gracies dominated the tournaments. One American female Olympic judo medalist, Rhonda Rousey went on to join a professional MMA promotion and had extraordinary success. UFC's owners recently relented to the market demand and hired women—including Rousey—to fight.

The Gracies were relative latecomers to the North American market compared with Japanese instructors like Oyama. That the UFC and other MMA contests reached an eager audience can be attributed at least as much to the work of the (mostly Japanese) martial artists as to Rorion and his advertising scheme. The reason for the North American interest in fighting arts is as much commercial as any other factor. Owing to the commercialization, deconstruction, and ultimate downfall of muscular Christianity in the early twentieth century, droves of young men reached adulthood without clear social definitions of manhood and a means by which to understand and express their masculinity. For many of these men, the martial arts offered a foreign, pre-legitimized way to negotiate such an identity crisis.

The legitimacy and authenticity needed came out of the zeitgeist rather than age-old tradition. The spread of "Asian" martial arts in North America and, subsequently, the West as a whole, mirrors the invention of tradition (in this case *budo*) seen in Japan during the Meiji Period. Kano's initial movement based on self-cultivation and creating a harmonious society was co-opted by Japanese nationalists who utilized *budo* as a tool to fulfill their own interests regarding the enactment of masculinity. After the war, dedicated martial artists like Mas Oyama looked overseas—as well as domestically—for ways to spread their industry and influence. North America proved a fertile market for a packaged concept of *budo* and *bushido* that had been tested and fitted to a youth demographic in Japan during the prior generation. Seeing the opportunity to attract a ready-made audience, the Gracies brought their brand of "Japanese" martial arts from Brazil via the clever sales pitch of an ostensibly fair contest of products. Besides personal financial windfall, this also led to the development of MMA into a government-regulated spectator sport with an international audience, many of whom are young men.

Negotiating Identity

The paradox of late-twentieth and early-twenty-first century American culture provided an impossible problem for young men to solve: Aggressive men in movies, television, and the military were heroes; however, the expression of aggression in daily life was taboo.[16] Building a muscular, unnaturally strong body was admirable, but the ideal continued to become more extreme and the purpose of the bodybuilder's efforts was display rather than application. By adopting the image of an adventurous, physically capable, aggressive yet socially conscious man via participation in the martial arts, these contradictory messages could be more easily negotiated.

Hirose and Pih (2009), in a study of the vocabulary of numerous fighters, see a distinction between men who engage in striking-focused styles of martial arts (e.g., karate, kickboxing) and grappling styles (judo, jiujitsu) in terms of public perception of relative manliness. That is, in a North American context, MMA matches have historically pitted a "striker" against a "grappler" and, in post-fight interviews, color commentary, and crowd reactions it is apparent that winning via submission (forcing an opponent to surrender due to a joint lock rather than a knockout) is seen as "cheating," "not fighting like a man," and generally disappointing, as opposed to a Japanese MMA context in which victory by technical mastery of grappling is well-respected. In contemporary, pragmatic terms, though, it is unusual for a professional MMA fighter anywhere to eschew training in both striking and grappling techniques if only to maximize opportunities for victory.[17]

Also useful for our purposes is the dissertation of Jaime Holthuysen, who conducted anthropological field work with MMA fighters in Arizona and shows a deep understanding of how such identity issues manifest in daily reality. She found that the matter of body image, for instance, involved a great deal more than interest in attracting sexual attention. Due to the variation among weight classes, the only true universals of ideal body image among her subjects were low body fat and well-defined muscles. Although some subjects related these qualities (particularly visible abdominal muscles) to their attractiveness, a more frequent association was with professionalism. Those fighters who appeared to be in extraordinarily lean condition at a pre-fight weigh-in were seen as honoring their obligation to be fit for the performance.[18]

Her interviews with MMA participants revealed their formation of a group identity in a way that can easily mirror the advent of other fight-focused folk groups. Most interviewees, fans, trainers, and active fighters shared their perception of the public's MMA stereotypes that fighting is barbaric, the fighters are uneducated, and, therefore, the spectators are also barbaric and uneducated. None of these are, of course, especially true of MMA more so than any other contact sport and clearly reflect the interviewees' understanding of their own culture. By viewing themselves through such a lens, however, those who identify as fighters and/or martial artists then construct a sense of self-versus-other and, naturally, the creation of an in-group is necessarily defined by the existence of an out-group. This identity is dependent, too, on the narrative utilized in its formation.[19]

Holthuysen's subjects tended to describe themselves as "warriors going into battle."[20] This attachment to the warrior image is prevalent in the culture of Western martial arts, and the samurai, especially, are invoked in this way. "Samurai" is attached to the names of countless martial arts clubs and academies, as well as providing themes for competitions (in 2011 a professional Brazilian jiu-jitsu tournament called Samurai Pro was held in California), narratives explaining the formation of the arts (the official Gracie Jiu-Jitsu Academy website claims that judo may have been formulated in an effort to hide the more effective combat techniques from American soldiers), and even the background for movies like 1992's *American Samurai* starring Mark Dacascos.[21] This demonstrates a reemergence of the imagined Japan found in narratives of American martial artists from the 1940s through the 1960s, though now merged with the desire for greater levels of perceived reality and realism when embodying a fantasy of violent power through the community of practice.

It is interesting how the male body has changed with regards to fighting, effectiveness, ideals, and personal mythology. Through the 1980s, men's muscles in popular media venues simply grew larger. Onscreen bodies like that of Arnold Schwarzenegger and Jean-Claude Van Damme showed that bigger muscles equaled power and achievement. I propose that, by the early 1990s, the limits of the human body had been reached in terms of how much tissue could be acquired, even through the use of anabolic steroids. The men in virtually every study of MMA to date have generally ignored the issue of size, instead emphasizing that leanness and skill are the true indicators of how hard one has worked to achieve one's goals. More pointedly, the world of American martial arts has, at least to some extent, seen the ideal body shrink in the past two decades in favor of less physically tangible qualities. The warrior myth is now the prime mover in the world of American fighting arts. In order to understand this psychosocial drive toward a warrior ethos (particularly the currently *en vogue*

MMA community), it proved helpful to conduct ethnographic work with active MMA fighters.

The Professionals' View

Thus far, the present book has taken a largely historical approach to the cultural creation of martial arts in the U.S. Any such study calls for the researcher to make interpretations and to present a filtered view of the material. Whenever possible, however, it is best to let people speak for themselves, and therefore the remainder of this chapter is dedicated to giving voice to the people who create and consume martial arts media. In the course of this project, I have interviewed quite an array of individuals, but not all of them were interested in being identified and, certainly, a compilation of transcripts alone would not be of interest to anyone without the accompanying historical and social context. Therefore, the following are interviews that have proven most representative of the themes and attitudes prevalent in my investigation.

It is a common source of humor among martial artists that practice facilities appear in some of the most unlikely places. Brazos Valley Mixed Martial Arts embodies this notion as it is situated in a shopping mall, next to a Sears department store and just around the corner from Toby Keith's I Love This Bar and Grill. The space includes wrestling mats on the ceiling and walls, a polygonal cage made of fence material, and motivational quotes painted on the walls. Near the entrance is a display case containing all manner of trophies, medals, old uniform belts, and a Captain America shield. The space is dense with the smell of disinfectant and old sweat. There are only a few places designated for sitting and it is fairly apparent that this is a place of business, but not commerce.

The owner of the shield and most of the case's other contents is a man possessed of both an intellect and biceps that are intimidatingly well-developed. William "Bubba" Bush has competed in combat sports since childhood, especially wrestling. When he found that the university he chose to attend did not have an established wrestling program, he turned his attention to mixed martial arts. Now, several years later, he is a professional fighter, having recently signed a contract with the Ultimate Fighting Championship. Bubba was very forthcoming with his thoughts on the state of martial arts in America and his insights are representative of both amateur and professional levels of involvement, as he has transitioned from one to the other. In terms of the warrior ethos among American martial artists and MMA audiences, he stated:

It points to something better inside of them. The same way that you desire The Force. You desire the ability, the confidence, the strength to defend your family, to defend yourself from the bullies…. And so you desire and admire the ability to do that. And any time you see someone with the ability to do that, you idolize them.

Bubba's statement cuts to the basis on which much marketing and invented tradition surrounding martial arts in the U.S. appears to be constructed. Promoters and propagators of the community, from Trias to Oyama to modern magazines like *Black Belt* and UFC advertising, all draw, fundamentally, on depicting individuals possessed of enviable power of one sort or another as the primary means of drawing interest from the general public.

Bubba was also quick to point out what he understands to be a major difference between MMA and Brazilian jiu-jitsu and other styles that became established earlier in the U.S.:

We had commercialized taekwondo much earlier than Brazilian jiu-jitsu, but you didn't actually strike each other, for the most part, in American taekwondo schools. In the ones that were popularized. So it was a difference between boxing, which takes a lot of dedication, a lot of work, a lot of damage to your body, you have to be tough to do it. But how many dads, say, or people, wanted to actually go in there and dedicate the time and energy to make it fun, versus just getting beaten up? So that was a lower income sport, but something that took passion, took commitment, but it was very small, very dedicated. Taekwondo became available to the masses as a commercialized martial art because it didn't have the pain involved, so it was more accessible to people, but it didn't solve the original problem, necessarily, of instilling manhood or being pragmatic, or practical, in the most basic of situations. So you run into people who've been point sparring for ten years, but punch them in the face and it's different.

For Bubba and many of his generation, there was a decision to be made between an unrealistic fighting art and one involving a great deal of time, dedication, and physical danger. He sees Brazilian jiu-jitsu (and MMA, by extension) as a martial art grounded in realistic scenarios, but without the distasteful elements of boxing—in particular the toughness required of participants. One could enjoy the psychological, physical, and social benefits of practicing a martial art without the danger of permanent damage or being pushed into greater levels of competition.

Community is central to his appreciation of MMA:

MMA gyms are quickly becoming the new golf courses…. It used to be this men's club where you'd go over and golf and hang out, and now it's more diverse. You know, men, women, and children. But there have been a lot of nights where we've been here until midnight because people just want to talk and socialize through the sport of Brazilian jiu-jitsu or fighting.

It is important to note that the socialization dimension is not simply the physical performance in a group setting of an individual endeavor.

Rather, having a common activity in a shared space is equally important to the practice of technique itself. Bush sees his martial arts academy as a place that fosters social bonds and, therefore, the fighter identity. This identity, it seems, is not exclusive to men in the way that he juxtaposes it with an earlier era of golf courses as a "men's club," but as more "diverse" and egalitarian in its appeal.

Diversity, efficacy, and purity were major themes that came up repeatedly during our conversation:

> Purity also encompasses what works. What works in the environment with the least restrictions. The least artificial restrictions. You know, artificial light, right? We talked about that and how it affects you. Well, artificial rule sets also change your life. Like we have an artificial sense of security. In life, because it is the way it is, when you get into an elevator with someone who's bigger than you, your life is in their hands. If you don't know more than they do, then you're just assuming that … societal repercussions are going to save you. When you get into the fighting world, we're now dealing with the most basic form of "what is self-defense?" and "what is combat capability?" and so we want to go to the purest version of that. Boxing has unrealistic rule sets, where if you take a boxer and you stick them in a muay thai fight, they will get kicked in the leg until they can't walk.

As with many of those who practice and/or watch MMA, Bush has no qualms about discussing his interpretation of the signals sent during a match or sparring session. For him, modern American life has resulted in a pervasive artificiality that is, for the most part, undesirable. He referenced an earlier part of our conversation in which we talked about the effect of artificial lighting on circadian rhythm, causing disruptions to sleep patterns. In the same way, he sees "artificial" sets of rules for competition as somehow damaging to the final goal of becoming strong and capable.

This element of "purity" also extends to the philosophy and even metaphysical dimensions of his training:

> I was reading about Aristotle talk about rhetoric the other day and he was saying how … a lot of people say rhetoric is dangerous because it's persuasion. It's the art of persuasion and talk. He said it's only as dangerous as anything else. You have to know how to use it dangerously or how to use it defensively. So we have to be skilled as fighters, able to hurt other people and defend those we love. So, yeah, it's very, unavoidably pure. And then the spiritual aspect of it, which has always been tied [to] it, I think, is there and is so strong because you are in a life-or-death situation. Anyone that's been in the cage has had to think about their life.

Here Bush likens physical antagonism to philosophical antagonism. As in *Fight Club*, realism seems to give way to hyper-realism which, in turn, leads one to address internal metaphysical quandaries. By returning to what he understands as a more naturalistic state (in this case, of violence), Bush, along with like-minded members of his community, create a psycho-social space in which they are given license and perhaps impetus to explore existential quandaries without the need to justify their contemplations as so much navel-gazing.

Given the prevalence of this new brand of neo-primitivism, it seems almost inevitable that the topic of masculinity and its expression would be another key topic:

> As far as bravado and machismo in the U.S., it's always been kind of, you know, a black belt in taekwondo has carried that attitude. It's a braggadocios thing. Growing up, I looked at a lot of people, "I've got a black belt in this or that" and I'm like, I don't care. You're a seven-year-old girl [*laughter*]. The thing in the [MMA] gym that I really enjoy, is that that is wiped out. Now, you go out to a bar or social setting, there's still a lot of vying for position, ego, and those sorts of things. But you get in the gym, and, well, that's Machado's tagline: Leave your ego at the door. We adopt it as well. Even if you don't preach it, it happens, because what you end up with is fifty men in a room ... that all know where they stand. It's not, "Man, if I got in a fight I would knock you out in one punch." There's none of that talk. It's, "Well, we sparred last week and you did knock me out, or you didn't, or we're very close." And so you know where you stand. Your relationships aren't just ethereal.

Addressing internal psychological struggles gives way to absorbing and identifying with the MMA community's tenet of realism and efficacy in all realms. For Bush, the bar scene is representative of modern artificiality and goes hand in hand with a manufactured sense of security and an unnatural social order. The gym, a place of primitive purity, is safe from such artificiality because both the community members and the practice itself are inherently opposed to an inflated sense of self-importance. Exposure to one's flaws, he makes clear, inevitably results in a reduction of self-aggrandizement because "ego" is the consequence of an unnatural bent in American society. This powerfully echoes—and even amplifies—masculine discourses of earlier generations that also called for neo-primitivism. Bush's statement is specifically critical of the taekwondo black belt as an indicator of both rank and ability because it is, like the bar setting, inherently artificial, and therefore lacks real meaning. In order to remedy this pervasive unreality, then, just as in *Fight Club*, it is necessary to practice fighting and to do so in a way that carries out a hyper-reality, thereby correcting the imbalance.

David McClung, an MMA coach with over thirty years of experience in combat sports and who participated in what may have been Texas' first legal mixed martial arts contest, generally agrees with Bush's assertions about the nature of fighting arts *vis-à-vis* social relationships and identity formation. In particular, the issue of "purity" as a descriptor of both combat efficacy and naturalistic lifestyle came up time and again as major themes in our conversation:

Personally, the thing that I've always loved about combat sports: There's a purity to it … there's a simple-ness to it. You do it, and everything else in the world gets the volume turned down…. It's a very simple thing, so everything else feels unnatural.

Again, a sort of neo-primitivism in the spirit of early twentieth century masculine discourse appears to be the main driving force behind and benefit from engaging in a fighting art that is perceived as having few artificial strictures placed on it. He also extends the artificiality of rules that govern more historically established combat sports to the associated cultural environment:

When you talk about boxing culture, it gets pretty ugly at the top. I think in certain areas you would see cultures within certain gyms. But I think those are natural male cultures, I don't think there's a lot of history behind them. They're sort of in their "teenage years," so to speak.

Interestingly, boxing, a fighting art with a very long history in the West, is seen here as possessing a largely undeveloped culture of community at the local level, while the professional realm is seen as established, but decidedly corrupt. By contrast, then, MMA gyms are seen to bring about a more robust community of practice.

Also like Bush, McClung sees training in the fighting arts as an avenue for the personal improvement of the individual in both a physical and a spiritual sense:

Training is easy. You can teach people technique and it gets easier over time. What never gets easy is the personal stuff. You're going to see it, and I'll tell you why you're going to see it. There is no negative human emotion that you will not see in this gym. It's all going to come out and you don't get to hide it from the people around you. If somebody beats the snot out of you and you've had a horrible day, it's just not going the way you want…. We've had grown men shed a tear in the corner, get really upset. You either leave the gym and never come back or you just accept that these people are, sort of by proxy, your family because they're going through something you're going through, that nobody else is experiencing, and they're seeing every single side of your personality. So, I would argue that we know each other as people far more than you would ever know your regular co-workers … or anything else because not only do you become a better fighter, but you become a more well-rounded person.

For McClung, then, the primal nature of frustration elicited by failing to conquer another fighter physically becomes the key to unlocking more complex emotional struggles within the individual. As he makes clear with the statement "We've had grown men shed a tear," crying is not an emotional response typically expected of men—at least not the type of men who participate in martial arts—and the power of the activity to bring out underlying issues and lead to their eventual resolution is meaningful in terms of social bonding. In this case, the community is formed around shared exhibits of vulnerability as well as strength. Returning to a perceived primitivism allows men to be "pure" and genuine in their relationships without surrendering the tough fighter identity.

McClung has seen patterns in the way a given martial art can come and go with the fickle desires of consumerism. He worries about the future of Brazilian jiu-jitsu in a nation where all physical pastimes seem to become competitive sports:

> [Brazilian jiu-jitsu] is going the way of taekwondo. It's becoming too sportish.... Any fighting art that got here [the U.S.] was generally embraced by early adopters. Generally tough guys looking for a way to fight. When I started fighting I searched gyms and sparred with instructors ... finally found one that just ripped me a new one. I went, "You're the guy." This is the guy who I'm going to learn from because, obviously, he knows what he's doing.

The process becomes cyclically predictable, though, as isolated incidents and media exposure draw more public interest:

> Other people see that. It's exciting. It's like, "Wow, okay, this karate thing." Maybe some little guy on the street beats somebody up. You know, someone tries to rob this guy and he ends up kicking him in the face. It draws in more people. There is a limit to the number, in its purest form, of people who are actually going to do it because, it turns out, people just don't like pain.

Purity is equated with pain and unpleasantness as well as combative effectiveness, indicating that those who aren't genuine in their desire to practice a fighting art are guilty of perpetuating an "impure" form. The process is finalized with the weakening of the original, "pure" style:

> This happens over and over and over. You can see it starting in the '60s with the judo thing, the '70s with the karate thing, and the '80s with the taekwondo thing, and the '80s and '90s with jiu-jitsu. And what's next? Who knows. Sumo [*laughter*]. But that's what happens. The sports have to be watered down to get enough people to make them monetarily viable, and therein lies their demise.

This "watering down" of a once-pure fighting art is seen as akin to death. In McClung's scenario, as in Bush's rendering of the historical narrative of American martial arts, commercialism is a necessary evil that leads to the popularity needed to sustain "pure" fighters and their art alongside a larger group of quasi-fighters, who may still identify as such, but do not comprise the core of the group identity.

In this cosmological view of the fighting arts as they are currently depicted and experienced in American popular culture, the genuine fighters operate at the highest level and, in order to survive in a capitalist system, participate in professional fights. Outside of this core, amateur fighters and others who attend training gyms make up a semi-pure community of practice, and this spectrum of involvement extends to spectators, whose money is necessary to support the core of pure, monetarily disinterested fighters:

> The sport doesn't exist without the fans, so I wouldn't say they're an annoyance. But I would say that in the moment of the fight, you're doing everything you can to tune that out. There are those fighters that absolutely embrace it. We call those "second place." In the long term they don't do as well. You learn to deal with it. You come to terms with it. But to me it was always a distraction.

In McClung's experience of professional fighting, fans are inconvenient, but also make positive contributions through their money and attendance at fights, although the pure fighter sees their presence as a distraction from the central activity. Paradoxically, the only reason for a professional bout to take place is the entertainment of the audience, and yet the audience itself stands in the way of the fighters performing optimally.

While the fighters at the core are interested in the combat as a pure activity and those comprising the rest of the local community of practice vary in degrees of purity and involvement, the outermost spectator who chooses not to be involved with the training side of combat sports, in McClung's estimation, likely holds different motivations altogether from the pure fighter:

> Why do people watch gladiatorial games? Why do they sit and throw beer bottles when their team doesn't do well? Because they want something transcendent. There's a primal aspect of it ... there's this idea that something primal is not cerebral. But primal man developed the cerebral. That's part of survival, having a sharp brain. It takes a sharp mind to do this [MMA]. People don't realize it, but it does.

As with the fighter whose identification with the activity is so strong that failure drives him to tears, the spectator identifies in the same way, though through the proxy of others in the fight. The desire for a primitive experience of transcendence is not unique to MMA, as can be seen with the golden age of boxing in the U.S. In both cases, the non-participant observer seeks to mitigate his own social frustration and anxiety by fantastically projecting himself onto the active fighter, whether the venue is a ring, cage, or other platform. Pointing to the importance of media and personal mythologizing in the world of American martial artists, McClung references a film to illustrate his point, *Vision Quest* (1985):

> That scene can answer very eloquently some of the questions you're asking. Why do people sit and watch? Because all of the sudden they feel like part of something so much greater than they were before they did it. That's a big part of MMA, too.

In the scene in question, the protagonist, a high school wrestler in the final hours before his match against a larger, nearly inhuman opponent, visits his mentor figure for advice to find him putting on a suit for the occasion. Asked for an explanation, the mentor tells him about watching a televised soccer match in which he experienced a transcendental moment as Brazilian superstar athlete "Pele" Edson Arantes do Nascimento scored a goal in an acrobatic manner. The implication of the scene is that the spectator of any situation in which other humans accomplish extraordinary physical feats provides the opportunity for a spiritual experience.

As seen during the 1960s and 1970s, the spread of Asian martial arts in the U.S. also instigated their association with all manner of mystical, frequently supernatural qualities to the point of exotification and orientalism. This indicates a general desire by spectators and participants alike for the transcendence to which McClung refers and, for him, is connected with America's age as a nation and the lack of a more established set of defined traditions:

> It goes back, I think, to being almost tradition-less. Almost without culture. So when you see a culture like that, it seems like maybe they know something we don't. So people start to quickly pantomime those things in the hope that.... How many times have you gone to a gym somewhere and seen them counting drills in the language of the thing they're doing?

The example of "pantomiming" a foreign tradition by counting in a non-English language (e.g., American karate students counting drills in Japanese) is used here to demonstrate that exotification of foreign settings—that is, not necessarily overseas, but socially foreign as in a martial arts academy—is essentially akin to a cargo cult in which carrying out gestures without full knowledge of the background helps to establish traditionalization and a sense of identity even when that tradition is manufactured as a product of the gesturing. This is precisely the means by which objects of knowledge can be transferred from one culture to another and result in different textures of knowledge, given enough time.

A desire for transcendence is universal, in McClung's view, and the martial arts aren't always embodiments of that experience, but can act as a gateway to other selective elements of foreign cultures that are then grafted onto the texture of knowledge:

> People love to think they're doing something exotic or outside of their everyday, so when it comes to spirituality, they're looking for an answer and they think, hey, maybe if I look to the Eastern arts.... Then they start reading Eastern philosophy. That's how I did it. Martial arts first, then somebody said, hey, read this book, it'll really help your state of mind when you're fighting. I read it, and it did.... In their mind, there's a crane flying overhead and a pan flute playing in the background as they sit. If you've ever seen somebody fake meditate, it's the most hilarious thing in the world. I almost feel bad for them. But they're still reaching for something. They're still looking for

that place inside themselves where the modern world has emptied them. And it's not going to fill it, but they're going to try.

In this case, the Asian martial arts (and the cultures from which they derive) are already subject to exotification by the individual in question prior to being sought out. It isn't necessarily the art or philosophy itself, then, that leads to transcendence or other personal changes, but the perception thereof. Inventing traditions, crafting explanatory narratives, and personal mythologizing are central to this American encounter with Asian martial arts.

As for the generation of experts like Draeger and Smith, whose efforts in relaying a fuller picture of the Asian martial arts as they existed in a cultural and historical context, the few who remain active today seem polarized in their opinions of MMA's popularity. Most have remained silent, but a few influential voices from the days of Draeger's Tokyo consortium have spoken out on the subject. Robert Smith wrote in his memoir, "To me this sorry activity reflects nothing so much as the nihilism of current America." This assertion contrasts sharply with the views of those directly involved with MMA, although Smith's rationale draws on the same features of the sport that fighters like Bush and McClung see as beneficial:

> Ultimate Fighting is ridiculous. It has minimal regulation, making for a brutal, dangerous hash that most competent fighters avoid, although their technical competence is much higher than the rag-tag participants Ultimate pulls, and they would have a fairly easy time of it if they entered…. The competent fighters see Ultimate as a beastly activity reflecting nothing so much as a terribly neurotic insecurity in participants and fans.[22]

That Smith saw the supposed openness of MMA regulations as a matter of brutality that appeals only to bloodthirsty nihilists points to an apparent miscommunication between generations. The same aspect of MMA is what the participants consider "pure"; where Smith saw brutality, they see unfiltered naturalism. Perhaps both parties would agree that the concept is an expression of neo-primitivism, but whether or not that is beneficial to society would almost certainly remain a point of contention.

Smith was also outspoken on matters related to violence in general. He decried hunting as unsportsmanlike and called for a ban on professional boxing. Bluming, whose "all-around" style (mixing Kyokushin karate and judo) preempted the Ultimate Fighting Championship by at least four decades, is much more specific in his feelings about modern MMA:

> The current style is more like a drunken brawl in a bar and has most of the time *nothing* to do with real technique. I don't even watch it anymore. Why people like the

UFC, it beats me and since I am 81 and full of injuries I don't give a damn anymore. I just still teach my ideas and my students.

It is telling that one of the men most central to spreading Asian martial arts to the Western nations through both personal instruction and by helping to introduce judo to the Olympics holds hostile sentiments toward the modern incarnation of the same open-style contests in which he once participated. Like Smith, he is critical of what he sees as a lack of refined technique among MMA fighters, although this does not seem to be the case upon visiting Bush's gym, where technical drills are polished with the same intensity that one sees in more "traditional" settings, such as judo and karate clubs. Rather, I would posit that a cultural gap is evident between the generation that produced martial artists willing to travel overseas and undertake scholarly as well as kinetic research into the textures of knowledge that produced Asian fighting styles and the current generation that sees rationalism and neo-primitivism in the fighting arts as socially beneficial and feel disinclined to concern themselves with cultural context at the expense of combative efficacy. In this respect, it could be said that the pioneers of the 1950s and '60s were outward-looking while the present MMA community is focused inward.

Reemergence of Asian Exoticism

The Western fascination with—and mythologizing of—the samurai runs deep in popular culture. A fitness craze was even founded on the basis of "the samurai sword workout." In her book detailing the program, Montagnani, the inventor, wrote:

> In the samurai philosophy, the sword symbolized a tool for cutting down your own ego, cutting down your faults, fighting an internal battle with the aspects of yourself that are undesirable, and making you more altruistic, caring, understanding of the world around you."[23]

While there were, certainly, some Warring States Period thinkers who would have supported this concept, in general the samurai class existed to conduct warfare; efficiency in mechanisms of killing was paramount among their concerns. Self-cultivation and the internal struggle with personal faults resonate much more strongly with the amorphous *budo* espoused by Kano and others who, it must be reiterated, were inventing and reinventing tradition. The idea that, as Montagnani suggests, hours of repetitive practice "forge rightness within us just as they did for the ancient samurai men and women" may be historically inaccurate, but keenly illustrates the Western reconceptualization of Japanese martial culture.[24]

Such a reconceptualization was necessary in order to create a sense of authenticity and a veneer of legitimacy for the purposes of those men who came to adopt Japanese martial culture as a means of negotiating masculinity in a postmodern Western setting wherein their perceived native traditions of manliness were marginalized and made self-contradictory. As Montagnani's romanticizing implies and Holthuysen's interviews confirm, the sense of self generated by identifying as a "fighter" or "martial artist" can provide a moral compass, community, and feeling of community connectedness to men who otherwise experience a feeling of purposelessness.[25]

Kung Fu Comics

Japanese culture is not alone in being reconceptualized for American purposes, however, as evidenced by the Chinese-inspired work of graphic novelist Ben Costa, whose *Shi Long Pang* (2013, 2014)—winner of the prestigious Xeric Award—follows the adventures of a seventeenth-century Shaolin monk and is very much situated in a background of American interpretations of Asian martial culture. Costa is a rather unassuming figure; his demeanor is very even-keeled and he has a love of traditional, pen-and-paper role-playing games. He has even gone on to design his own game systems in the Dungeons and Dragons mode, with one based on his comic soon to be released. He also co-produces a popular web-based comic, *Rickety Stitch and the Gelatinous Goo*, with James Parks. Costa's art style is reflective of the era in which he was raised, with vibrant colors, loose, thick lines, and characters reminiscent of 1980s and 1990s animation. His primary influences in terms of graphic novels are the *Teenage Mutant Ninja Turtles* franchise and Stan Sakai's *Usagi Yojimbo* series, both of which lampoon the exotification of martial arts in America while alternately producing quite serious dramatic dialogue and frank, sometimes disconcertingly violent action sequences. Other media, however, shaped Costa's choices in storytelling:

> It all started out by watching kung fu movies. My brother loved Bruce Lee, and also started amassing a big collection of Jackie Chan movies during a time when such films weren't widely available. I was fascinated by the aesthetic of kung fu movies more than anything. Later on, I began practicing martial arts, and that's when I really took an interest in Shaolin history and Chinese culture in general. Before that I had never pursued any specific interest in history outside of a mandatory school assignment. For one reason or another, the classroom never piqued my curiosity.

Costa's statement regarding history and schoolwork are in reference to his unique tendency to provide explanatory footnotes and bibliographies at the end of each volume. In this way, as a media producer his work represents a turn in the popular perception of Asian martial arts in American culture. Although it has grown apparent that orientalist approaches to inventing traditions and weaving mythologies around the objects of knowledge like kung fu and karate has resulted in a new texture of knowledge alien to the arts' places of birth, Costa and others of his generation choose to embrace that Americanized Asian tradition, even blending it with verifiable historical reality. Here the influence of earnest scholarly pioneers like Smith and Draeger operates in tandem with that of outrageous characters like Count Dante.

Although part of the generation that has made MMA one of the most lucrative professional sports enterprises, Costa is not a fan, preferring to patronize the styled films of Jackie Chan and reading about Chinese martial arts history. He favors Chan and other Hong Kong filmmakers over most contemporary American martial arts media because "I dislike how there is usually some mystic, magical element attached to most depictions of martial arts, as if they can't stand on their own. This applies to comics as well. Also, there's almost never an Asian lead character in mainstream media, which is just ridiculous."

His comment here indicates that, like Bush and McClung, Costa is disillusioned with the notion of the unrealistically extraordinary being manifest in the Asian martial arts. While his interests are markedly more artistic, historically oriented, and entertainment-driven, he shares the desire for the arts themselves to be the focal point of media and involvement, rather than any supernatural abilities promised or implied by promoters. Compared with Oyama and Trias advertising inner peace and superhuman invulnerability as results of their training, this more realistic worldview appears to be common among the current generation of the American martial arts community. Costa goes on to explain:

> Knowing that Shaolin history itself is quite legendary and "inventive," I wanted to ground that in reality. I felt there was no way that I could avoid historical inaccuracies when exploring Shaolin, so it was my responsibility to depict the cultural backdrop as accurately as I could. The setting and period in most kung fu movies is very nebulous, and that's something that usually bothered me. I think this is where *Usagi Yojimbo* influenced me the most. Stan Sakai has married a highly researched depiction of feudal Japan with a world full of funny animals. So in my case, Shaolin history is the funny animals.

Again, he sees a need to provide an accurate historical setting for highly unrealistic fight scenes. He even goes to the extent of criticizing

Hong Kong-made kung fu films for their lack of historical setting, pointing to a willingness to adopt and adapt some source material while ignoring others in order to fashion a uniquely American product that remains true to a newly established tradition of martial arts narrative fiction.

Costa also approaches the question of the tough-guy image in American martial arts media with a combination of breaking from a perceived trend while firmly couching himself within the recent narrative tradition:

> I didn't want to write about a stoic, badass character solely bent on revenge, which is what martial artists are often like in media. While that can be great, it's been done. And it's not something most people can relate to. People might think super-masculine characters are "cool," but what percentage of people actually identifies with that character? I wanted a character that was capable but unsure of himself, smart but completely naive. An actual human being…. It's a construct, and I wanted Pang to struggle with that. In Volume 2, I wanted the struggle to focus more on learning what it is to be a monk outside the temple. And I think that is also at odds with a conventional masculine identity.

By going against what he perceives to be a trend of "super-masculine" characters, he links his work to a much more established tradition of Buddhist monastic life, which, while being more historically accurate, also aligns his characters with the ideals espoused by MMA fighters that vulnerability is desirable in the appropriate context and a return to a state of realistic, naturalistic lifestyle is preferable to modern masculine artifice.

Graphic novels are important in this regard, not because they enjoy as large an audience as major motion pictures or even, necessarily, as televised fighting, but because they are frequently the field in which popular ideas germinate. Summer blockbuster films, highly rated television shows, and some of the world's best-selling video games are based on comic books. They are as much the avant-garde of every generation since the 1940s as any other art form, if not more so. That being the case, it is important in a study of cultural zeitgeist to inquire about the state of the most successful and influential graphic novels.

Since the 1960s, the American martial arts identity has gone from describing a small collective of dedicated individuals, through several periods of waxing-and-waning prominence in the popular media, and it is currently comprised of diverse and disparate communities of practice. These local communities are spread across a spectrum of involvement, from non-participant fans of combat sports and martial arts cinema to fighters in the arena, experienced instructors, and media content creators. Asian martial arts in particular have been depicted in a number of ways that reflect more so the unique social needs and situation of Americans in any given period than the social arrangements in their places of origin. Likely because of their nature as systems of stylized and controlled violence, masculinity has been a running theme in the American treatment of fighting arts, regardless of their historical backgrounds. Currently, there appears to be an impetus among many active members of the community to both depict and practice martial arts with a greater concentration on realism, as reflected in the hyper-realism of media like *Fight Club*, in which neo-primitivism has again come to the fore of male social activity.

Conclusion

At first this may be a kind of belief, but later it is something the student feels or already has. Physical practice and rules are not so easy to understand, maybe especially for Americans.

—Suzuki Shunryu

Historically, in an American context, masculine identity was mainly based on one's ties to the local community during the nineteenth century. Vocational apprenticeship was highly valued as a means by which to build an external persona that established the individual man as a contributing and responsible member of his immediate social environs. Situated in this way, the center of community life was often the church, especially in rural communities. A well-regarded man within the local population, then, tended to lead a life focused on activities related to the church, work, or both. Even where entertainment and sport were concerned, middle- and upper-class American men centered their leisurely pursuits on church and vocational acceptability, with some exceptions. In the antebellum southern states, for instance, cockfighting and fisticuffs, even when explicitly illegal, remained relatively popular pastimes among men, to the extent that fathers were known to bring their sons to such events. This came to constitute a rite of passage in many cases. Still, nationwide, violence as an entertainment medium was broadly looked down upon by moralists. Boxing was still outlawed in most locales.

As the century turned and new technological and scientific innovations led to the growth of centralized production in urban areas, young men migrated away from home to seek their fortunes as industrialists. Community continued to be seen as essential to success, however, and the YMCA identified itself as one means of joining together under a common set of ideals and behavioral regulations that eased the stresses of city life, provided informal business connections, organized leisure activity, and involvement in religious life, all under a single roof. As the century wore on, the YMCA's membership began to decline in the face of increasing consumerism brought about by the industrialized lifestyle of the city and an increased focus on the value of the individual—chiefly the result of transplants from rural areas finding the city a more isolating arrangement. In response, the YMCA leadership turned more to sports and other play activities to attract young men. Although numerically successful, this led to a de-emphasis on the religious message of the YMCA-as-church and, eventually, to near-total secularization, with some YMCA gymnasiums even having a separate entrance that allowed the unsavory likes of boxers and bodybuilders to avoid the churchgoing set.

That sports became the YMCA's main attraction for young men (and, later, women) can be tied to a greater shift in American consumer habits of the early twentieth century, culminating in the extreme and unabashed consumerism of the 1920s. With community life no longer the primary determining factor in the value of the individual, secularization of society as a whole rose and even public health reformers like Kellogg found that their messages of fitness and salubrious living, though ultimately derived from religious beliefs, could not be advertised as such because the general public would ignore proselyting. Rather, consumerism and individualism converged on the body, making it a target for advertisers and creating an entirely new market for health food, exercise machines, and fitness magazines.

With women, too, gaining independence and a sense of agency within American society, men found that their identity as sole breadwinner and head of the household, and their physical dominance over their partners, was beginning to slip. At the same time, a general anxiety over work-related conditions also spread. As white-collar workers let slip their physical states, the rhetoric of health advocates and fear of effeminization took hold. This led social reformers like Theodore Roosevelt to call for a greater concentration on breeding masculinity among the nation's men. Many sought to do so through the implementation of neo-primitivism, a perceived return to more traditional ways of life which were often represented by imagined versions of foreign and past cultures, including Native Americans, Asians, and early American settlers. The primitive activities included camping, hiking, hunting, exercise, sports, and organized fighting. The circulation of men's fitness magazines shot upward, with many expanding their coverage to include self-improvement more widely. Strongmen, once relegated to circus performances, found steady employment as instructors of physical education, even within the YMCA, where their theological credentials were often overlooked. Likewise, state after state legalized and took to regulating professional boxing.

With men seeking to negotiate new definitions of masculinity in the face of a general anxiety over effeminization, the body became a ground for individual control and personal mythologizing. By engaging in body-building and gymnastic exercises, it became possible to exert one's will over real-world circumstances. This way of thinking, along with control of the diet and a prevalence of advertising that indicated the perpetually unsatisfactory nature of the consumer's health, created a carnal culture in which the body became the direct enemy of the self, constantly trapped in a struggle with disease and weakness. With their own physical states not being satisfactory—and frequently, too, because white-collar jobs were regimented and under the command of others—men also turned their leisure-time attention to spectatorship of prizefights. By projecting oneself on professional fighters, anxious men could weave personal mythologies, seeing an ideal self reflected in the bodies of top-level athletes who, even when they lost, retained a sort of dignity in their ability to absorb punishment. Consumerism and anxiety combined in this way to create a golden age of American prizefighting during the 1930s and 1940s.

While men were renegotiating the state of masculinity in early twentieth century America, the newly created nation of Japan was establishing itself as an imperial power on par with Western nations. Having borne witness to the impact of the opium trade and colonialism in China as a consequence of several unequal treaties with Western nations, Japanese leaders responded to the forced opening of trade ports by the U.S. in 1854 and the Meiji reforms in 1868 by instituting a European-style constitution, modernizing its military forces, disarming the hereditary samurai class, and rapidly improving domestic infrastructure. Within a few years, Japan became a country capable of matching any established Western country in terms of technological ability. But this confederation left the new national leadership with a cultural problem in the form of a disparate society that, only a few generations prior, had been locked in intense civil war. The invention of a national identity was needed.

As domestic forces vied for control of Japan's direction, it became apparent that the Western colonial powers segmenting China may very well move east and pose a greater threat to Japanese sovereignty. Both individual political leaders and much of the public at large agreed that practicing colonialism was the most logical solution, and justified this decision by noting that an Asian power would be most fit to administer Asian colonies. The first targets for Japanese expansionism were Manchuria and the Korean peninsula. Territory was won through the Sino-Japanese and Russo-Japanese wars, the latter of which served to show the world that Japan's military capacity was on a level with even the largest of Western forces. More specifically, the claim was that Japan, though small and with limited natural resources, could command greater efficiency and that the individual Japanese was superior in most ways to any Western opponent. After its victory in the Russo-Japanese War, mandatory judo training was most notably credited as the source of such efficiency.

Nationalist forces took up the reins of Japan's government soon after the turn of the century, heeding public calls for greater protection from foreign threats and expansion into mainland Asia. These ultra-conservatives saw their indigenous fighting arts as a means to inculcate youths with imperial fervor and patriotism, but the classical martial arts were not suited to preparation for Western-style military training, nor to working with large groups in a regulated manner. From the turn of the century and into the 1910s and 1920s, a forward-thinking professor of education, Kano Jigoro, carried out an intensive study of the classical Japanese martial arts and formulated a system that he called "judo," which conformed to the demands of the national government's needs in terms of physical education, could be taught *en masse*, and could be quickly modified to fit the nationalist cause. Kano, responding to official critiques as he petitioned to have judo implemented in the school system, altered his original system in a number of ways. The reforms continued over the following years and by the end of the 1930s judo practitioners wore standardized uniforms, had military-style ranks indicated by their belt colors, and could follow a set of regimented exercises under the auspices of a central authority, Kano's Kodokan Institute.

Kano was also responsible for bringing another martial art to the attention of the educational authorities. An Okinawan schoolteacher, Funakoshi Gichin, had studied karate for much of his life and, like Kano, felt that (with some modifications) it warranted a place within the physical education curriculum. Although it was later incorporated as a full prefecture of Japan, at the time Okinawa was still essentially a foreign culture and Kano's sponsorship of Funakoshi proved the most tactful way of introducing karate to the central government. Also like Kano, Funakoshi was able to appease a nationalist audience by having karate students wear judo-style uniforms and rank belts and practice in block formations; many of the techniques were altered and renamed to make them simpler to acquire. Even the name of the art, originally written with characters meaning "Chinese hand," were subtly changed to retain the same pronunciation, but with the meaning of "empty hand."

The value of martial arts as tools for social control was fundamental enough to the imperial cause that the government established a teacher education college specifically to prepare physical educators for instruction in the fighting arts. Kano saw, too, that public support for new martial disciplines would hinge on perceived tradition, so he stressed that judo was simply a continuation, like other martial arts of the era, of the proud samurai heritage so vital to the expansionist movement into mainland Asia. The education system, then, was honed into a mechanistic process whereby both classroom and physical education teachers inculcated young men with a nationalist discourse in which martial heritage formed the backbone of the national identity, which could be enacted in the world by spreading Japanese leadership and values across Asia, through violence when necessary. This rhetoric was supported outside of schools in boys' magazines that featured adventure stories about young men journeying into Manchuria as Asia's saviors, battling bandits and troublesome Western conquerors. The message must have seemed universal to Japanese youths of the early twentieth century: Masculinity and success depend on one's love of country, which is best expressed by carrying superior Japanese values to fellow (and unfortunate) Asian neighbors.

After the Japanese surrendered to Allied occupation, Douglas MacArthur's General Headquarters, fully aware that Japanese martial arts had been utilized in the years leading up to the war as tools of social control, banned their practice. To prevent a return of the grass roots support on which nationalists initially relied, these arts could not be allowed to publicly flourish as they posed an obvious danger to U.S. hegemony on the islands and would provide a physical space for plotting against MacArthur's occupation as well as a psychological space for occult retention of pre-war sentiments toward the outside world. Curiously, karate was exempt from the martial arts ban, most likely due to its Okinawan origins, which could be emphasized in order to present the art as decidedly un-Japanese and, therefore, acceptable to the American occupiers.

Consequently, while karate was growing in popularity prior to the war thanks to Kano and Funakoshi's promotional efforts, the immediate postwar period saw an extraordinary growth in practice and even attracted a number of foreign soldiers looking for a means to pass the time in what proved to be a rather placid nation that offered almost no violent resistance to the occupiers. Because of pre-war changes made by Japanese nationalists, karate was highly accessible to Western military men who were already accustomed to moving in formation according to rank, wearing uniforms, paying obeisance to the national flag, and following all manner of standards and regulations. Even without a strong command of the Japanese language, soldiers and sailors were quickly able to acquire the body culture of karate. This allowed many Americans to feel confident in founding their own clubs and academies upon their return home.

While they were physically competent, however, the majority of these men lacked both the linguistic and cultural understanding to have a sense of the arts within their own context. The process, as discussed in Chapter 4, led to a transfer of objects of knowledge (technical components of the fighting arts) to the West without their being embedded in the original texture of knowledge (those social, cultural, and historical components that cause otherwise illogical elements to be understood as fully rational). Taken out of context, then, the martial arts that these men acquired in Japan and, to a much lesser extent, other regions of East and Southeast Asia— see Chapter 3 for an explanation of why Chinese martial arts did not reach American audiences until much later—were plastic enough that they could be mythologized and affixed with fantastical narratives. Ultimately they offered a nearly blank slate for American social needs to be negotiated via the construction of a cultural "other" in which the exotic and legendary acted as a means of reflecting the contemporary experiences of practitioners.

During the years of the American postwar economic boom, the middle class continue to burgeon as improving technology, social conditions, and the G.I. Bill afforded many veterans the chance to acquire training and education not previously available. The growth in white-collar positions directly impacted the number of prospective prizefighters as fewer young men saw fighting as an attractive alternative to physical labor. Amateur recreational boxing also declined in this period thanks, in part, to new standards and expectation of male social behavior. Men's magazines, social critics, and politicians expressed distaste for "association men" who sought camaraderie with others as weak and lacking independence. Physical culture in general went out of public favor at this time, giving way to a man-of-leisure aesthetic in which spectating was acceptable, but visiting the gym oneself was akin to work, which did not fit the lifestyle espoused in publications like *Playboy* and, in its early years, *Look*.

Lack of involvement in physical entertainment, combined with a rise in office-based occupations, correlated with an epidemic of weight gain and related health problems in American middle-class men. By the late 1950s and 1960s this resulted in a general anxiety akin to that which had been prevalent after the turn of the century, and for similar reasons. As women attained greater levels of autonomy and equality in all areas of life, men, no longer able to identify their masculinity by means of vocation, turned to their bodies which, in a now primarily secular social environment, came to be highly commoditized. With the body once again seen as the enemy and boxing no longer a viable retreat, many young men of the post-war generation sought personal power by identifying with the Asian martial arts as made available by returning servicemen like Robert Trias, as well as Japanese instructors with international ambitions like Mas Oyama. Both sets offered a tightly packaged, invented tradition of holistic masculinity alternative to the now-stigmatized world of Western boxing.

Markedly Western (and especially American) narrative structures were melded with the body culture of Asian martial arts in the U.S. to produce fertile ground for acting out a mythology of the lone warrior, which is essentially the same figure seen in other narrative genres of the American psyche, such as Western films and novels and frontiersman tales. Hollywood latched onto this shift in male folk culture and, by the 1970s, movie heroes were not only muscular individualists, but almost always employed some manner of stylized fighting art. The process of bringing erstwhile exotic products to mainstream American attention, though, typically requires both a significant measure of media exposure and the public presence of individuals understood to be experts on the topic. While films, magazines, and graphic novels acted as fertile soil for the projection of personal mythologies, expertise came in the form of two very different groups of martial artists.

In domestic popular culture of the 1960s, 1970s, and even into the 1980s, one could find instructional books, articles, and videos for martial arts techniques espoused by self-appointed experts, frequently with flamboyant personalities. John Keehan, alias Count Dante, perhaps the most notorious such figure, is useful as a demonstrative. A hairdresser and used car salesman based in Chicago, he claimed to be a master of several different Asian martial arts. He supposedly acquired his training during his world travels as an apprentice to the secretive leaders of the Black Dragon Fighting Society. He sold a series of how-to pamphlets by mail through advertisements in graphic novels, complete with imaginative explanations of both techniques and a wholly fictive history of both himself and East Asia in general. He was succeeded by later generations of mail-order mystics whose books now fill retailers' shelves; they even run their own training camps for would-be ninja, samurai, kung fu monks, and any other imaginary construct for which their readership is willing to pay. Count Dante represented one type of attempt to commercialize the interest that young American men were developing for exotic fighting arts of the East, but there were other, more scholarly efforts.

The other source of experts was smaller and perhaps less visible given their lack of flamboyancy. Men like Donn Draeger, Robert W. Smith, and Jon Bluming actually traveled to Japan and elsewhere (Smith later moved to Taiwan and Draeger is known for having mounted expeditions all over Southeast Asia) to study the highly exoticized martial arts in their own contexts. Though they were less commercially successful than characters like Count Dante, the quality of their work continues to be on par with any research produced today. Draeger and Smith's *Asian Fighting Arts* (1969) remains a standard reference. In addition to being more scholarly rigorous than men like Keehan, the pioneer martial arts researchers in Asia also held verifiable records of their exploits. Bluming won innumerable honors in both judo and karate. Draeger was so well-known among classical Japanese martial artists that he was invited to join the Butoku-kai and served as cultural consultant for a James Bond film. Smith was an employee of the CIA—although in an analytical capacity only, never as a field operative.

The latter group of researchers conducting scholarly rigorous study in Asia was aware of and frequently irritated by the extraordinary claims of Count Dante and his ilk, to say nothing of the political squabbles from which each would eventually renounce himself as regards the world of competitive fighting (especially judo). To satirize such shameless commercialists, Smith, Draeger, and Bluming created the abovementioned John F. Gilbey, a sort of portmanteau of the unbelievable qualities and exploits with which each of them had been attributed over the years. Gilbey was a giant of a man possessed with near-superhuman strength, and his vast bank account supported full-time globe-hopping as he searched for martial arts masters. Gilbey authored two books and a few articles (actually penned by Smith) which were clearly intended for humor, including one specifically dedicated to the art of the knock-knock joke. It says a lot about American perceptions of the Asian fighting arts that Gilbey not only received fan mail, but was treated seriously in a number of books and magazines, his ludicrous adventures apparently having been taken at face value.

By the late 1980s these experts—even Gilbey—were responsible along with the entertainment media for normalizing Asian martial arts in the broader American social environment. What began as a folk movement toward the arts as a means of negotiating new standards of masculinity was commoditized to such an extent that Hollywood action heroes became hyper-masculine, with bodybuilders being cast as boxers and soldiers, professions in which being overly muscular is typically seen as a detriment.

By the end of the 1980s, the ideal masculine image for a large number of American men involved total conquest of the body leading to an unnaturally large musculature that at once differentiated the sexes in a way that vocation and civic activity no longer could, and that lent intimidating physical power to the owner. Even where the protagonist of a given story invited personal identification through lack of physical prowess (e.g., *The Karate Kid*), Asian martial arts could be acquired as a tool to achieve the same ends of physical power and independent agency.

During the 1990s, a curious change took place as American men practicing Asian martial arts and consuming related media became disillusioned with the hyper-masculine action hero image. This can partly be attributed to the rise of child enrollment in martial arts schools, thereby damaging the ability of adult men to successfully embody fantasies of fistic achievement. As a social barometer, one may look to the popularity of martial arts comedies, such as those starring Jackie Chan. Chan frequently lampooned the more serious socially critical work of Bruce Lee, making light of his own lack of toughness and capacity for violence. The most extreme of these media outlets was probably the Teenage Mutant Ninja Turtles, a group of adolescent human-turtle hybrids who commanded (and continue to enjoy) enormous success in comic books, films, and television. This franchise makes light of how Americans have a mental construct of Asia and its martial heritage so far removed from reality that it can only be adequately expressed through mutated turtle ninja.

At the same time, a new group of martial artists emerged under the banner of rationalism. The rationalists looked to reintegrate empiricism within the context of fighting arts competitions by patronizing mixed-style contests with regulations that allowed for the most diverse array of techniques possible. The first Ultimate Fighting Championship was held in 1993 and the franchise was the focus of extraordinary public attention. The main selling point of mixed martial arts tournaments proved to be a question that dated back to the mixed contests in nineteenth and early twentieth century Japan that pitted boxers against judo practitioners and, frequently, Americans against Japanese: Which fighting style would prove superior in an open setting? Although mixed martial arts bouts in the U.S. are, in fact, subject to rules and regulations mandated by governmental authorities, both the fictive history shared by participants and spectators as well as the self-mythologizing that takes place in the community of practice sets the stage as one in which there are "no holds barred," thereby allowing all involved to believe that the victor of an MMA match truly is the better combatant.

Practitioners sometimes compare the current style of MMA with professional boxing, which they see as corrupt and lacking in the type of supportive community necessary for the proper functioning of an MMA gym. Where boxing is perceived as a male-exclusive activity that may even be tied to class- and race-based distinction, MMA is described as egalitarian and rationalistic in the community's acceptance of all methods that prove applicable. One wall of William Bush's gym features a banner with a quotation from Bruce Lee, "Accept that which is useful. Reject that which is useless. Add what is essentially your own." Whereas sports like boxing and golf are seen as men's clubs, the MMA community is understood by practitioners to be diverse on all fronts, although still strongly associated with expressions and negotiations of an essential masculinity.

The negotiation of this masculine discourse appears to be as much the result of tertiary aspects of fight training as it is embodied in the direct application of force. The MMA gym setting provides a psycho-social and physical space in which it is acceptable for men to demonstrate powerful emotions, even crying at times when the emotive process of technique acquisition yields to outside frustrations from individuals' lives. In this way—and from an analytical perspective—MMA serves more or less the same social function that boxing did during its golden age and exoticized Asian martial arts did for a period from the late '60s through the '80s. Men (and some women) seek a rationalistic, neo-primitive escape from the anxieties of modern life by projecting themselves onto professional fighters, navigate their own emotional struggles by bonding with one another in a community wherein displays of weakness are accepted, and acquire or strengthen shared beliefs by embodying a shared experience, the act of which provides fertile soil for self-mythologizing. Interestingly, the cyclical nature of this primitivism phenomenon can be seen in popular discourse about diet and exercise in the second decade of the twenty-first century. Wellness books and websites urging readers to adopt a lifestyle inspired by their Paleolithic ancestors are legion.

In the visual and non-combative performing arts, too, invented traditions of the Asian martial arts in America have come to be combined with rationalistic historical research to create a uniquely Western representation of Asian martial cultures. Graphic novels like *Shi Long Pang* and *Usagi Yojimbo* reimagine dimensions of the lone warrior myth so prevalent in American martial arts imagery to be at once consummately accurate (*Shi Long Pang* includes an extensive bibliography and footnotes) and patently artificial (*Usagi Yojimbo*'s protagonist is an anthropomorphic rabbit samurai). While depictions of fighting in this context is certainly stylized, it also tends toward a more rationalized approach, with either the stated goal of aesthetic appeal or an attempt to approximate the reality of combat through exaggeration: *Shi Long Pang*'s fight scenes are florid affairs while *Usagi Yojimbo*'s are frank and violent. Even outside of professional fighting, then, the Asian martial arts in America have continued to follow the path of rationalization. Even when discursive masculinity is less outright, the undertone of navigating a masculine identity in a world with few exclusively male realms is still prevalent.

Interpretations and Implications

Some men choose to fight. They do so in innumerable ways and capacities, always stylizing and crafting the activity into an artistic endeavor. Art has two fundamental aims: to express the self and to allow the audience to use it as a means to understand the self. In the U.S., it has been a matter of not only appropriation, but also interpretation and innovation to make of the Asian fighting disciplines what one will. This has brought about a century of unpredictable twists and turns and affected nearly every area of American life in one way or another. It would be difficult to locate an American town of much size that does not have at least one martial arts club. The fighting arts are a part of our everyday speech, as when we are nice and "wear kid gloves," when a politician looks to be "leaning on the ropes," a comment has "cut deep," or a when someone engages in a bit of "verbal jujitsu." From graphic novels to films, literature to music, the martial arts are a fundamental fabric of American life.

Now that we have seen the development and trends in American martial arts media and practice since the dawn of the twentieth century, consider what it says about Americans, men, and the world at large. It is telling that the U.S. military has taken to funding martial arts programs for troops who, in the age of bombs and automatic weapons, do not have much direct use for these skills. The army outsourced its combatives program to the Gracie family and so, unsurprisingly, the product looks like MMA, with soldiers rolling on the ground, applying chokes and joint locks, and competing with others in tournaments sponsored by their units. The Marine Corps developed its own proprietary system, known as the Marine Corps Martial Arts Program (MCMAP), often referred to more poignantly as "semper fu."

The military is not concerned that its technology will suddenly fail on every level and that warfare will immediate degenerate to hand-to-hand fighting. Rather, the purpose of these programs is psychological. The thinking appears to be that soldiers who feel confident without a weapon in hand will be more relaxed in a stressful situation. The MCMAP system also features a reading list, and Marines are tested as much on their synthesis of the ethical and historical imperatives of the program as they are the ability to disarm a knife-wielding adversary. True to form, the Marine Corps program is hierarchical, with each participant memorizing sets of techniques in order to earn various colored belts. In that way, little has changed since the advent of the colored belt system in the 1920s. The program is obviously designed to capitalize on American perceptions of the martial arts. The term is used, the thinking goes, and so certain accouterments are called for: belts, uniforms, ethical and philosophical treatises, and perhaps competitions.

One could speculate endlessly on how Kano would feel about the U.S. military adopting a system from his judo curriculum that was initially intended only to designate which students had enough experience to offer advice. As a peace-loving man, he might be disgusted. On the other hand, he may appreciate that his principle of mutual assistance and high morality seems to have transferred with it. He would likely be less than impressed, though, with the state of his other inventions in the hands of American popular culture. It wasn't until years after his passing, for instance, that blue uniforms were permitted for use in international judo tournaments so that judges could better distinguish between contestants. These days, it is possible to purchase uniforms in every color of the rainbow, patterned with camouflage, and covered in patches designating everything from rank to perfect attendance. In what may be the single most succinct way to sum up the journey of Asian martial arts in the U.S., there are companies advertising judo jackets in a set with *hakama* (a kind of traditional Japanese pleated trouser with very wide legs), both of which are colored to look like the American flag.

Are these martial arts still Asian, then? One of the largest operators of studios nationwide, the American Taekwondo Association (ATA) is a franchise system in which local instructors essentially purchase a package that covers all needs, including advertising, sales training, and bookkeeping. In what but the shallowest ways are such enterprises Asian? Here I return to a point made at the beginning of this book: In this capacity, "Asia" is not a real place. Instead, it embodies an exotic, Orientalized mythos, a far-off place where the phenomenal is commonplace, and designates social behaviors and objects of culture as being acceptable for transmutation. When the martial arts are treated in this way, Americans give themselves permission to treat them as bricolage, the concept of using whatever is handy to form what needs to exist. The martial arts, collectively, are not really about combat. As a category, they are vessels for the transmission and dissemination of culture. They are crafts onto which folklore, traditions, and beliefs are loaded so that they may arrive in other minds and other lands. In this way, the martial arts have truly conquered the world.

None of this has settled the matter of why people choose to fight, however. For that, we must look at the patterns apparent in our historical investigation. The fighters are overwhelmingly male, generally anxious about the state of masculinity in their given timeframe, and have been exposed to bodily ideals that tend not to mesh well with reality. Bartitsu— the British-Japanese concoction of Barton-Wright—was popular enough in its day because it was understood to be more physically effective than whatever other options existed (that is, one concerned for his safety could have learned to box, though its familiarity and limited scope certainly paled in comparison to the more robust Bartitsu). Sherlock Holmes adopts it and, in so doing, overcomes his greatest opponent. When James Cagney uses judo or James Bond becomes a ninja, those suddenly appear to be the most viable options because they are so effectively employed. These days, young men (and an increasing number of women) see mixed martial arts on television and films and conclude that MMA must be the best option in order to achieve their goals.

The question, then, is not which style is most effective—that changes with the tide of popular culture—but what drives people to seek out a community of practice. Historically, it is apparent that, if a broad stroke is to be used and idiosyncratic reasons abandoned, concern for masculinity and social power is the most important element. Films, television, graphic novels, and even word-of-mouth tales fulfill men's needs for belief in mentorship, the ability to earn respect and power, self-mythologizing, and the extraordinary. Without formal apprenticeship as a part of most daily life, the prospect of being guided to achievement by an exotic master is vastly appealing, hence the cultural cache of the Mr. Miyagi character. Even a recent rehash of *The Karate Kid*, titled *Never Back Down* (2008), revolves around the relationship between an adolescent who moves to a new town and a dark-skinned martial arts teacher with an accent (in this case, Brazilian). This all circles back to a primary element of Campbell's heroic journey as every hero requires an unusual mentor.

When women took hold of their social and political agency during the 1960s and 1970s, there was a fair amount of backlash against the movement by those who feared for their "traditional" social roles. One way in which this issue was circumnavigated involved taking up the martial arts as life-ways. When Robert Trias explains that the Occidental man has lost the ability to think in an abstract spiritual manner, he is appealing to a fear that something more tangible—that is, social power—has gone missing. The same dynamic is at work in the writing of Masutatsu Oyama, who emphasized his karate as an art for men. Thanks to a far-reaching orientalist streak in American culture, it became acceptable for men to reinitiate older forms of respect and power by practicing them under the guise of exotic Asian systems of living. The same was true of boxing during its golden age, when women first began their movement toward improved agency and the vote. Men, anxious already over white-collar degeneration and the U.S. entry into global conflict with the First World War, perceived a threat to their hierarchical positioning and took to the gym to build themselves in the manner of Theodore Roosevelt.

Personal myth-making is a valuable tool for negotiating everyday life, and doubly so when under stress. The strategy of projecting oneself onto a character like a larger-than-life boxer or a highly capable movie martial artist is useful as a psychological coping strategy. Myth-making is a universal human adaptation—perhaps even biological to some extent, given its prevalence in every culture and society. It allows us to identify with and, in some ways, become great figures who are able to deal with situations and challenges perhaps too trying for any normal person. For men, the mechanism was employed repeatedly throughout the last hundred years or so to address the amorphous, ethereal threats presented by general anxiety, loss of power and prestige, and disputes over tradition that distinguished the decades of the tumultuous twentieth and early twenty-first century by clinging to the martial artist identity. It allowed them to reinterpret themselves and their surroundings in a comforting and empowering way without posing a direct conflict against social movements. By giving themselves permission to enact their masculinity as a collective within the auspices of gyms, academies, movie theaters, and the pages of graphic novels, men were able to work through their potentially catastrophic impulses and worries without appearing vulnerable to themselves or others thanks to the legitimizing force of community.

These endeavors also allowed Americans broadly and men especially to accept the possibility of the extraordinary. Young men did not send away for the Black Dragon Fighting Society pamphlet or read Donn Draeger's judo weightlifting articles because they found the subject matter silly or pointless. The desire for personal power, whatever one's initial motivation, is inevitably about believing that human beings are able to manipulate their world and themselves. As David McClung explained in his interview when referencing the film *Vision Quest*, there is an innate yearning to believe that the extraordinary is possible. That same longing, unfulfilled, can lead to either positive or disastrous ends. When presented with a mundane world that failed to preserve their values and traditions, many American men during the course of the twentieth century went to great lengths (and often expense) to locate the extraordinary in the exotic, mysterious, non-existent East. They searched for mystical energy fields and superhuman masters of the human body. Their inexistence was and continues to be irrelevant. That which doesn't exist in the real Asia is simply invented in the minds of those who desire it, then passed on to the next generation, and so on in perpetuity.

All of this points to another trope of invented martial traditions and folklore that continues to be an underlying issue in the genre: the fallacy of a golden age. While the term may be used in reference to a period of exceptional prosperity (as in the golden age of boxing), in this case I use it to mean a prelapsarian rhetoric. It is often the case that the mysterious East, which globalism and technology have made highly accessible, is no longer simply far away geographically, but also chronologically. With the advent of the Internet, machine translation, international education and commerce, it isn't unusual in today's world to make a holiday visit to Japan, China, Korea, or places yet farther afield like Bhutan and Myanmar/Burma. Even Easter Island is now a vacation destination. This level of availability makes such locales less exotic, and so those with a predilection toward orientalism are forced to concoct an Asia that exists only in the past, before whatever fall led to the present state of civilization. Insisting that past masters of the martial arts possessed superior skills makes them satisfactorily unreachable in the same way that claims of underground death matches and secret ninja training had done for prior generations. This process is aided by euhemerism, the apotheosis of historically real personalities like Masutatsu Oyama and Ueshiba Morhei, to say nothing of the tales now told about Robert W. Smith and Donn Draeger. As he has mentioned in numerous interviews, Jon Bluming was informed of his own amazing exploits in Japan during the 1950s and 1960s, only to find that he does not live up to the legend. Even Jon Bluming is not as impressive as Jon Bluming.

This may be merely interesting and a bit entertaining for many of those observing the phenomenon of modern American orientalism, but there is also a very dangerous side to the golden age concept. In recent years, Japan has seen a rise in anti-foreign nationalism of the type not prevalent since just before World War II. While not a large portion of the population, those demonstrating by marching through the streets of Tokyo with imperial flags, driving black vans while shouting racist messages, and even defacing library copies of Anne Frank's *Diary of a Young Girl* (1947) are raising the hackles of an international community that still hasn't fully come to terms with the effects of the war. The pre-war ancestors of these groups are those who leveraged judo, karate, and other martial arts to nationalistic ends, fomenting a pro-expansionist youth culture in order to populate the Japanese colonies in Manchuria. If it has not already taken place, commandeering the martial arts in order to spread their message is a virtual inevitability. Now the issue has another layer, however, in that so few veterans survive to speak out against them that Japan of the early twentieth century can be treated as a golden age, before the great fall that ended in our current economic conundrum. Naturally, such talk will be accompanied by accusations against the U.S., China, and the rest of those who acted as opponents during the war and occupation.

The potential for inflammatory pro-imperial hate speech is very real. It would be unwise to avoid addressing the issue simply because the demonstrators are few and counter to the current public opinion. We must recall that the most extreme nationalists of Japan's pre-war era were also a small minority, but they managed to gain sufficient power in the right governmental positions to hijack otherwise humanistic martial disciplines to the ends of cultivating a culture of violence. Preventing such a possible repeat of history requires two actions, both relatively undemanding. First, education about the process leading up to imperial expansion and the subsequent war must be thorough, and realistic. A holistic examination of the pre-war period should include intentional outlining of the extreme nationalist agenda that was made to appeal to young people through various modes, including the seemingly innocent martial arts. Second, the educated public should pay attention to how free speech is being abused by such extremist groups and stand against such inculcation of its youth not only in schools and town halls, but also in martial arts academies and entertainment venues.

So much for Japan, but this manner of anti-foreign sentiment is also present in the U.S., and equally disconcerting. The same solutions apply, though there is an added dimension to the threat of commandeered recreational settings: domestic racism. At least one well-known professional MMA fighter and a slew of amateurs sport racist tattoos and have even spoken publicly on their negative views of non-white minorities. In the professional fighting world, there are rumors of poor backstage treatment for fighters of color, women, and homosexuals. For a time, there was a mixed martial arts gym in Maryland that proudly professed a neo-Nazi membership. Although such matters are likely to occur in any industry and have certainly been an issue in show business from the start, it is still worth considering the hazards of allowing the martial arts to be tied with hate speech of any kind. As seen in pre-war Japan, young people studying a fighting discipline are acutely open to absorbing other information when presented simultaneously. Skill in enacting violence aside, giving voice to hateful messages in an arena where droves of young people are already primed to absorb information is potentially perilous. Education is the key to preventing repeats of history. Outside of the formal education system, martial arts communities will need to police themselves with regards to the rhetoric being presented. One way in which this may be accomplished is through the concept of intangible cultural heritage (ICH).

Intangible Cultural Heritage

In 2003 the United Nations Educational, Scientific and Cultural Organization (UNESCO) established the Convention for the Safeguarding of Intangible Cultural Heritage, thereby bringing to fruition some thirty years of efforts to officially recognize member states' intangible contributions to world culture and in the interest of protecting those traditions that stand in immediate danger of disappearing from the collective repertoire of human knowledge. The initial practices, traditions, and other "intangibles" listed as warranting UNESCO recognition primarily consisted of public performance arts (especially music and dance), festivals, a system of divination, and methods of painting and storytelling. The 2011 expansion of the list featured the first martial art to receive ICH designation, a Korean style called *taekkyeon*.

UNESCO's decision to include the martial arts as a genre of intangible cultural heritage carries important implications given the global popularity of martial practices collectively. To preserve and show value for all forms of martial arts as a means of intangible cultural heritage (including those generated in the U.S. following after Asian inspiration and/or derivation), it may be worth considering the value of supporting the UNESCO project. Some key issues that should be addressed by the martial arts studies community with regards to advising interlocutors, governmental and partner organizations, and others to whom advice, both formal and not, may be given in the future.

According to the UNESCO convention, intangible cultural heritage refers to any and all "practices, representations, expressions, knowledge, skills—as well as the instruments, objects, artefacts [sic] and cultural spaces associated therewith—that communities, groups and, in some cases, individuals recognize as part of their cultural heritage."[1] Apparently broad by design, ICH as a category for protection and promotion has become something of a catch-all. Initially planned to complement the notion of tangible heritage—which refers primarily to buildings and monuments—ICH can now encompass physical structures as "cultural spaces" in addition to ephemeral practices such as dance and musical performance that can only exist in the moment.

The conservation of tangible heritage as practiced by most members of the United Nations can be traced to the European Enlightenment and the consequent rise of rationalistic inquiry. Scholars active in the art community like John Ruskin (1819–1900) advocated the value of conserving pre-industrial arts and architecture. But he and those who followed took this to mean conservation of the material product rather than the method and way of producing it. The result became a Western European focus on the value of buildings and artifacts, almost wholly ignoring the performative act of creation and, often, "preservation" included partial destruction of the artifacts themselves so that they could be maintained using newer materials and techniques, such as chipping away at worn stone to renew its appearance and replacing sections of masonry with man-made building supplies.[2]

This was the world into which the idea of intangible heritage was introduced. The debate within UNESCO began in earnest in the 1960s and led to the drafting of the 1972 World Heritage Convention, which focused primarily on tangible heritage. The discussion continued for three decades, driven, in large part, by non-Western member states' desire to protect the cultural properties that they considered as valuable as any building or monument, but that lacked the legal (and therefore monetary) means to do so. The 2003 convention remedied this lack of recognition, however generally, thereby providing avenues for global recognition and funding for the protection of non-material properties. UNESCO was not the first governmental (or quasi-governmental) body to emphasize conservation of the intangible, however.[3] Intriguingly, the modern Japanese government began dedicating resources to that end decades ago, going so far as to designate some people as special holders of ICH and providing funds to preserve their traditions.

The role of the convention is to preserve the "identification, documentation, research, preservation, protection, promotion, enhancement, transmission, particularly through formal and non-formal education, as well as the revitalization of the various aspects of [intangible cultural] heritage." The document goes on to state that UNESCO itself will take a secondary role, whenever possible, to local organizations as they are assumed to be in a better position to safeguard such heritage. Logically, the representatives of each member state cannot be expected to serve as subject matter experts on the diverse range of intangible heritages presented for support, so the system of recognition is built around the designation of advisory bodies that serve to make highly influential recommendations to the committee.

Before a given property is presented to UNESCO, it is expected to (generally) have undergone recognition at the national level, where safeguarding efforts have already been implemented. Only when the need for international involvement becomes apparent is an advisory body designated and the best means by which to aid in the property's conservation, promotion, and/or revitalization recommended. UNESCO committee members then vote on the recommendation. The goals of inviting UNESCO involvement form a relatively short list: to establish international cooperation when the property is present in multiple states, to obtain needed funding and/or other support (chiefly infrastructural) from the international community where a state does not have sufficient resources, to obtain emergency assistance when a property is in immediate danger, and/or to request the aid of experts in ICH conservation when a state does not have any of its own.

Although UNESCO ICH designation is central to any discussion of cultural property conservation, the process of applying official (that is, public) channels to the protection of cultural properties begins at the local level before moving on to the provincial and state governments, then calls for international recognition form the highest level of public interest. Depending on one's interpretation, the 2003 convention seems to focus on two types of ICH: those properties that are nearly extinct and require significant resources to survive and those that are of such value and importance to a given people's identity that they feel international recognition would benefit the role of the United Nations in establishing stronger bonds and intercultural understanding. In the case of each cultural property, the question is how and to what degree the heritage in question benefits from UNESCO and governmental support.

For properties in immediate danger, the primary benefits are advocacy, infrastructural support, and financial assistance. When the Japanese government becomes involved in the conservation of folk traditions, it often simply means that local representatives aid the tradition holders in obtaining the materials needed to continue their practice as well as locating appropriate trainees to carry on the heritage. This would seem to be both efficient and cost-effective, barring materials that require great expense.

In the case of properties that are not in immediate danger, the benefits of ICH designation for the tradition holders are less pronounced. The aforementioned instance of UNESCO adding *taekkyeon* to its official register serves as an intriguing example. Given the heated debate over the origins of taekwondo, especially since its selection as an Olympic sport, the desire by many Korean practitioners of the style for ties to an older tradition have become pronounced, with any number of taekwondo academies around the world claiming a history that dates back over two thousand years. For taekwondo practitioners (and, indeed, Korean nationalists seeking to free their country's most prominent combative art from its modern origins in Japanese and Okinawan karate), the legitimization of *taekkyeon* would serve to then establish taekwondo as independent from karate and wholly Korean.

In this way, Korean identity is directly connected with taekwondo as a national pastime, especially given its international popularity, and its legitimacy may be seen as a kind of "soft power" in the same mode as popular music and films. However, the ability to manipulate such power relies on being viewed as inherited from a legitimate tradition, just as the very existence of the nation-state requires that a novel identity be formed from disparate groups in a way that allows those within the national boundaries to agree on a singular concept of self. In order for taekwondo to be seen as a legitimate Korean art form on the global stage, it is necessary for an older tradition with some ancient basis to act as a sort of "missing link." That link is *taekkyeon*.[4]

The application process for UNESCO ICH recognition calls for investigation by the designated advisory body (generally an NGO or other third-party promotional organization), written descriptions of the cultural property including history, practice, and social role, as well as testimony from subject matter experts as to the value of the tradition and need for intervention to conserve it. In addition, the sponsoring government, tradition holders, and advisory body must produce a video, approximately ten minutes in length, detailing the cultural property. Put together, these materials form a narrative relating not simply facts about a given tradition, but its meaning to those interested in its protection.

In the *taekkyeon* example, the promotional video suggests that there was a prelapsarian time in which the art was enjoyed by a great many Koreans;

however, political turmoil caused the suppression of this traditional cultural expression, almost leading to its extinction. As fortune would have it, a single master survived through to the period of national independence and passed his skills on to a protégé, who set about establishing an organization to again disperse the art to the Korean people. As discussed in the introductory chapter, martial arts, like all folk practices, often feature such creation narratives that at once explain and justify the existence of the tradition, and *taekkyeon* is no exception. The value in such a story is not to be found in its historical veracity, but in the meaning it holds for the tradition bearers, as with other folk narratives. It is apparent that the story shared in the UNESCO promotional materials is intended to relate the importance to the Korean people (or at least those represented by the sponsoring agencies) that this particular narrative and the practice to which it is tied be recognized as legitimate and meaningful by the international community, both because of its implications for taekwondo specifically and Korean identity in general.

In addition to legitimizing tradition, there are monetary incentives to ICH status, especially when conferred by UNESCO. This happens on at least three fronts. First, when working with local governmental and advisory organizations, there are public funds to be considered. The NGO selected by UNESCO to advise on matters pertaining to the martial arts is the World Martial Arts Union (WoMAU). Founded in 2002, WoMAU's chief stated purpose is to "promote exchange and cooperation between martial arts organizations, promotion and conservation of each country's traditional martial arts, research and study of martial arts and contribution positively to the world peace." WoMAU's affiliation process is fairly liberal, allowing for an extraordinarily diverse representation of martial arts from all corners of the globe. One of their activities with the greatest international exposure is the annual Chungju World Martial Arts Festival, which features public presentations and activities focused on the member groups, but with a heavy emphasis on Korean martial arts.[5]

To accomplish its goals, WoMAU receives donations and endowments from several sources, including the Korea Foundation, an independent quasi-governmental group associated with the Ministry of Foreign Affairs. The Korea Foundation presents WoMAU with an annual budget of $500,000 (U.S.) to cover the cost of the festival and other activities, such as making presentations for UNESCO. In this way, *taekkyeon* practitioners (that is, members of the Korean Taekkyeon Association as it was selected by WoMAU for cooperation) have benefitted directly via increased membership due to economic intervention aimed at researching the history of the art as well as promoting it to the public, which then draws greater membership and, therefore, increases revenue from membership fees (this not accounting for equipment sales, etc.).

In other instances, the funding comes from UNESCO itself in the form of the Fund for the Safeguarding of the Intangible Cultural Heritage. This fund receives mandatory contributions at least every two years from the states that choose to be party to the ICH convention and can be applied to any of the aims stated in the guiding document. The flow of money in this case can be seen as representative of the convention's goals as all member states are essentially supporting (and thus recognizing) the intangible cultural heritage of the other states, affirming each nation's people's identity through what is essentially a consumerist activity.

The risk of placing a heritage tradition on display for public consumption—and in particular in a market context—inevitably leads to exposure that can be detrimental to the often-fragile nature of the heritage community and its interaction with conservationists, governments, and the consumer. It is the responsibility of the conservation agency, consulting body, and/or individual conservationist to maintain connections with the tradition holders and ensure that they receive continued support and guidance.

The danger of market influence to change a heritage property beyond recognition is very real. The development of *taekkyeon* will be educational in this regard as the effect of UNESCO ICH status is seen on a martial art for the first time. It is entirely possible that public exposure and increased membership revenue for the Korean Taekkyeon Association will cause the group to hold larger tournaments and exhibitions, to sell merchandise, alter requirements for practitioners that will encourage yet more international involvement, license academies and clubs overseas, and raise the cost of official licensing to boost income. If this were to occur, it may only be a matter of years before the *taekkyeon* presented to UNESCO exists in name only. This, of course, is a sort of worst-case scenario; however, prudence may be the best approach in this instance.

In instances of dangerous nationalism like pre-war Japan, local and state-level involvement can be questionable while UNESCO intervention may actually mitigate the problem. The Japanese government was able, in large part, to abuse martial culture by preventing international feedback, such as the German advisory council that helped to shape judo. Assuming that intercultural exchange truly does lessen the likelihood of conflict, the cooperation of martial artists from different countries, yet representing the same style, could very well lessen that style's chances of being made a tool for nationalist propaganda. At the same time, however, one cannot help but notice that the Korea Foundation, created by and cooperating closely with the South Korean Ministry of Foreign Affairs, funds much of WoMAU's activities, the first of which, with regards to ICH, was to promote a Korean martial art for UNESCO recognition and holds its annual festival in a Korean city and much of the scheduled events focus on Korean martial culture. The question of objectivity should be raised in such instances.

Festivals like WoMAU's present another danger for the hosting region: buildup in anticipation of a sudden burden followed by economic collapse. This phenomenon has been witnessed surrounding the Olympic Games, which may function here as a sort of ethnographic analogy. Hosting a major spectator event like the Olympics is fiscally dangerous and often causes a depression following their conclusion as multimillion dollar structures stand unused in already-put-upon urban spaces. To be fair, there are also cases in which the rebuilding of a city has led to positive changes. But this is where the Olympic analogy breaks down; such an event dedicated solely to the cultural promotion of martial arts (as opposed to an MMA tournament) will not only attract fewer spectators by several orders of magnitude, but the likelihood of local officials and taxpayers agreeing to fund the construction of entire venues to house it is extremely low. Assuming that a martial arts festival could garner sufficient public attention to prove profitable, the question arises, again, of the degree to which authenticity and tradition may be sacrificed in the interest of the bottom line.

Assuming that no conflicts of interest are apparent and that the art and its attendant community would benefit from increased public exposure, governmental funding, or other intervention, the next step should be to determine the minimum level of action needed to preserve and/or promote the property in such a way that it maintains cultural integrity. The intervention is best kept to a minimum due to the dangers outlined in the above section; essentially, the less outsider involvement, the less likely it is to irrevocably transform the tradition in a negative or damaging way.

After the necessary level of intervention has been determined by tradition holders and agreed upon by the outside agency, it would then be worthwhile to establish a protective assembly of practitioners to advise on the impact of virtually any action as it relates to the tradition's well-being. From the outside agent's standpoint, it is best to allow, to the extent possible, the tradition bearers to direct and carry out their own conservation activities. The conservationist should recognize that cultural properties change in the face of any stimulus and, therefore, the amount of outsider direction has an immediate and lasting effect that cannot be taken lightly.

If the community in question is to be depicted to the general public, it may be necessary for the conservation professional to assist in the organization and definition of a cultural identity that can be readily expressed in the form of a narrative that adheres to the community's sense of self. The videos that UNESCO requires for its application process are a reliable example of the value that this practice has for public relations. As with festivals, the representation of a given group to the greater public sphere is often difficult, especially for isolated communities, necessitating the assistance of a professional. Narrative creation carries with it the added benefit of greater group cohesion since it allows group members to express in short the value they place on the cultural property. Well-crafted, the narrative representation can take into account all or most members' perceptions of the tradition and, therefore, bring about greater unity, which is inimitably useful when faced with additional outside scrutiny.

Meanings and Values

Here we return to the questions raised in this book's introduction. Who are martial artists? Without being too flippant, this is a massive category of people who choose to identify as such. Many of them actively pursue some manner of fighting discipline. Some of them do not. They are not, it turns out, a single unified subculture. Martial artists carve out folk groups within folk groups, differentiate themselves to an astonishing degree, run the gamut from casual observer to full-time professional, and simultaneously enjoy social prestige for their dedication and social criticism for enacting violence. Some are quite spiritual, even to the extent of identifying their styles and schools with particular religions and deities. United Martial Artists for Christ, for instance, boasts a healthy membership roster. The same is true of the Gospel Martial Arts Union. At the same time, there are those who take the opposite route, such as the famous atheist writer Sam Harris, who has spoken at length of his martial arts practice.

To what end do people practice these skills? There are, of course, as many reasons to study the fighting disciplines as there are individuals. To paint with a broad brush, though, one must first consider the historical uses. Men have used them as escapes from a seemingly hostile zeitgeist, as a way to accrue agency and personal empowerment, as a tie to an imagined place that still possesses a sense of mystery and potential, and simply as a way to exercise that seems more intellectually stimulating than a treadmill. There is no short or simple answer to the question of why, with one slightly truistic phrase: The purpose of the martial arts is to meet whatever need the traditional holders have at the time. They are the stuff of bricolage, infinitely malleable depending on the situation. They can be used to turn young people into imperialist crusaders, but also to show the masses the virtue of passivism. They are fun sports for health and recreation, but can also take a deadly turn, and can even serve as the catalyst for entry into cults and religions.

Because of this malleability and the universal existence of martial arts in human societies everywhere, its social and historical importance cannot be overlooked. It is tempting for someone investigating a cultural region to ignore the martial arts found there as nothing more than amusing ways to fill the time between more important activities, but that would be remiss. Suppose one were intent on studying the history and culture of Brazil. There is a unique system there, called *capoeira*, which has its roots in both West Africa and South America and resembles a form of breakdancing. Instead of looking elsewhere for information about the Brazilian people, one should also inquire about the role played by *capoeira* in the nation's history. It turns out to have important implications for ethnic conflict, for instance, as one of the ways through which slaves rose up against their captors. One would never know this by dismissing it as a simple game.

For the general public, too, martial arts work as vessels for cultural transmission. It would be challenging these days to visit a cinema and not find at least one film featuring stylized martial arts action. They comprise an entire movie genre, and common storylines like *The Karate Kid* and *Bloodsport* see reincarnations every few years. These certainly fall within what we may call the "gutsy sports hero" variety in which the protagonist works hard to achieve a goal, then achieves the goal and, in so doing, receives the boon, wins the affection of a love interest, and/or learns a valuable lesson about personal confidence or self-worth. This, again, corresponds to Joseph Campbell. The same pattern is true of graphic novels. Even when not explicitly the theme of a given title, one need only flip through any action-related comic to see the influence of martial arts films. The same is true of video games and even novels, many of which use characters' training experiences as plot devices or the occasional *deus ex machina*. Almost always, though, the martial arts as depicted in entertainment venues like these have another unifying feature: They all carry some degree of philosophical tinge.

The philosophies may vary (although they are surprisingly uniform), but any training sequence will likely include dialogue with much broader implications than simply fisticuffs. Although hardly the first instance of martial philosophizing, *Kung Fu* may be the most well-known example, and with good reason. It is notable that the nuggets of knowledge dispensed by the protagonist's teacher, the blind Master Po, exhibit traditional Western approaches to existential dilemmas rather than markedly Chinese ones. In more recent years, *The Last Samurai* shows Tom Cruise's character—an American stranded in a rural samurai village—learning fistic philosophy from a supposedly ancient Japanese tradition. It is curious, then, that the message ends up being one of self-sacrifice for the cause of liberty and independence, which are most certainly not in keeping with Japanese philosophical thought of the late Edo and early Meiji periods.

Here lies the very heart of the American martial arts invention. *The Last Samurai* is about an American soldier who, disgusted with himself and his people over their domestic actions and violent tendencies, ventures to the exotic East out of necessity, rather than choice. There, he meets mysterious figures, sees spiritual experiences that are never fully explained, and learns philosophical thought and self-worth through martial disciplines. In the end, we find that he has become perhaps more American, with stronger beliefs in liberty and the Western brand of justice than he held before setting out on his heroic journey. It is even suggested at the film's conclusion that he somehow survives the catastrophic final battle when more capable warriors do not and, naturally, returns to the samurai village and gets the girl. There are few storylines more American than this and it demonstrates succinctly the meaning of martial arts in America: Their purpose is to tell ourselves stories about ourselves.

Chapter Notes

Introduction

1. Geertz, Clifford. 1972. "Deep Play: Notes on the Balinese Cockfight," pg. 29.
2. Elias, Norbert and Eric Dunning. 1986. *Quest for Excitement: Sport and Leisure in the Civilizing Process*, pg. 4.
3. Hobsbawm, Eric. 1983. "Introduction: Inventing Traditions," pg. 1.
4. Cetina, Karin Knorr. 1997. "Sociality with Objects: Social Relations in Postsocial Knowledge Societies."
5. Krug, G. J. 2001. "The Feet of the Master: Three Stages in the Appropriation of Okinawan Karate Into Anglo-American Culture."
6. Featherstone, Mike. 1991. "The Body in Consumer Culture," pg. 170.
7. De Caro, Frank and Rosan Augusta Jordan. 2004. *Re-Situating Folklore: Folk Contexts and Twentieth-Century Literature and Art*, pg. 15.
8. Campbell, Joseph. 1973. *The Hero with a Thousand Faces*, pg. 15–16.

Chapter 1

1. Boon, Kevin Alexander. 2003. "Men and Nostalgia for Violence: Culture and Culpability in Chuck Palahniuk's Fight Club," pg. 267–268.
2. Hall, Donald E. 1994. "Introduction," pg. 6.
3. Hall, pg. 7–8.
4. Hall, pg. 9.
5. Roberson, Susan L. 1994. "Degenerate Effeminacy," pg. 156.
6. Garnham, Neal. 2001. "Both Praying and Playing: 'Muscular Christianity' and the YMCA in North Durham," pg. 297–298.
7. Hopkins, Howard. 1951. *History of the YMCA in North America*, pg. 15.

8. Hopkins, pg. 199.
9. Hopkins, pg. 389.
10. Green, Harvey. 1986. *Fit for America: Health, Fitness, and American Society*, pg. 214.
11. Hopkins, pg. 248–249.
12. Gorn, Elliott J. 1986. *The Manly Art: Bare-Knuckle Prize Fighting in America*, pg. 113–119.
13. Green 1986, pg. 215.
14. Garnham, pg. 400–401.
15. Pennington, John. 1994. "Muscular Spirituality in George MacDonald's Curdie Books," pg. 141.
16. Hoganson, Kristin L. 1998. *Fighting for American Manhood: How Gender Politics Provoked the Spanish-American and Philippine-American Wars*, pg. 8–9.
17. Rotundo, Anthony E. 1983. "Body and Soul: Changing Ideals of American Middle-Class Manhood, 1770–1920," pg. 6.
18. Rotundo, pg. 225–226.
19. Hoganson, pg. 34.
20. Rotundo, pg. 232
21. Putney, Clifford. 2001. *Muscular Christianity: Manhood and Sports in Protestant America, 1880–1920*, pg. 44.
22. Svinth, Joseph R. 2003. "The Spirit of Manliness: Boxing in Imperial Japan, 1868–1945," pg. 54.
23. Putney, pg. 73.
24. e.g., Hoganson 1998.
25. Rotundo, pg. 242.
26. Green 1986, pg. 206.
27. Hoganson, pg. 35.
28. Green 1986, pg. 32.
29. Green 1986, pg. 154.
30. Rotundo, pg. 241.
31. Black, Jonathan. 2009. "Charles Atlas: Muscle Man."
32. Pope, Harrison G., et al. 1998. "Evolving Ideals of Male Body Image as Seen Through Action Toys" pg. 68.

33. Bederman, Gail. 1995. *Manliness and Civilization*, pg. 15.
34. Hopkins, pg. 248.
35. Green 1986, pg. 199–201.
36. Bederman, pg. 13.
37. Rotundo, pg. 29–30.
38. Hopkins, pg. 256.
39. Hopkins, pg. 244.
40. Hopkins, pg. 391.
41. Rotundo, pg. 283.
42. Green 1986, pg. 249–250.
43. Bederman, pg. 217.
44. Rotundo, pg. 32.
45. Connell, R. W. 1998. "Masculinities and Globalization," pg. 6.
46. Rotundo, pg. 32.
47. Green 1986, pg. 255.
48. Godfrey, Emelyne. 2010. "Jujusuffragettes," pg. 633–634.
49. Godfrey, pg. 635.
50. Connell, pg. 5–6.
51. Silver, Mike. 2008. *The Arc of Boxing: The Rise and Decline of the Sweet Science*, pg. 24–25.
52. Ownby, Ted. 1990. *Subduing Satan: Religion, Recreation, and Manhood in the Rural South, 1865–1920*, pg. 2.
53. Featherstone, Mike. 1991. "The Body in Consumer Culture," pg. 172.
54. Putney, pg. 163.
55. Putney, pg. 126.
56. Green 1986, pg. 312–317.
57. Toon, Elizabeth and Janet Lynne Golden. 2002. "'Live Clean, Think Clean, and Don't Go to Burlesque Shows': Charles Atlas as Health Advisor," pg. 48.
58. Green 1986, pg. 323.
59. Black 2009.
60. Wolf-Meye, Matthew. 2003. "The World Ozymandias Made: Utopias in the Superhero Comic, Subculture, and the Conservation of Difference," pg. 498.
61. Silver, pg. 28–29.
62. Ownby, pg. 136.
63. Featherstone, pg. 186.

Chapter 2

1. Hobsbawm, Eric. 1983. "Introduction: Inventing Traditions."
2. Nitobe, Inazo. 1972. *The Works of Inazo Nitobe*.
3. Maeshima, Kazuhiro. 2004. "Tocqueville's Democracy and Samurai: Inazo Nitobe's Attempt to Apply American Democracy to the Feudal Tradition of Japan," pg. 103.
4. Abe, Ikuo, et al. 1992. "Fascism, Sport and Society in Japan," pg. 4–5.
5. Karlin, Jason G. 2002. "The Gender of Nationalism: Competing Masculinities in Meiji Japan," pg. 62–68.
6. Karlin, pg. 71.
7. Abe, et al., pg. 5.
8. Abe, et al., pg. 8.
9. Inoue, Shun. 1998. "The Invention of the Martial Arts: Kano Jigoro and Kodokan Judo," pg. 164–165.
10. Inoue, pg. 170–172.
11. Karlin, pg. 77.
12. Inoue, pg. 172.
13. Gordon, Andrew. 2003. *A Modern History of Japan: From Tokugawa Times to the Present*, pg. 49.
14. Gordon, pg. 53–57.
15. Gordon, pg. 179.
16. Green 1986, pg. 260–274.
17. Thomson, James C., et al. 1981. *Sentimental Imperialists: The American Experience in East Asia*, pg. 137.
18. Thomson, et al., pg. 77.
19. Nakajima, Tetsuya, and Lee Thompson. 2012. "Judo and the process of nation-building in Japan: Kano Jigoro and the formation of Kodokan judo," pg. 99.
20. Nakajima and Thompson, pg. 101–102.
21. Nakajima and Thompson, pg. 106–108.
22. Inoue, pg. 106–107.
23. Lowry, Dave. 2006. *In the Dojo: A Guide to the Rituals and Etiquette of the Japanese Martial Arts*, pg. 39.
24. Inoue, pg. 107.
25. Inoue, pg. 171.
26. Tan, Kevin S. Y. 2004. "Constructing a Martial Tradition: Rethinking a Popular History of Karate-Dou," pg. 173–175.
27. Draeger, Donn F. and Robert W. Smith. 1980 [1969]. *Comprehensive Asian Fighting Arts*, pg. 59.
28. Draeger and Smith, pg. 60.
29. Tan, pg. 183.
30. Draeger and Smith, pg. 60.
31. Tan, pg. 183.
32. Gordon, pg. 176.
33. Karlin, pg. 71.
34. Gordon, pg. 181–183.
35. Kleeman, Faye Yuan. 2005. "Inscribing Manchuria: Gender, Ideology, and Popular Imagination," pg. 55.
36. Gordon, pg. 183.
37. Kleeman, pg. 55.
38. Harootunian, Harry D. 1959. "The Progress of Japan and the Samurai Class, 1868–1882," pg. 256.
39. Kleeman, pg. 55.
40. Bazylko, Andrzej. 2004. "'Master of Masters'—Morihei Ueshiba (1883–1969)."
41. Kleeman, pg. 63.
42. Donohue, John J. 1994. *Warrior Dreams:*

The Martial Arts and the American Imagination, pg. 28.

43. Svinth, pg. 37–39.
44. Svinth, pg. 39–42.
45. Svinth, pg. 45–46.
46. Henning, Stanley E. 1981. "The Chinese Martial Arts in Historical Perspective," pg. 176.
47. Perry, Elizabeth J. 1985. "Rural Violence in Socialist China," pg. 436–440.
48. Henning 1981, pg. 176.
49. Perry, pg. 440.
50. Eberhard, Wolfram. 1975. "Foreigners and Foreign Wars in Chinese Folk Novels," pg. 67.
51. Kleeman, pg. 50–51; Eberhard, pg. 66.
52. Draeger and Smith, pg. 18–19.
53. Henning 1981, pg. 177.
54. Draeger and Smith, pg. 19.
55. Henning, Stanley E. 2003. "The Martial Arts in Chinese Physical Culture, 1865–1965," pg. 19–21.
56. Gordon, pg. 187.
57. Henning 2003, pg. 24.
58. Thomson, et al., pg. 160.
59. Henning 1981, pg. 177.
60. Henning 2003, pg. 27.
61. Donohue, pg. 28.

Chapter 3

1. Henning 2003, pg. 30.
2. Henning 2003, pg. 32.
3. Henning 1981, pg. 177.
4. Thomson et al. 1981, pg. 194.
5. Baber, John W. (AFC 2001/001/50101) Interview.
6. Romano, Salvatore "Sam" (AFC 2001/001/58343) Interview.
7. Carlson, Glenn (AFC 2001/001/86048) Interview.
8. Van Skiver, Raymond (AFC 2001/001/12540) Interview.
9. Inoue 1998, pg. 173.
10. Oyama, Masutatsu. 1979. *The Kyokushin Way*, pg. 5.
11. Oyama, pg. 33.
12. Oyama, pg. 15.
13. Matthews, Gordon. 2003. "Can a 'Real Man' Live for His Family?" pg. 109.
14. Matthew, pg. 121.
15. Cox, Rupert A. 2003. *The Zen Arts: An Anthropological Study of the Culture of Aesthetic Form in Japan*, pg. 57–58.
16. Oyama, pg. 105.
17. Oyama, pg. 107.
18. Oyama, pg. 5.
19. Oyama, pg. 110.
20. Bluming, Johannes "Jon" Cornelius. 1998. Interview transcript.
21. Cox, pg. 186.
22. Iwabuchi, Koichi. 1994. "Complicit Exoticism: Japan and its Other," pg. 4.
23. Benedict, Ruth. 1946. *The Chrysanthemum and the Sword: Patterns of Japanese Culture*, pg. 10.
24. Iwabuchi, pg. 6.
25. Benedict, pg. 2.
26. Iwabuchi, pg. 6.
27. Iwabuchi, pg. 15.
28. Connell, R. W. 1993. "The Big Picture: Masculinities in Recent World History," pg. 606.
29. Iwabuchi, pg. 25.
30. Oyama, pg. 23.
31. Svinth 2003.
32. Krug, G. J. 2001. "The Feet of the Master: Three Stages in the Appropriation of Okinawan Karate Into Anglo-American Culture," pg. 395–396.
33. Oyama, pg. 89.
34. Donohue 1994, pg. 41.
35. Donohue, pg. 10.
36. Krug, pg. 401–402.
37. Krug, pg. 402–403.
38. Donohue, pg. 54.
39. Trias, Robert A. 1973. *The Hand Is My Sword: A Karate Handbook*, pg. 15.
40. Trias, pg. 141.
41. Trias, pg. 140.
42. Littlewood, Roland. 1998. "Living Gods: In (Partial) Defence of Euhemerus," pg. 8–9.
43. Donohue, pg. 53.
44. Donohue, pg. 56–62.
45. Trias, pg. 17.
46. Trias, pg. 9.
47. Trias, pg. 18.
48. Green, Thomas A. 2003a. "Sense in Nonsense: The Role of Folk History in the Martial Arts," pg. 5.
49. Green 2003a, pg. 5.
50. Trias, pg. 22.
51. Cuordileone, K.A. 2000. "'Politics in the Age of Anxiety': Cold War Political Culture and the Crisis in American Masculinity, 1949–1960," pg. 539.
52. Cuordileone, pg. 542–543.
53. Berrett, Jesse. 1997. "Feeding the Organization Man: Diet and Masculinity in Postwar America," pg. 805.
54. Osgerby, Bill. 2003. "A Pedigree of the Consuming Male: Masculinity, Consumption and the American 'Leisure Class,'" pg. 76.
55. Berrett, 811–813.
56. Silver 2008, pg. 36–37.
57. Silver, pg. 37.
58. Connell, pg. 597.
59. Purdy, Ken W. 1961. "Karate: Japan's Spectacular Art of Handmade Mayhem," pg. 72.
60. Purdy, pg. 72.

61. Purdy, pg. 66.
62. Krug, pg. 62.

Chapter 4

1. Toelken, Barre. 1996. *The Dynamics of Folklore*, pg. 234.
2. Letter to Smith, 7 October 1974.
3. Smith, Robert W. 1964. *Secrets of Shaolin Temple Boxing*, pg. 15.
4. Letter to Smith, 27 December 1974.
5. Letter to Smith, 20 November 1973.
6. Letter to Smith, 12 July 1968.
7. Letter to Smith, 20 November 1973.
8. Smith, Robert W. 1999. *Martial Musings: A Portrayal of Martial Arts in the 20th Century*, pg. 21.
9. Smith 1999, pg. 98.
10. Letter to Smith, 9 July 1974.
11. Letter to Smith, 9 July 1974.
12. Smith 1999, pg. 99.
13. Letter, 8 September 1974.
14. Interview, 10 February 1998.
15. Interview, 10 February 1998.
16. Letter to Smith, 7 November 1974.
17. Letter, 4 November 1972.
18. Letter, 4 August 1967.
19. Harrington, letter to Smith, 2 June 1997.
20. Bluming interview transcript, 20–21 February 1998.
21. Bluming, personal communication.
22. Smith 1999, pg. 108.
23. Bluming interview transcript, 20–21 February 1998.
24. Letter, 9 July 1974.
25. Bluming, personal communication.
26. Bluming interview transcript, 20–21 February 1998.
27. Smith 1999, pg. 111.
28. Bluming interview transcript, 20–21 February 1998.
29. Bluming interview transcript, 20–21 February 1998.
30. Masutatsuoyama.com. 2013. "Bulls, Challengers, and the Godhand."
31. Bluming interview transcript, 20–21 February 1998.
32. Masutatsuoyama.com
33. Bluming interview transcript, 20–21 February 1998.
34. Bluming, personal communication.
35. Bluming, personal communication.
36. Bluming interview transcript, 20–21 February 1998.
37. Godfrey, pg. 29.
38. Smith 1999, pg. 113.
39. Gilbey, John F. 1983. *The Way of a Warrior*, pg. 29.
40. Letter to Smith, 5 December 1997.
41. Letter to Smith, 5 December 1997.

42. Letter to Smith 10 March 1963.
43. Letter, 2 June 1972.
44. Letter, 4 November 1972.
45. Letter to Smith, 1 July 1973.
46. Letter to Geoff Wilcher, 3 December 1981.
47. Bates, letter to Smith, 8 November 1996.
48. Draeger and Smith, pg. 22.
49. Smith 1999, pg. 195.
50. Smith 1999, pg. 201.
51. Lad, letter to Smith, 25 January 1983.
52. Smith 1999, pg. 223.
53. Toelken, pg. 209–210.
54. Dante, Count. 2014. *World's Deadliest Fighting Secrets*, pg. 11.
55. Letter to Smith, 21 June 1965.
56. Roy, T.L. 2010. *Deadliest Man Alive! The Strange Saga of Count Dante and the Black Dragon Fighting Society*, pg. 19.
57. Roy, pg. 27.
58. Roy, pg. 57–58.
59. Time. 1942. "U.S. at War: Takcihashi's Blacks."

Chapter 5

1. Nagashima, Akira. 1970. "A Comparison of Japanese and U.S. Attitudes Toward Foreign Products," pg. 74.
2. Savran, David. 1998. *Taking It Like a Man: White Masculinity, Masochism, and Contemporary American Culture*, pg. 114.
3. Savran 1998, pg. 137.
4. Savran 1998, pg. 119.
5. Connell 1993, pg. 198–199.
6. Savran 1998, pg. 194.
7. Singer, Mark. 1986. "Osu!"
8. Boon 2003, pg. 270.
9. Boon 2003, pg. 273.
10. Jones, Gerard. 2003. *Killing Monsters: Why Children Need Fantasy, Superheroes, and Make-Believe Violence*, pg. 11.
11. Campbell, Joseph. 1973. *The Hero with a Thousand Faces*, pg. 72–73.
12. Svinth 2003, pg. 63–64.
13. Svinth 2003, pg. 65–68.
14. Svinth 2003, pg. 67.
15. Svinth 2003, pg. 69–70.
16. Boon 2003, pg. 269.
17. Hirose, A., and K. K. H. Pih. 2009. "Men Who Strike and Men Who Submit: Hegemonic and Marginalized Masculinities in Mixed Martial Arts," pg. 199–200.
18. Holthuysen, Jaime. 2011. "Embattled Identities: Construction of Contemporary American Masculinity Amongst Mixed Martial Arts Cagefighters," pg. 121.
19. Holthuysen 2011, pg. 212.
20. Holthuysen 2011, pg. 156.
21. Graciemag.com. 2011. "From Kayron to

Galvao, the Stars Meet Up at Samurai Pro"; Brajitsu, Inc. 2013. "The Origins of Jiu-Jitsu."
22. Smith 1999, pg. 352.
23. Montagnani, Ilaria. 2005. *Forza: The Samurai Sword Workout*, pg. 10.
24. Montagnani 2005, pg. 10.
25. Holthuysen 2011, pg. 177.

Conclusion

1. UNESCO. 2003. "Convention for the Safeguarding of Intangible Cultural Heritage."
2. Hassard, Frank. 2009. "Intangible Her-itage in the United Kingdom: The Dark Side of Englightenment?" pg. 270.
3. Blake, Janet. 2009. "UNESCO's 2003 Convention on Intangible Cultural Heritage: the Implications of Community Involvement in 'Safeguarding.'"
4. Ahn, Jeong Deok, Suck ho Hong, and Yeong Kil Park. 2009. "The Historical and Cultural Identity of Taekwondo as a Tradi-tional Korean Martial Art," pg. 1717.
5. WoMAU. 2012. "WoMAU and its Role Reviewed with Decision of Taekkyon for Inscription on the List as a Momentum."

Bibliography

Abe, Ikuo, Yasuharu Kiyohara, and Ken Nakajima. 1992. "Fascism, Sport and Society in Japan." *The International Journal of the History of Sport* 9 (1):1–28.

Ahn, Jeong Deok, Suck ho Hong, and Yeong Kil Park. 2009. "The Historical and Cultural Identity of Taekwondo as a Traditional Korean Martial Art." *The International Journal of the History of Sport* 26(11):1716–1734.

Amdur, Ellis. 1998. "Letter." Texas A&M University, College Station, TX.

Baber, John W. (AFC 2001/001/50101). Veterans History Project. American Folklife Center: Library of Congress.

Bairner, Alan. 2012a. "Sport, Social Science and the Asia Pacific." *Asia Pacific Journal of Sport and Social Science* 1 (1):1–7. doi: 10.1080/21640599.2012.714920.

_____. 2012b. "When 'East' Meets 'West': Reflections on Cultural Exchange." *Asia Pacific Journal of Sport and Social Science* 1 (2–3):87–96. doi: 10.1080/21640599.2012.758923.

Bates, Christopher. 1996. "Letter." Texas A&M University, College Station, TX.

Bazylko, Andrzej. 2004. "'Master of Master'—Morihei Ueshiba (1883–1969)." *Budojo*,

Bederman, Gail. 1995. *Manliness and Civilization*. Chicago: University of Chicago Press.

Benedict, Ruth. 1946. *The Chrysanthemum and the Sword: Patterns of Japanese Culture*. Boston: Houghton Mifflin.

Berrett, Jesse. 1997. "Feeding the Organization Man: Diet and Masculinity in Postwar America." *Journal of Social History* 30 (4):805–825.

Black Dragon Fighting Society, 1968. *Advertisement*.

Black, Jonathan. 2009. "Muscle Man: With His Send-away Fitness Program, Charles Atlas Turned 97-Pound Weaklings into First Class Males." *Smithsonian* 40 (5):64–71.

Blake, Janet. 2009. "Unesco's 2003 Convention on Intangible Cultural Heritage: The Implications of Community Involvement in 'Safeguarding.'" In *Intangible Heritage*, edited by Laurajane Smith and Natsuko Akagawa, 45–73. New York: Routledge.

Bluming, Johannes "Jon" Cornelius. 1997–1998. "Letters." Texas A&M University, College Station, TX.

_____. 1998. Interview transcript, edited by Graham Noble. Texas A&M University, College Station, TX: Cushing Memorial Library and Archives, Robert W. Smith Martial Arts Collection.

_____. 2014. Personal Interview.

Boon, Kevin Alexander. 2003. "Men and Nostalgia for Violence: Culture and Culpability in Chuck Palahniuk's Fight Club." *The Journal of Men's Studies* 11 (3):267–276.

Brajitsu, Inc. 2013. "The Origins of Jiu-Jitsu." Accessed 19 July 2013. http://www.gracie academy.com/history.asp.

Bush, William "Bubba." 2014. Personal Interview.

Campbell, Joseph. 1973. *The Hero with a Thousand Faces*. Princeton, NJ: Princeton University Press.

Carlson, Glenn (AFC 2001/001/86048). Veterans History Project. American Folklife Center: Library of Congress.

Carpenter Collection. before 1927. Boys, and Toys. Library of Congress, Carpenter Collection.

_____. no date. Patriotic Children with Flags. Library of Congress, Carpenter Collection (1885–1972).

Cetina, Karin Knorr. 1997. "Sociality with Objects: Social Relations in Postsocial Knowledge Societies." *Theory, Culture & Society* 14 (4):1–43.

Channon, Alex. 2012. "Western Men and Eastern Arts: The Significance of Eastern Martial Arts Disciplines in British Men's Narratives of Masculinity." *Asia Pacific Journal of Sport and Social Science* 1 (2):111–127.

Chapman, Kris. 2004. "Ossu! Sporting Masculinities in a Japanese Karatedōjō." *Japan Forum* 16 (2):315–335. doi: 10.1080/0955580042000222709.

Connell, R.W. 1993. "The Big Picture: Masculinities in Recent World History." *Theory and Society* 22 (5):597–623.

_____.1998. "Masculinities and Globalization." *Men and Masculinities* 1 (1):3–23. doi: 10.1177/1097184x98001001001.

Costa, Ben. 2014. Personal Interview.

Cox, Rupert A. 2003. *The Zen Arts: An Anthropological Study of the Culture of Aesthetic Form in Japan*. New York: RoutledgeCurzon.

Cuordileone, K.A. 2000. ""Politics in the Age of Anxiety": Cold War Political Culture and the Crisis in American Masculinity, 1949–1960." *The Journal of American History* 87 (2):515–545.

Dante, Count. 2014 [Black Dragon Fighting Society edition 1968]. *World's Deadliest Fighting Secrets*. Edited by Annette Hellingrath. North Hills, CA: Rising Sun Productions.

De Caro, Frank, and Rosan Augusta Jordan. 2004. *Re-Situating Folklore: Folk Contexts and Twentieth-Century Literature and Art*. Knoxville: University of Tennessee Press.

Donohue, John J. 1994. *Warrior Dreams: The Martial Arts and the American Imagination*. Westport, CT: Bergin & Garvey.

Draeger, Donn F. 1963–1974. "Letters." Texas A&M University, College Station, TX.

_____. 1981. "Letter." Texas A&M University, College Station, TX.

_____, and Robert W. Smith. 1980 [1969]. *Comprehensive Asian Fighting Arts*. New York: Kodansha.

Eberhard, Wolfram. 1975. "Foreigners and Foreign Wars in Chinese Folk Novels." *Journal of the Folklore Institute* 12 (1):65–81.

Elias, Norbert, and Eric Dunning. 1986. *Quest for Excitement: Sport and Leisure in the Civilizing Process*. New York: Basil Blackwell.

Featherstone, Mike. 1991. "The Body in Consumer Culture." In *The Body: Social Process and Cultural Theory*, edited by Mike Hepworth, Mike Featherstone, and Bryan S. Turner, 170–196. London: Sage Publications.

Friedman, Harris. 2005. "Problems of Romanticism in Transpersonal Psychology: A Case Study of Aikido." *The Humanistic Psychologist* 33 (1):3–24. doi: 10.1207/s15473333thp 3301_2.

Garnham, Neal. 2001. "Both Praying and Playing: "Muscular Christianity" and the YMCA in North Durham." *Journal of Social History* 35 (2):397–407.

Geertz, Clifford. 1972. "Deep Play: Notes on the Balinese Cockfight." *Daedalus* 101 (1):1–37.

Gilbey, John F. 1983. *The Way of a Warrior*. [Place of publication not identified]: North Atlantic Bks., U.S.

Godfrey, Emelyne. 2010. "Juju Suffragettes." In *Martial Arts of the World*, edited by Thomas A. Green and Joseph R. Svinth. Santa Barbara, CA: ABC-CLIO.

Godfrey, John. n.d. "Donn Draeger: Man with the Deadliest Hands in the World." 29, 68–69.

Gordon, Andrew. 2003. *A Modern History of Japan: From Tokugawa Times to the Present*. New York: Oxford University Press.

Gorn, Elliott J. 1986. *The Manly Art: Bare-Knuckle Prize Fighting in America*. Ithaca, NY: Cornell University Press.

Graciemag.com. 2011. "From Kayron to Galvao, the Stars Meet Up at Samurai Pro." Accessed 19 July 2013. http://www.graciemag.com/2011/05/from-kayron-to-galvao-the-stars-meet-up-at-samurai-pro.

Green, Harvey. 1986. *Fit for America: Health, Fitness, and American Society*. New York: Pantheon Books.

Green, Thomas A. 2003a. "Sense in Nonsense: The Role of Folk History in the Martial Arts." In *Martial Arts in the Modern World*, edited by Thomas A. Green and Joseph R. Svinth, 1–12. Westport, CT: Praeger.

_____, and Joseph R. Svinth. 2003b. "The Circle and the Octagon: Maeda's Judo and Gracie's Jiu-Jitsu." In *Martial Arts in the Modern World*, edited by Thomas A. Green and Joseph R. Svinth, 61–70. Westport, CT: Praeger.

Hall, Donald E. 1994. "Introduction." In *Muscular Christianity*, edited by Donald E. Hall. New York: Cambridge University Press.

Harootunian, Harry D. 1959. "The Progress of Japan and the Samurai Class, 1868–1882." *Pacific Historical Review* 28 (3):255–266.

Harrington, Patrick. 1997. "Letter." Texas A&M University, College Station, TX.

Hassard, Frank. 2009. "Intangible Heritage in the United Kingdom: The Dark Side of Enlightenment?" In *Intangible Heritage*, edited by Laurajane Smith and Natsuko Akagawa, 270–288. New York: Routledge.

Henning, Stanley E. 1981. "The Chinese Martial Arts in Historical Perspective." *Military Affairs* 45 (4):173–179.

_____. 2003. "The Martial Arts in Chinese Physical Culture, 1865–1965." In *Martial Arts in the Modern World*, edited by Thomas A. Green and Joseph R. Svinth, 13–36. Westport, CT: Praeger.

Hirose, A., and K.K. h Pih. 2009. "Men Who Strike and Men Who Submit: Hegemonic and Marginalized Masculinities in Mixed Martial Arts." *Men and Masculinities* 13 (2):190–209. doi: 10.1177/1097184x09344417.

Hoberek, Andrew. 1997. "The "Work" of Science Fiction: Philip K. Dick and Occupational Masculinity in the Post-World War II United States." *Modern Fiction Studies* 43 (2):374–404.

Hobsbawm, Eric. 1983. "Introduction: Inventing Traditions." In *The Invention of Tradition*, edited by Eric Hobsbawm and Terence Ranger, 1–14. New York: Cambridge University Press.

Hoganson, Kristin L. 1998. *Fighting for American Manhood: How Gender Politics Provoked the Spanish-American and Philippine-American Wars*. New Haven: Yale University Press.

Holthuysen, Jaime. 2011. "Embattled Identities: Construction of Contemporary American Masculinity Amongst Mixed Martial Arts Cagefighters." Ph.D., Department of Anthropology, Arizona State University.

Hopkins, Howard. 1951. *History of the YMCA in North America*. New York: Association Press.

Inokuchi, Hiromitsu, and Yoshiko Nozaki. 2005. "'Different than Us': Othering, Orientalism, and US middle school students' discourses on Japan." *Asia Pacific Journal of Education* 25 (1):61–74. doi: 10.1080/02188790500032533.

Inoue, Shun. 1998. "The Invention of the Martial Arts: Kano Jigoro and Kodokan Judo." In *Mirror of Modernity: Invented Traditions of Modern Japan*, edited by Stephen Vlastos, 163–173. Berkeley: University of California Press.

Iwabuchi, Koichi. 1994. "Complicit Exoticism: Japan and Its Other." *The Australian Journal of Media and Culture* 8 (2):1–24.

Jefferson, T. 1998. "Muscle, 'Hard Men' and 'Iron' Mike Tyson: Reflections on Desire, Anxiety and the Embodiment of Masculinity." *Body & Society* 4 (1):77–98. doi: 10.1177/1357034x 98004001005.

Jennings, George. 2012. "Learning, Mastery and Ageing: Alternative Narratives Among British Practitioners of Traditionalist Chinese Martial Arts." *Asia Pacific Journal of Sport and Social Science* 1 (2–3):128–142. doi: 10.1080/21640599.2012.742312.

Johnson, Sheila K. 1988. *The Japanese Through American Eyes.* Stanford, CA: Stanford University Press.

Karlin, Jason G. 2002. "The Gender of Nationalism: Competing Masculinities in Meiji Japan." *Journal of Japanese Studies* 28 (1):41–77.

Kimura, Ihei. 1937a. *Boy's Exercises.* Tokyo: Kokusai Bunka Shinkokai.

_____. 1937b. *Fencing.* Tokyo: Kokusai Bunka Shinkokai.

Kleeman, Faye Yuan. 2005. "Inscribing Manchuria: Gender, Ideology, and Popular Imagination." *East Asian History* 30:37–66.

Krug, G.J. 2001. "The Feet of the Master: Three Stages in the Appropriation of Okinawan Karate into Anglo-American Culture." *Cultural Studies—Critical Methodologies* 1 (4):395–410. doi: 10.1177/153270860100100401.

Kusz, K.W. 2001. "'I Want to Be the Minority': The Politics of Youthful White Masculinities in Sport and Popular Culture in 1990s America." *Journal of Sport & Social Issues* 25 (4):390–416. doi: 10.1177/0193723501254004.

Lange, Dorothea. 1939. *US Highway 99, Between Tulare and Fresno, California*: U.S. Department of Agriculture, Farm Security Administration.

Lau, Kimberly J. 2000. *New Age Capitalism: Making Money East of Eden.* Philadelphia: University of Pennsylvania Press.

Littlewood, Roland. 1998. "Living Gods: In (Partial) Defence of Euhemerus." *Anthropology Today* 14 (2):6–14.

Lowry, Dave. 2006. *In the Dojo: A Guide to the Rituals and Etiquette of the Japanese Martial Arts.* Boston: Weatherhill.

Maeshima, Kazuhiro. 2004. Tocqueville's Democracy, and Samurai: Inazo Notbe's Attempt to Apply American Democracty to the Feudal Tradition of Japan. In *Departmental Bulletin Paper*: Keiwa College.

Masutatsuoyama.com. "Bulls, Challengers, and the Godhand." Accessed 13 June 2014. http://www.masutatsuoyama.com/en/home/masoyama.htm.

Matthews, Gordon. 2003. "Can a 'Real Man' Live for His Family?" In *Men and Masculinities in Contemporary Japan*, edited by James E. Roberson and Nobue Suzuki, 109–125. New York: RoutledgeCurzon.

McClung, David. 2014. Personal Interview.

McFarlane, Stewart. 1991. "The Mystique of Martial Arts: A Reply to Professor Keenan's Response." *Japanese Journal of Religious Studies* 18 (4):355–368.

Messner, M.A. 2007. "The Masculinity of the Governor: Muscle and Compassion in American Politics." *Gender & Amp; Society* 21 (4):461–480. doi: 10.1177/0891243207303166.

Montagnani, Ilaria. 2005. *Forza: The Samurai Sword Workout.* Berkeley: Ulysses Press.

Nagashima, Akira. 1970. "A Comparison of Japanese and U.S. Attitudes Toward Foreign Products." *Journal of Marketing* 34 (1):68–74.

Nakajima, Tetsuya, and Lee Thompson. 2012. "Judo and the Process of Nation-Building in Japan: Kanō Jigorō and the Formation of Kōdōkan Judo." *Asia Pacific Journal of Sport and Social Science* 1 (2–3):97–110. doi: 10.1080/13854046.2012.743701.

Nitobe, Inazo. 1972. *The Works of Inazo Nitobe.* Tokyo: University of Tokyo Press.

Oates, Joyce Carol. 2006. *On Boxing.* New York: Harper Perennial.

Osgerby, Bill. 2003. "A Pedigree of the Consuming Male: Masculinity, Consumption and the American 'Leisure Class.'" *The Sociological Review* 51 (1):57–85.

Ownby, Ted. 1990. *Subduing Satan: Religion, Recreation, and Manhood in the Rural South, 1865–1920.* Chapel Hill: University of North Carolina Press.

Oyama, Masutatsu. 1979. *The Kyokushin Way.* Tokyo: Japan Publications.

Pennington, John. 1994. "Muscular Spirituality in George Macdonald's Curdie Books." In *Muscular Christianity: Embodying the Victorian Age*, edited by Donald E. Hall, 133–149. New York: Cambridge University Press.

Perry, Elizabeth J. 1985. "Rural Violence in Socialist China." *The China Quarterly* 103 (September):414–440.

Pope, Harrison G., Jr., Roberto Olivardia, Amanda Gruber, and John Borowiecki. 1998. "Evolving Ideals of Male Body Image as Seen Through Action Toys." *International Journal of Eating Disorders* 26 (1):65–72.

Purdy, Ken W. 1961. "Karate: Japan's Spectacular Art of Handmade Mayhem." *Look*, 66–72.

Putney, Clifford. 2001. *Muscular Christianity: Manhood and Sports in Protestant America, 1880–1920.* Cambridge: Harvard University Press.

Roberson, Susan L. 1994. "Degenerate Effeminacy." In *Muscular Christianity*, edited by Donald E. Hall, 150–172. New York: Cambridge University Press.

Romano, Salvatore "Sam" (AFC 2001/001/58343). Veterans History Project. American Folklife Center: Library of Congress.

Rotundo, Anthony E. 1983. "Body and Soul: Changing Ideals of American Middle-Class Manhood, 1770–1920." *Journal of Social History* 16 (4):23–38.

_____.1993. *American Manhood: Transformations in Masculinity from the Revolution to the Modern Era.* New York: Basic Books.

Rowbotham, Sheila. 1974. *Women, Resistance and Revolution: A History of Women and Revolution in the Modern World.* New York: Vintage.

Roy, T.L. 2010. *Deadliest Man Alive! The Strange Saga of Count Dante and the Black Dragon Fighting Society*: Cerebus Books.

Ryan, Alexandra. 2009. "Globalisation and the 'Internal Alchemy' in Chinese Martial Arts:The Transmission of *Taiji*quan to Britain." *East Asian Science, Technology and Society: An International Journal* 2 (4):525–543. doi: 10.1007/s12280–009–9073-x.

Savran, David. 1998. *Taking It Like a Man: White Masculinity, Masochism, and Contemporary American Culture.* Princeton, NJ: Princeton University Press.

Shah, Hemant. 2003. "'Asian Culture' and Asian American Identities in the Television and Film Industries of the United States." *SIMILE: Studies in Media & Information Literacy Education* 3 (3):1 10. doi: 10.3138/sim.3.3.002.

Shu, Yuan. 2003. "Reading the Kung Fu Film in an American Context: From Bruce Lee to Jackie Chan." *Journal of Popular Film and Television* 31 (2):50–59. doi: 10.1080/01956050309603666.

Silver, Mike. 2008. *The Arc of Boxing: The Rise and Decline of the Sweet Science.* Jefferson, NC: McFarland.

Singer, Mark. 1986. "Osu!" *The New Yorker*, May 25.

Smith, Robert W. 1960. *Jon Bluming at the Kodokan.* Texas A&M University, College Station, TX: Cushing Memorial Library and Archives, Robert W. Smith Martial Arts Collection.

_____.1964. *Secrets of Shaolin Temple Boxing.* Rutland, VT: Charles E. Tuttle Co.

_____.1999. *Martial Musings: A Portrayal of Martial Arts in the 20th Century.* Erie, PA: Via Media Publishing Company.

_____.no date. *Draeger Posing.* Texas A&M University, College Station, TX: Cushing Memorial Library and Archives, Robert W. Smith Collection.

Social Register. no date. *Society Sluggers—Youngsters of the Elite Hold Boxing Tournament at Piping Rock Club*: Social Register.

Spencer, D.C. 2009. "Habit(Us), Body Techniques and Body Callusing: An Ethnography of Mixed Martial Arts." *Body & Society* 15 (4):119–143. doi: 10.1177/1357034x09347224.

Studio, Bilger. 1920. *Boxing Exhibition at Y.M.C.A.* Freeport, IL.

Svinth, Joseph R. 2003. "The Spirit of Manliness: Boxing in Imperial Japan, 1868–1945." In *Martial Arts in the Modern World*, edited by Thomas A. Green and Joseph R. Svinth, 37–46. Westport, CT: Praeger.

Ta, Lynn M. 2006. "Hurt So Good: Fight Club, Masculine Violence, and the Crisis of Capitalism." *The Journal of American Culture* 29 (3):265–277.

Tan, Kevin S.Y. 2004. "Constructing a Martial Tradition: Rethinking a Popular History of Karate-Dou." *Journal of Sport & Social Issues* 28 (2):169–192. doi: 10.1177/0193723504264772.

Thomson, James C., Jr., Peter W. Stanley, and John Cutis Perry. 1981. *Sentimental Imperialists: The American Experience in East Asia*. New York: Harper & Row.

Time. 1942. "U.S. at War: Takcihashi's Blacks." *Time Magazine*, October 5, 1942, Vol. XL No. 14.

Toelken, Barre. 1996. *The Dynamics of Folklore*. Logan: Utah State University Press.

Toon, Elizabeth, and Janet Lynne Golden. 2002. "'Live Clean, Think Clean, and Don't Go to Burlesque Shows': Charles Atlas as Health Advisor." *Journal of the History of Medicine and Allied Sciences* 57 (1):39–60.

Trias, Robert A. 1973. *The Hand Is My Sword: A Karate Handbook*. Rutland, VT: Charles E. Tuttle Co.

UNESCO. 2003. "Convention for the Safeguarding of Intangible Cultural Heritage." Available at http://www.unesco.org/culture/ich/en/convention

Vaccaro, C.A., D.P. Schrock, and J.M. McCabe. 2011. "Managing Emotional Manhood: Fighting and Fostering Fear in Mixed Martial Arts." *Social Psychology Quarterly* 74 (4):414–437. doi: 10.1177/0190272511415554.

Van Skiver, Raymond (AFC 2001/001/12540). Veterans History Project. American Folklife Center: Library of Congress.

Wakins, John Edward (AFC 2001/001/67247). Veterans History Project. American Folklife Center: Library of Congress.

Watson, Nick J., and Stephen Friend. 2005. "The Development of Muscular Christianity in Victorian Britain and Beyond." *Journal of Religion and Society* 7:1–21.

Wolf-Meye, Matthew. 2003. "The World Ozymandias Made: Utopias in the Superhero Comic, Subculture, and the Conservation of Difference." *The Journal of Popular Culture* 36 (3):497–517.

WoMAU. 2012. "Womau and Its Role Reviewed with Decision of Taekkyon for Inscription on the List as a Momentum." http://www.womau.org/bbs/board.php?bo_table=e_b4x3&wr_id=16

Index

187